Providence

Providence, Piety and Power

John Petley

RoperPenberthy Publishing

Published by RoperPenberthy Publishing Ltd, Springfield House,
23 Oatlands Drive, Weybridge, Surrey KT13 9LZ

Text copyright © John Petley, 2012

ISBN 978 1 903905 75 3

Typeset by Avocet Typeset, Chilton, Aylesbury, Bucks.
Printed in England

CONTENTS

CONTENTS

Foreword

For much of the twentieth century fashionable philosophers in the English-speaking world, particularly in Oxford and Cambridge, were attracted to 'logical positivism'. To simplify for the sake of rapid exposition, logical positivism claimed that only two kinds of statement could be made about reality. These were analytic statements, which were true by definition, and synthetic statements, which were valid only because they could be subjected to an empirical test. In his celebrated 1936 book on *Language, Truth and Logic* Ayer developed the distinction between the two types of statement into a larger claim about the ambit of philosophical inquiry. In Ayer's view only logic, mathematics, and the empirical sciences offered meaningful propositions. All other spheres of knowledge – including metaphysics, religion, and traditional ethics – lacked intellectual validity. Theology was reduced to hocus-pocus. By implication, the Church had nothing to say about contemporary political and economic debates, and its messages could and should be ignored.

John Petley's book is a powerful, well-argued and fascinating response to this kind of plausible atheism. Petley is not afraid to assert the relevance of Holy Scripture to current problems. He is prepared to invoke God's will as a relevant variable in judging today's politicians. He also believes that an overarching divine Providence is watching us and weighing us in the balance, and that – whether we are conscious of it or not – our apparently secular society is imbued with religious motives and understandings. He sees the Bible and the patristic literature as having continuing relevance to key public policy decisions. His perspective is essentially that of an Evangelical Christian, with a somewhat conservative stance on the major issues of our times.

I am a sceptic by inclination. As a sceptic, I am suspicious of both extremes. I dislike logical positivism's repudiation of religion and Petley's occasional appeals in *Providence, Piety and Power* to a superior divinity to settle our problems. At any rate, *Providence, Piety and Power* raises an important question. Would we prefer living in societies in which most people have an active religious life of some sort or in societies that are wholly secular in outlook? *Providence, Piety and Power* has made me think hard about this question, and I am grateful to Petley for making me debate with myself and worry about where I stand. I commend *Providence, Piety and Power* to the general reader, particularly if he or she believes that religion has a vital role to play in modern political and social affairs.

Professor Tim Congdon, CBE

Introduction

The inspiration for this book can be traced back to the time I spent as a researcher in Brussels. I was still a relative newcomer to politics at this time, never having been a member of a political party before joining the UK Independence Party in 2001, having become convinced by several Christian friends that it was in Britain's best interest to withdraw from the European Union. Several months before making my way to Brussels, I had been asked to stand as the party's candidate for the Lewes constituency in the 2005 General Election, and I must admit, I now look back with horror at how ill-prepared I was! I could hold my own if the subject of the European Union came up, but frequently felt out of my depth in the hustings when domestic policy issues were discussed.

The years in Brussels confirmed me in my opinion that whatever the economic logic for the UK joining the European Union – or Common Market as it then was – back in 1973, it is no longer in our interest to remain part of the top-down bureaucratic nightmare that the EU has become. In addition, my work required me to get to grips with the wider political scene, including acquiring an understanding of domestic politics in the UK, and as I looked at one policy area after another, a pattern slowly emerged:– the vast majority of the political and economic woes currently facing Britain and many other Western nations can be laid fairly and squarely at the doors of an ideology that has saddled us with a large, costly and intrusive state.

Before arriving in Brussels, I had read only one or two books written by Christians about political issues. I guess this is hardly surprising, for there are very few such books in existence, certainly on my side of the Atlantic. I had been aware of terms like "the Messianic state" and can recall how one or two Christians had told me how the state had usurped many functions that had hitherto been the domain of the Church or private philanthropy. However, my time in Brussels confronted me head on with the tremendous damage that socialism – the main driving force behind the increase in both the size and the power of the state in the last 100 years – has done to the UK, and indeed elsewhere.

About the same time, I made another discovery – that I had hitherto failed to think consistently as a Christian and apply any sort of Biblical thinking to the political arena. Indeed, up to this point I had neither appreciated that the Bible has so much to say about what would now be termed political issues nor had I been of the political thinking of Christians in the past, particularly among the reformers and Puritans – the spiritual giants of the 16th and 17th centuries. So began a journey of discovery trying to determine what constitutes a Christian worldview. One thing became clear very quickly – it would have very little in common with socialism, which in spite of some apparent similarities, is as different from Christianity as chalk is from cheese.

It may appear that a book that attempts to put socialism under the spotlight of scripture is a strange topic in the early 21st century. Is such an analysis needed when the classic socialist policy of public ownership of the means of production is so widely discredited among Western democracies? Venezuela's Hugo Chávez may still be nationalising everything he can lay his hands on, and the ANC's youth wing were still giving enthusiastic support for state ownership of the means of production in South Africa as recently as January 2011, but such attitudes seem like a strange throwback to the past. Anthony Giddens, former Director of the London School of Economics and a great influence on Tony Blair, wrote of "the death of socialism" as far back as 1998 in his book *The Third Way*. After all, even the People's Republic of China, still a one-party state under the rule of a party calling itself the Communist Party of China, has opened up to private enterprise.

In reality, the fundamental socialist belief in the big state is far from dead. Socialism has moved on significantly from its initial emphasis on state ownership – indeed Blairite socialism in particular has conceded considerable ground in its thinking on the right to private property – but after shifting its focus onto state-enforced compulsory wealth redistribution in order to equalise material prosperity, socialism is now dominated by a wider equality agenda – an agenda which grew out of Marxism, and which is increasingly meddling in the day-to-day lives of ordinary people. Of particular relevance to this book, the "nanny state" of Margaret Hodge and Harriet Harman is proving a far more deadly enemy to the Gospel that the seminal socialist 1945–51 administration of Clement Attlee. What is particularly tragic is that even though Gordon Brown was thankfully toppled from power in the May 2010 General Election, the new coalition government seems unwilling to reverse many of Labour's damaging social policies, and consequently, the hard-won freedoms for Bible-believing Christians to practise their faith unmolested are still under as great a threat in countries like the UK than at any time since the late 17th Century.

I have met a good few Christians who seem instinctively uncomfortable with socialism and the big state in general, without being to articulate the reason why. This book will prove that there are sound theological reasons for their unease, and my earnest desire is that it will be a means of guiding others along the same road that it has taken me so many years to find. Socialism has been undermined by politicians like Margaret Thatcher and Ronald Reagan, and by economists like FA Hayek and Milton Friedman, but I am not aware of any book that has attempted to evaluate it from a Biblical perspective.

I believe the timing of this book is significant – the unpopular but essential attempts to cut government spending in Britain, the growing disillusion with the EU as a result of the Eurozone sovereign debt crisis and the widespread cynicism felt towards politicians in all three main British parties suggests that the coming decade may well see a significant shake-up of the political landscape in the UK, and offers a chance for the status quo to be challenged in many areas. The mind-boggling deficits run up by governments across the Western world are generating serious concerns about whether the state should be entrusted with such power and so much of our money. To this question, as will be shown, the Bible replies with an unequivocal "no." Any nation whose leaders seek guidance from the Bible will end up with a far smaller and less intrusive state than is currently the norm – indeed, a government that takes the Bible's teaching seriously will aim to reinvigorate the sense of community and personal responsibility which in turn will allow the state to be shrunk even further than proposed by many advocates of limited government.

In this book, *Providence, Piety and Power,* I will look at the development of Christian political thinking down the ages and use it as a yardstick with which to compare and contrast socialism from its inception to the present day. A subsequent volume, *Weighed and found Wanting*, will take the form of case studies showing the fundamental anti-Christian impetus that drives socialist thinking in a number of significant areas of policy, including the welfare state, education and the green agenda, and will attempt to offer Biblically-based alternatives.

Evidence of the repeated failure of socialism, whether in the guise of classic social democracy, Marxism-Leninism or its more sinister "politically correct" postmodern variant is there for all to see and is being increasingly acknowledged. The recent impact of the TEA Party movement in the USA and the Republican gains in the 2010 mid-term Congressional elections are indicative of a growing recognition among the American electorate of the errors of big state policies in that country. In the UK – which is the main although not exclusive focus of the latter chapters of this book – opposition is less organised at the moment, although commendable work has been undertaken by several think tanks and campaign groups like the Institute of Economic Affairs, the Centre for Policy Studies, the Taxpayers' Alliance and The Freedom Association. It is therefore surely only a matter of time before supporters of small government will have more choice at the ballot box this side of the Atlantic too. The tide is beginning to turn against the big state, which has proven itself to benefit only whingers, the indolent and control freaks, while penalising aspiration, hard work and thrift. In the coming years, this sentiment may well develop into a momentum which could destroy socialism once for all as a serious political force.

This book encourages Christians to add their voices to those seeking to restrict the size of the state, and to restrict it to perform only those functions ordained for it in the Bible. Christians who take up the challenge of its message will find themselves treading a path which was well-worn many years ago, but has become very overgrown, with only a few pioneering individuals having walked along it in recent years. They will find themselves facing opposition, as supporters of the current variant of socialism are reluctant to engage with its opponents in open and fair debate, while controlling significant sections of the media and much of the education system. Consequently, alternative viewpoints can find it hard to get a fair hearing, and anyone daring to tackle socialism head on will find themselves derided as an extremist or totally mad. However, if we have any concern for God's glory, that His will may be done on earth as it is in Heaven, and if we are to obey our Saviour's injuction to love our neighbour – and thus to save our land from the squalid barbarism of the state worship with which socialism in all its variants is always intimately associated – we cannot stand idly by.

May God use this book for His glory.

John Petley
May Hill, Gloucestershire, August 2012

Chapter 1:

Monarchy, Democracy and Theocracy: Providence, Politics and the concept of restraint.

By me kings reign and princes decree justice[1]

Sola Scriptura and politics

"It's the fault of those greedy bankers!" So ran the consensus among the media, politicians and even some church leaders when more than a decade of solid economic growth came to an abrupt end in 2007. However, as the second phase of the crisis developed from 2010 onwards, with the focus shifting to excessive government borrowing and the Eurozone sovereign debt crisis in particular, the blame is now beginning to shift to where it truly belongs – "It's the fault of those bloated governments!" While the behaviour of certain members of the banking profession cannot be condoned, the prime culprits for the woes we are currently facing are governments which have become too big and consequentially spend too much taxpayers' money. The sovereign debt crisis has proved once and for all that the trend throughout the 20th century for an increased role for the state was a disastrous mistake. In fact, one could go further still:– what has happened right across the Western world in the last few years is the inevitable consequence of politicians not following the Maker's instructions. The state, in other words, has gone far beyond its God-given mandate, assuming a role for itself unwarranted by the scriptures while at the same time failing to fulfil the tasks which God has allotted to it

The purpose of this book is to study from an Evangelical Christian perspective how we have arrived at this unfortunate situation. A second volume will attempt to outline some sort of remedy. In so doing both volumes will in some instances adopt a very different line from the recent pronouncements of many British and European church leaders, including Rowan Williams, the Archbishop of Canterbury and Pope Benedict XVI. Everyone views the world from a particular perspective, which will be a framework of their ideas and beliefs. Such frameworks are known as worldviews. Among other things, worldviews analyse what is wrong with the world, and propose solutions. An Evangelical Christian will build his or her worldview around the Bible's teaching, and will therefore inevitably arrive at different answers to these men because of their differing views on the inspiration of the Holy Bible. Neither Dr Williams nor the Pope regard the Bible as the final authority "for doctrine, for reproof, for correction, for instruction in righteousness.[2]" On the one hand, the Roman Catholic Church, while acknowledging the divine authorship of the scriptures, has assigned an equal authority to its own traditions – including its interpretation of the Bible – which in practise can lead to a stifling of the authentic voice of God's Word. On the other hand, theological liberalism, as represented by Dr. Williams, has sought since the 18th Century to interpret the Bible through the filter of human reason, denying its unity and divine inspiration and therefore rejecting as mythical anything that cannot be easily reconciled with everyday human experience, such as the miracles recorded in the Gospels.

By contrast, Evangelicals are characterised by their unshakeable belief in the authority of the Bible – its inerrancy and unique status as a book given by God. The reformers and the Puritans in particular sought to apply its teaching to every area of life – in other words, to develop a comprehensive Christian worldview – and of especial importance for this book was their Bible-based approach to politics. Bearing in mind the distinctive Evangelical emphasis on *Sola Scriptura* (the Bible as the only infallible authority) it is inevitable that an Evangelical political perspective will be distinctive from that of a Roman Catholic or a theological liberal. This is not to deny that one can find support for many aspects of Christian political thought among Roman Catholics, theological liberals and indeed outright atheists for the simple reason that where governments have been influenced by Christian political thinking – notably in Britain, the Netherlands and the USA, the blessings that followed have been appreciated by men and women of many faiths and none. Deuteronomy 28 is a long chapter, which may be summed up in a single sentence: "Obey my law and you will be blessed, disobey it an you will suffer the consequences." Although the Israelites were a nation with a unique covenant relationship to God, and the sacrificial system contained in the Mosaic Law is no longer needed, there is an important principle to learn from this chapter, which this book will attempt to bring out: those nations whose laws have been the most influenced by God's Word have historically enjoyed the smallest government, the greatest freedom, the lowest taxes and the highest level of prosperity. If the fashionable "Happy Planet" or "Gross National Happiness" indices had been in existence in the 16th-19th centuries, these same nations would have been at the very top here too. These blessings are surely proof that the manifestations of Evangelical political thought considered in this book are truly from God.

It must be pointed out that Evangelicals have not always agreed with each other on every single point of interpretation, and even some of the greatest saints have adopted positions on certain issues, notably on the degree to which godliness can be enforced by the state, that subsequent Evangelical thinking has felt uncomfortable with. Furthermore, the period from the Reformation to the late 17th Century, during which Christian political thinking reached its zenith, was a different age in many aspects from that in which we now live. Christians in politics today will need to apply the Bible to address issues which were unknown 400

17

years ago, such as political correctness or assisted suicide. Consequently it would be impossible to write one definitive manifesto setting out in precise detail for all time how God has set forth in the Bible exactly how a nation should be governed. Nonetheless, there is a broad consensus on a number of fundamental principles that can be applied to the 21st Century as much as the 16th or 17th Centuries.

One intriguing question to which it is hard to provide a satisfactory answer is why, having been at the cutting edge of political development for over 100 years, Christian political thinking, having reached something of a consensus by 1700, suddenly went into a long period of decline from which it is now only beginning to recover. Such has been the scale and the length of the Christian retreat from the political arena that any idea of there being such a thing as distinctive Christian politics is quite new to many Evangelicals today. It has taken the introduction of a raft of disturbing legislation onto the statute books of countries like the UK and the USA during the last 50 years to force Christians – in some cases rather reluctantly – back into the political arena in order to confront what is clearly unchristian politics. Even without a well thought out Christian worldview, Christians know instinctively that what is being advocated in areas like abortion, euthanasia and homosexuality is contrary to God's will. Nonetheless, we are only at the beginning of a recovery of clear Christian thinking in the political realm. The Bible does not merely speak about the sanctity of life and the importance of marriage. It also addresses issues such as the right to private property, inheritance, the size of the state, crime and punishment, care for the poor and marginalised, to name just a few. It is vital for the church to get to grips with the whole counsel of God in the area of politics, for in the early 21st century Christians are in a battle, and whether we like it or not, in the very forefront. With socialism we are faced with a system of political thought which was born in rebellion against God and not only disregards but actually opposes what the Bible teaches. It has undergone frequent metamorphoses in the last 100 years, but has not changed in this fundamental area. Initially it appeared to be compassionate and to offer the best way forward for mankind in an age of extreme inequality. Its moral bankruptcy is now apparent to any open-minded person, albeit only after many years of deceiving good and honest men, including some Evangelical Christians, while its malign influence has seeped out far beyond such explicitly socialist organisations as the British Labour Party or the trade unions, affecting the thinking of many people without them even realising it.

Only by taking a systematic look at Biblical teaching in all areas relating to politics and studying how the Christian political worldview has developed over the years will Christians be equipped with the yardstick that is needed if the battle with socialism is to be won.

Providence – the Biblical context for government

The starting point of any attempt to formulate some Biblical principles for politics is to establish how this subject fits into the overall message of the scriptures. At first glance the affairs and governments of the nations of the earth seem something of a sideshow in terms of the dominant theme of the Bible – the message of salvation through Jesus Christ which permeates its pages from Genesis to Revelation. The Old Testament predicts His coming, while the New tells of His life and death. That death on behalf of sinners is set forth as the great act of reconciliation whereby men and women who have all sinned and come short of the glory of God may, by trusting solely in Jesus Christ for salvation and not in their own works, be pardoned, declared righteous and spared the condemnation and punishment they deserve. Christians have the glorious hope of eternal life in the new heaven and new earth "wherein dwelleth righteousness[3]" to look forward to. Why should we be sidetracked with the affairs of this present world? The answer is that although the great narrative of redemption of undeserving sinners through Jesus Christ unquestionably is the dominant message of the Bible, it is not the only theme, and it is in two significant and interconnected doctrines – creation and providence – where any study of Christian politics must begin.

The very first verse in the Bible introduces the reader to God as creator. He brought a vast universe into being out of nothing. Psalm 33:6 states that "By the word of the Lord were the Heavens made, and all the host of them by the breath of his mouth." And the reason He did so, just like the reason He chose to save undeserving sinners, was to display His glory[4]. Indeed, creation in its beauty and intricacy still does indeed display that glory.

However, the created world that we inhabit now is not in the pristine condition in which it was created. As a result of the Fall – the sin of Adam and Eve in the Garden of Eden – God placed a curse on the earth – a curse that affected not just man, but the whole created order[5]. The curse brought death to mankind, pain in childbirth for women and a harsher and less productive environment in which to labour. There was nonetheless mercy in the midst of judgement, notably the first promise of the coming of Jesus Christ to redeem man from the curse – the seed of the woman who would bruise the serpent's head[6]. However, alongside God's great plan of salvation, there were other notes of mercy too. God did not turn His back on the world He created. It still retains a great deal of beauty, and man, made in the image and likeness of God as His steward or vice-regent to "replenish the earth,...subdue it and have dominion[7]" has been allowed, in spite of his sin, to retain this creation mandate. Furthermore, God did not leave man to fulfil this task unaided. He continued to be active in the world – sustaining and directing it, while setting out guidelines in the Bible which tell man how to govern it. This on-going care for the world at large is known as the doctrine of providence, or common grace. The American theologian Wayne Grudem defines God's providence as follows: "God is continually involved with all created things in such a way that he (1) keeps them existing and maintaining the properties with which he created them (2) cooperates with created things in every action, directing their distinctive properties to cause them to act as they do, and (3) directs them to fulfil his purposes.[8]" It is the third of these points which is particularly relevant to the theme of this book.

The doctrine of providence does not enjoy the prominence in Evangelical thought which it once did, in spite of being widely taught in both the Old and New Testaments. While it is true that many Christians today accept God's providential dealings at an individual level – for instance when a material need is wonderfully answered in response to prayer – few Christians give much thought to how much God actually blesses mankind as a whole. As Evangelical Christianity since the late 19th century has focussed so strongly on the message of salvation and retreated from any wider concern for mankind as a whole, some Christians today, when considering the subject of providence for the first time, find it bizarre that God should bless in any way those who never once thank Him for these mercies and who die bound for eternal condemnation, missing out on redemption due to never having professed faith in Jesus. However, God's ways are not our ways, and the Scriptures are quite clear about the reality of these temporal blessings which are shared by all mankind. Jesus Christ Himself talks in the Sermon on the Mount of God's goodness to mankind, elect and reprobate alike, making: "His sun to rise on the evil and on the good" and sending "rain on the just and on the unjust.[9]" Christians, as has been noted, have the glorious hope of spending eternity with God in glory. For non-Christians however, the far more limited temporal blessings of providence are the only blessings they will ever enjoy. If Christians are to do good to all men[10], it is part of our responsibility not only to point sinners to the Saviour, but also to maximise their opportunity to enjoy the blessings of providence.

Government forms one major area of God's providence. What level of government mankind would have required had Adam and Eve not sinned is a speculative question we cannot answer in detail, although the answer is probably very little. This is because all the principal functions of government specifically identified by Christians – and indeed those which are almost universally acknowledged, such as the preservation of law and order and national security – are only needed because of the effects of the Fall. Of course, many governments themselves have been headed by godless men and some have been incredibly evil, but this does not negate the fact that government is a gift from God and a good thing. Even tyrannical government is better than no government at all for it brings stability and some sort of order through the restraint of wickedness. Without it, a fallen world, full of men and women tainted by sin, would degenerate into violent, lawless chaos. One only has to consider the total collapse of law and order in present-day Somalia, which has been without effective government for nearly two decades, to prove the point. Although the potential for evil within government has caused some Christians to question whether it is a gift from God, in a fallen world, we should not make perfection the yardstick when deciding whether something is from God or not. The cycle of nature, including the sunshine and rain referred to above, is another aspect of God's providence, and in most circumstances is a blessing to mankind. However, sunshine can cause drought and famine, while the monsoon rains can bring devastation to countries like Pakistan or Bangladesh. It is significant that one of the most important passages addressing the subject of the state, Romans 13:1–6, was written by the apostle Paul at a time when government for millions in Europe, North Africa and parts of Asia meant the Roman Empire and in particular the wicked emperor Nero, who in the latter years of his reign began a vicious persecution of Christians. Paul would have been under no illusions about his character, yet he wrote that "He is the minister of God to thee for good.[11]" Paul is saying that although in his individual character Nero may have been a most unpleasant man, in his capacity as part of a government, he was still a blessing, because his government, through its legal system and its strong army, kept a degree of law and order and restrained evil internally and externally.

Obviously, the more God's guidelines are followed by a government, the more this restraint will prove a very real blessing to all the governed. We can only admire God's kindness when considering the degree to which restraint operates across society, thanks to family and peer pressure as well as government. The prophet Jeremiah, contemplating the depth to which humanity has fallen as a result of the sin of Adam and Eve paints a bleak picture indeed: "The heart (*of man*) is deceitful above all things and desperately wicked; Who can know it?[12]" Yet in spite of this, very few men or women achieve a fraction of the evil of which their rebellious hearts are capable – indeed, many men who lived and died enemies of God in their hearts have been graciously allowed to leave a legacy which has been a blessing to mankind, such as the music of Mozart or the engineering feats of Isambard Kingdom Brunel.

While the doctrine of providence is self-evident, it is appropriate to pause to address a strand in Christian thinking since the 18th century which denies the role of earthly government in the restraint of evil. Supporters of this view go beyond questioning whether government can be from God because of the sinfulness of kings and politicians. They teach that Christians should have nothing whatever to do with politics as earthly government is outside of God's jurisdiction and therefore irrelevant for the Christian. The most prominent advocate of this position today is the American pastor Greg Boyd, who states, "All human governments...are actually ruled by Satan[13]" His basis for this statement is to take at face value Satan's words in Luke 4:5–7 where he tells Jesus that "All this power (*i.e. over the kingdoms of the world*) I will give thee and the glory of them; for that is delivered unto me and to whomsoever I will, I give it." Quite apart from the fact that Jesus Himself said of Satan "When he speaketh a lie, he speaketh of his own, for he is a liar and the father of it,[14]" Satan's words can only possibly be taken at face value if other scriptures such as Romans 13 or the verse quoted at the head of this chapter are ignored. Furthermore, Jeremiah 29:7, a verse in which the prophet tells the Jews exiled in Babylon to seek the peace of the city to which they had been carried away and to pray for it, can be applied in the present age as a guideline for the Christian's attitude to the world, in which he too can regard himself an exile, Our citizenship may be in heaven[15], but we are to get involved, and pray for our political leaders[16] – a strange injunction if all human government is under the rule of the Devil. Boyd's teaching hardly squares up with the overall message of the Bible, especially as it makes God less than omnipotent. For these reasons, it must be rejected.

Having therefore established the general principle that government is a gift from God for the restraint of evil, the next issue to address is what this restraint means in practise, and this can best be illustrated by considering how well it has operated in three very different models of government[17] which developed in the years before Jesus Christ. Two of these three are still very much with us – albeit in a considerably modified form – while the third, although an unique system applying to one nation only for a limited period of time, has been influential in shaping Christian political thought, even if it has long been extinct and cannot be replicated in the modern world. It is significant that Christian political thinkers through the ages do not offer a consensus of the best form of government – indeed, the Bible is not prescriptive on this point, and God's guidelines are sufficiently flexible to be accommodated quite widely. However, it is apparent that some types of government are more conducive to the principle of restraint than others.

Monarchy (rule by one person)

Monarchy is the oldest form of government mentioned in the Bible, and the most widespread, although this in itself does not imply divine sanction. It is a natural development of God creating human beings with different personalities. Strong individuals inevitably emerged as soon as men began to live in any sort of tight-knit community like a town or city which required a degree of communal organisation. There is no information in the Bible about the form of government in cities from Cain's pioneering construction of the city of

Enoch[18] to those destroyed in the Great Flood, but it would not be unreasonable to assume they were ruled by strong men. Rule by one man, whether called emperor, king, prince or some other title, was the norm through the Old Testament period and beyond, both in the lands mentioned in the Bible and those further afield.

Not all monarchs necessarily ruled over large territories – indeed in the account of the battle of the kings in Genesis 14, the word "king" does seem a bit overblown for men some of whom were top dogs in cities with a population possibly no larger than that of a small provincial town in our own time. However, at the other end of the scale, large countries including Egypt and China were ruled by monarchs well before the time of Abraham. In the Bible, the first mention of the word "kingdom" can be found in Genesis 10:10 in connection with Nimrod – a monarch who ruled over a substantial empire and is described as "a mighty one in the earth" and a "hunter before the Lord[19]" He located his imperial capital at Babel, and there were other large cities under his rule[20]. He was clearly an important figure, as his "hunting before the Lord" later became a legend. Commentators ancient and modern are unanimous in interpreting "hunting" as more than pursuing and killing animals for food. Calvin understands it as meaning that "He was a furious man, and approximated to beasts rather than man[21]" while James Montgomery Boice says that "he was a hunter of men-a warrior. It was through his ability to fight and kill and rule ruthlessly that his kingdom of Euphrates valley city states was consolidated.[22]"

Nimrod's tyranny highlights the principal weakness of monarchy. One consequence of the Fall is that men with dominant personalities can easily become despots. To put it another way, although government acts in a general sense as a restraint upon evil, the governors themselves need to be restrained. There are a number of ways by which this is accomplished. In the case of Nimrod's empire, God intervened directly. Although many today under the influence of an evolutionary worldview believe that our first ancestors were primitive savages, the Bible speaks of Nimrod's empire as an advanced civilisation capable of building "a tower whose top may reach unto Heaven.[23]" This great tower was built as an act of defiance against God, and God's response to the building project was miraculously to confuse the speech of the builders. This judgement brought an abrupt end to the construction of this great edifice and scattered the builders over the face of the earth. The spontaneous creation of different languages, besides helping delineate the different nations, was a merciful act of restraint, for it prevented "the creation of a rebellious one-world political tyranny.[24]" Great empires would come and go, but every would-be tyrant since Nimrod has been restrained by linguistic diversity.

Another welcome restraint God has placed on monarchy is that although the term "absolute monarch" is widely used to describe these ancient kings, no one man can rule over a vast empire single-handed. Ministers of state would inevitably be required in any decent sized kingdom. By the time of Israel's stay in Egypt, the Pharaoh needed the assistance of a Prime Minister who headed up a large civil service including a treasury and department of agriculture[25]. The Egyptian population naturally had no say in the choice either of their monarch or his advisors. Joseph's rise to become Prime Minister of Egypt was entirely Pharaoh's initiative[26]. In any absolute monarchy, only the officials had much opportunity to exercise restraint, although any reader of the book of Daniel cannot but observe how difficult it could be even for a godly and respected official to restrain a powerful headstrong monarch like Nebuchadnezzar of Babylon. Of course, a wicked official can make a bad king worse. It was Haman the Agagite, an official at the Persian court with a huge ego, who encouraged King Ahasuerus to exterminate the Jews,[27]while the unwise counsel of the young friends of Rehoboam, son of King Solomon, resulted in the fracturing of the Israelite state into two separate kingdoms[28]. Wicked monarchs and wicked officials seldom manage to remain united for too long, however. Sooner or later, a senior minister or army leader will break ranks to lead a coup d'état. The historical books of the Old Testament contain a number of accounts of such uprisings, both among the Jews and their neighbours[29], and the history of the monarchies of many European and Asian nations in more recent times is no different. Such bloody events are hardly the best way of restraining evil, as in all too many cases the net result is the replacement of one unsatisfactory ruler by another.

One way of pre-empting such violence was for the monarch to attempt to make himself untouchable by claiming divinity. Who would dare attack or criticise a living god? The Egyptian pharaohs and the Roman emperors were considered to be gods, and some of the latter in particular took their divinity very seriously. Even those who were less than convinced of their own deity recognised the value of religion as a tool of subjection. Mercifully, this form of tyranny – the ultimate in rebellion against God – has been confined to the history books, although as recently as 1928, the coronation service of the Japanese Emperor Hirohito allegedly elevated him to divine status[30]. Any monarch of a nation that has embraced a monotheistic religion would naturally regard such behaviour as blasphemous, but kings in such countries have found more subtle means of putting themselves beyond criticism. The Stuart kings believed that they were divinely ordained to their task and therefore not responsible to any other human being. This theory of the "divine right of kings" now seems as ludicrous as the concept of the monarch as a living god. It is certainly true that Saul and David, the first two Israelite kings, were divinely chosen by God[31], but could the same really be said of Charles I? The Stuarts may have had a point inasmuch as there are several passages in the Old Testament where God stresses the accountability of monarchs to Him. For example, in Psalm 2:10–12, rulers are told to rule wisely or face the consequences: "Kiss the Son, lest He be angry and ye perish from the way.[32]" Unfortunately, Charles I did not rule wisely; failing to recognise that his duplicity, his persecution of godly men, and his abuse of the tax system to finance ill-advised wars could not be swept under the carpet on the grounds that he was accountable only to God. His stubborn adherence to this doctrine led to civil war and ultimately cost him his head. Considering that the picture painted of monarchs ancient and modern has been so negative, it is vital to return to the point made by the Apostle Paul in Romans 13 that a king – even a tyrant – is God's minister for good. This still begs the question as to why monarchy was not quickly replaced by something better. Why submit to these unaccountable autocrats? The answer can be found by considering that the world of the Old Testament was a world of nations frequently at war. In these circumstances, leadership by a powerful king was viewed as essential if the land was to be defended against an aggressor. Better suffer the rule of a tyrant of one's own race who at least brings peace and stability rather than suffer invasion by a foreign power. These have often been the only two choices available. In certain cultures, particularly where Evangelical Christianity has made little impact, strong leadership is still valued today, even at the cost of liberty. Russia is a good example:– it has applied the epithet "The Great" to two thoroughly ruthless despots, the Czar Peter (1696–1727) and the Empress Catherine[33] (1762–1796), while its current despot, Vladimir Putin, still enjoys a considerable degree of support, if not on the same scale as ten years ago. Some countries have sat more comfortably under autocratic rule than others. In Britain and the USA, Gospel freedoms have generated a greater appreciation of political freedom. The most celebrated British defence of the voluntary surrender of individual liberty for the purpose of national security was Thomas Hobbes' *Leviathan*, published in 1651. Hobbes' views were widely criticised, and have never commanded widespread support in Britain, although it is surprising to find the Bible commentator Matthew Henry speaking very favourably of monarchy. Nimrod, he claimed, set a precedent as "other nations soon learned to incorporate under one head for their common safety and welfare, which, however it began, proved as great a blessing to the world that things were reckoned to go ill indeed when there was no king.[34]"

Of course, alongside the tyrants, history also boasts some noble and godly monarchs who took the principle of accountability before God very seriously. Biblical examples include Hezekiah, Josiah, and, above all, David, a man after God's own heart.[35] More recent examples include the English kings Alfred the Great and Edward VI, and France's Louis IX (St. Louis). Godly kings have recognised not only their accountability to God, but also their limitations. David, at the end of his reign, confessed his failings. "The Rock of Israel spake to me: 'He that ruleth over men must be just, ruling in the fear of God'....My house (is) not so with God.[36]" It is this recognition of frailty in even the best of kings that has inspired Christians, wherever they have had significant influence in a nation's life, to develop a political system less dependent on one single sinful human being.

Democracy (Rule by the people)

Today most Christians feel more comfortable with democracy than any other model of government. Of all models of government it best fits Proverbs 11:14 – "In the multitude of counsellors there is safety" while it is also more conducive to the idea of restraint than monarchy. A few hints of democracy can be found in the Bible. For instance, in the Old Testament, the Israelites were told to appoint their judges and officers[37], with the implication being that these men were to be elected by the people. In the New Testament, the word translated "ordained" (AV) or "appointed" (NKJV, NIV) in Acts 14:23, referring to the choosing of elders in the churches of Pamphylia, is the Greek word *Cheirotoneo*, meaning "to elect or vote by a show of hands" which was the word used for voting in the democracy of ancient Athens – the city associated above all with the earliest developments of this mode of government. While these ancient Greeks who pioneered democratic government were pagans, this should not cause Christians to reject democracy as part of God's providence in the area of government. If creative arts, another blessing of God's providence, originated in the wicked and ultimately doomed line of Cain[38] rather than the godly line of Seth, then cannot God be behind the concept of democracy, even if it originated among pagans rather than His chosen people?

Democracy has unquestionably proved to be the best bulwark against tyranny, as it has enabled the population to some degree to hold its rulers to account and limit their powers. Furthermore, very few wars have been fought between democracies. Democracy has its faults, as will any system of government in a fallen world, but few Christians would disagree with Winston Churchill's rather sarcastic description of it as "the worst form of government except for all the others that have been tried."

There are two principal variants of democracy, both of which have been alluded to above. The choosing of officials and judges in the Old Testament is an example of **representative democracy**, where the electorate – in this case the Israelites – chose others to act on their behalf and represent the entire nation. However, while the choosing of elders by the churches in Pamphylia was also a type of representative democracy, the Athenian democracy which also used the word *Cheirotoneo* was a **direct democracy – in** other words, the people voted on the issues themselves rather than elected representatives to vote on their behalf. There was also no real separation of executive and judicial power in ancient Athens, with the assembly both enacting laws and acting as jury. Only male citizens were allowed to vote, and indeed the only reason these citizens had the time to engage in this time-consuming democratic process was due to the considerable slave population who naturally were not allowed to take part in it, but whose labours provided their masters with the time necessary. Non-citizens likewise were also ineligible to participate.

A detailed study of the development of democracy is beyond the scope of this book[39] as well as a digression from its main theme. Suffice it to say that many features of democracy as we know it today are recent developments, such as the competition between different political parties, the idea of government and opposition, or heated debates about the merits of first-past-the-post versus the various systems of proportional representation. In the UK, Holland and Scandinavia, a democratic government coexists with a constitutional monarchy – in other words, the king or queen is little more than a figurehead with an elected goverment wielding the real power. This concept would have been unthinkable in the period before Christ, or indeed for many years afterwards.

From the perspective of the early 21ˢᵗ Century, democracy appears to have been a great success story. Even the Athenian democracy, for all its shortcomings, would be viewed today as enlightened and progressive for its time. Since 1500, in countries such as Britain, Switzerland, the Netherlands and the USA where Evangelical Christianity has been particularly influential, the governments have been among the most democratic in the world – either republics or constitutional monarchies. Bearing this in mind, it is surprising that it took so long for a political system so conducive to freedom and restraint of tyranny to be widely accepted. Early critics included the philosopher Plato, who questioned whether the rank and file, even among the citizens, had the capacity for government. Later critics included the Victorian writer and historian Thomas Carlyle (1795–1881) who believed that in an industrial age democracy was incapable of addressing the unsatisfactory living and working conditions of the poor, and that a benign dictatorship was the only answer. Democracy has proved both men wrong. Several 19ᵗʰ Century American presidents, including Abraham Lincoln (1809–1865), were born into modest families, and would therefore have been deemed unsuitable even to participate in government by Plato, yet they rose to the highest office in the land. Likewise, democracy has not impeded a gradual rise in living standards in industrialised nations – indeed, living standards have been higher in industrialised democracies than in non-democratic industrial countries, as émigrés from the Soviet Union were to discover on arrival in the West – not that one could remotely use the word "benign" to describe the dictatorship in the former Union of Soviet Socialist Republics!

What are democracy's failings? With a representative democracy, particularly since the rise of party politics, those who are elected to office can all too often be pressured into toeing the party line to the detriment of the views of the people they should be representing. There are several issues where the views of the majority of British MPs and those of the electorate are not in line. Opinion polls, particularly since the Eurozone debt crisis, suggest that more people wish to see Britain leave the EU than those who wish to stay in. None of the leaders of the three largest political parties, nor any members of the cabinet or shadow cabinet side with the majority on this issue. Likewise, opinion polls conducted as recently as 2010 showed a majority support for the death penalty for certain types of murder, over 40 years after it was abolished[40]. Needless to say, supporters of capital punishment form only a small minority in the House of Commons.

One way round this mismatch is the Swiss model where a representative democracy is held to account by a limited use of the referendum – i.e. direct democracy. Switzerland is perhaps the best example in the world today of how democracy can restrain the size and power of government, as by making room for bottom-up initiatives which trigger a binding referendum if there is sufficient support, the electorate have the capacity to overrule the government when it is out of step with popular sentiment.

Unfortunately, as was noted above, elected politicians can become as intoxicated by power as absolute monarchs. This may explain why the Swiss model has not caught on more widely. Referendums have been held elsewhere, of course, and their sad history in the European Union shows that direct democracy too has its limitation: the Danes, having rejected the Maastricht Treaty in a referendum in 1992, had to vote again, as they had delivered the "wrong" result. The Irish were treated exactly the same way when they rejected the Lisbon Treaty in a referendum in 2008. It is no coincidence that many of the founding fathers of the EU, notably Altiero Spinelli (1907–1986), Paul-Henri Spaak (1899–1972) and Jean Monnet (1888–1979) were either avowed socialists or sympathetic to socialism, and Monnet in particular was contemptuous of both the nation state and democracy[41]. Socialism has often proved an uncomfortable bedfellow to democracy because of this issue of accountability. It has a habit of generating politicians who think they know best. Naturally, any person in authority who struggles with being accountable to the people will be even less comfortable with the idea of accountability before God. "We don't do God", said Tony Blair's spindoctor Alastair Campbell in 2003. It is hardly surprising that socialism has created politicians who have been every bit as tyrannical as some absolute monarchs, as its roots, like Nimrod's empire, lie in rebellion against God – a recapitulation of the sin of our first forebears in the Garden of Eden, who were seduced by Satan into thinking above their station – "Ye shall be as God.[42]" Like Adam and Eve, socialists are not content with the God-given task of being His vice-regents on earth, ruling it according to His revealed will. They want to make their own rules according to human reason and fleshly lusts. They want to be in total control. However, such has been the allure of democracy that in recent times many regimes with serious democratic deficits, socialist, Islamist and fascist alike, have at least gone through the motions of pretending to seek a popular mandate, even if the consequences for an individual who chose not to vote for the ruling party or an approved candidate could be quite severe.

Is there an even better model of government than democracy? Certainly not at the present time, but some 3,500 years ago one nation was ruled by God Himself, – surely the ultimate in good government, as the Ruler is perfect and thus needs no restraint whatsoever. Unfortunately, the nation He ruled did not always appreciate their unique privilege.

Theocracy (Rule by God)

The Israelites, when they entered the Promised Land, were marked out as a nation by their mode of government. Unlike their neighbours, they were to have no earthly monarch; God Himself was to be their king. Provision was made as far back as the time of Moses for the eventual emergence of a monarchy[43], but for a period of several hundred years, the Israelites operated under this unique system.

God laid the foundations for the Jewish theocracy during the wilderness years when He revealed to Moses how the Israelites were to behave when they entered the land of Canaan. These rules are set out in parts of Genesis, the latter part of the book of Exodus and much of the next three books – Leviticus, Numbers and Deuteronomy. Some of the laws related to the sacrificial system and to the annual feasts the Israelites were to keep, while others dealt with social and moral issues – ranging from dietary rules, inheritance, how to deal with infectious diseases and the punishment of offenders. Some of these laws sound very harsh to modern ears – the stoning to death of a woman who has engaged in sex before marriage[44], for instance. On the other hand other laws are remarkably humane and advanced for the period – the requirement to be generous to the poor[45], the principle of impartiality in the administration of justice[46] and the requirement to cancel debts after seven years,[47] for example.

It is quite remarkable how small the "government" actually was in the theocratic period. While agrarian communities in general need fewer rules and regulations than industrial nations, the picture of Israelite society painted by the early books of the Bible is that of a remarkably decentralised nation, with a strong sense of community. Each tribe lived in its allotted area, with local elders and officials chosen by the people being largely responsible for the administration of justice[48], although it appears that in some areas, the whole community would be involved. The priests had powers in other areas, including determining if marital infidelity had taken place.[49] They also served as health officials[50]. Education was the responsibility of the family[51], with parents teaching their children the law, and thus imbuing into them a love for it, which should have resulted in a considerable restraint of evil throughout the land. There were no import duties, the only restriction on trade being its total prohibition on the Sabbath day – a principle that was not always strictly enforced[52]. From time to time, God raised up leaders known as judges, who led the nation in battle, but the position was not hereditary, nor was the death of one judge necessarily followed by the immediate appointment of a successor.

There is a fascinating glimpse of Israelite society in chapters 2–4 of the Book of Ruth, which shows how well a community can function without big government. Boaz, a wealthy man, provides willingly and generously for the poor[53] and the redemption of Ruth is accomplished amicably with the aid of the local elders and community[54]. When God's laws are obeyed, there is no need for compulsory wealth redistribution to succour the poor, nor a massive bureaucracy to determine a land ownership issue.

However, the Israelite theocracy did not always work so well. It was a covenant between God and His people, and although God always kept his side of the bargain, the people were more fickle. The final chapters of the book of Judges depict a period when the Israelites chose not to obey God's laws, and consequentially were left with anarchy – no government at all. It is significant that two variants of socialism – classic Marxism and Anarchism – sought to eliminate government completely, believing that the result would be utopia. Judges 18–21 paints a very different picture: theft, marital infidelity, attempted murder, gang rape and civil war. The book closes with the observation that "every man did that which was right in his own eyes.[55]" It proves the point made earlier: fallen men and women will always need some government for their own good, for where there is no restraint, the result is not utopia but violent chaos.

The last of the judges was the prophet Samuel. In his old age, much to his dismay, he found himself confronted by demands from the people to be ruled by a king, like the neighbouring nations. The reason they gave was rather bizarre – "Thou art old and thy sons walk not in thy ways.[56]" Why should this have been a problem when the position of judge was not hereditary? God could have quite easily raised up another judge from outside Samuel's family. Samuel was deeply distressed. He warned the people that moving away from God's ordained pattern would lead to a much larger and expensive mode of government. Indeed, his speech, recorded in 1 Samuel 8:7–18, is one of the proof texts Christians have used to show that large government is not God's will. Samuel warns the nation that the establishment of a monarchy will disrupt family and community life[57] and would force them to make a substantial contribution to the running of the state[58]. It is significant in these days when public spending in Britain amounts to some 50% of GDP that Samuel's definition of big government was a tithe, or 10% of GDP!

Sadly, the people would not listen[59]. God told Samuel that their demand for a king was a rejection not of Samuel's ministry (nor, for that matter, of small government *per se*) but of Him and the unique theocratic government He had ordained for them, He told them that nevertheless, their demand was to be met, and that the Israelite nation was to become a monarchy[60]. As noted above, God had already anticipated this situation. In Deuteronomy 17, guidelines had already been laid out many years earlier, decreeing that the Israelite kings were not to be like those in the surrounding nations who flaunted their wealth, but should rather be faithful students of God's Word[61]. God ensured that even when the monarchy was established, the theocratic element did not totally disappear, so although the kings may have wielded considerable authority, they never became "absolute monarchs" in the classic sense of the term, for there remained a considerable separation of powers in the land. The priesthood remained a strong independent voice – on several occasions boldly confronting kings who overstepped the mark.[62] God also raised up prophets like Elijah,

Elisha and Jeremiah, who were equally fearless in challenging kings, making it clear that they were ultimately responsible to God, and if they broke His law, God would remove them. In the case of Israel, the Northern Kingdom, this often resulted in their entire families dying with them[63], although in Judah to the South, God preserved the line of King David, even though few of his successors were of the same calibre. Unsurprisingly the more wicked kings resented these prophets[64] and the restraint they exercised on their power, for they spelt out in no uncertain terms that while the model of government had changed with the retirement of Samuel, God's law – His guidelines for rulers – had not.

Following the captivity and exile of first Israel and then Judah, the Jews found themselves under the rule successively of the Babylonians, Persians, Greeks and Romans with only brief periods of independence in between. The last prophets ministered in the Persian period, and the canon of the Old Testament scriptures was completed at the same time. While the Jews reverenced the scriptures, especially the Mosaic Law, the presence of foreign rulers precluded them from being complete masters of their own affairs. Their unique theocracy was finished, although the Law which had set out its terms was to remain influential not only in the life of their nation, but in shaping governments in other lands as well.

Notes
[1] Proverbs 8:15.
[2] 2 Timothy 3:16.
[3] 2 Peter 3:13.
[4] Revelation 4:11.
[5] Genesis 3:14–19, Romans 8:19–22.
[6] Genesis 3:15.
[7] Genesis 1:28.
[8] Grudem, W *Systematic Theology*, p315 Zondervan, Grand Rapids/ IVP, Leicester 1994.
[9] Matthew 5:45.
[10] Galatians 6:10.
[11] Romans 13:4.
[12] Jeremiah 17:9.

[13] http://gregboyd.blogspot.com/2008/01/satan-government-and-christian-anarchy.html Accessed 28/01/2011.
[14] John 8:44.
[15] Philippians 3:20.
[16] See also 1 Timothy 2:1–2.
[17] These three forms of government are not the only possible models. There is also oligarchy (rule by a few), aristocracy (rule by a group of elite citizens) and military dictatorship. In their outworkings, these systems tend to resemble monarchy more than the other models considered. Anarchy (no ruler) is briefly considered in the study of theocracy.
[18] Genesis 4:17.
[19] Genesis 10:8.
[20] Genesis 10:10.
[21] Calvin's commentaries, Volume 1 Genesis p317 (Genesis 9:8) Baker Books Grand Rapids 1998. Originally published in 1554.
[22] http://ldolphin.org/babel.html Accessed 09/03/2012.
[23] Genesis 11:4.
[24] North, Gary, (1982) Genesis, The Dominion Covenant, p152, Tyler, Texas.
[25] Beyer, William C, (1959) The Civil Service of the Ancient World, Public Adminstrative Review XIX (3) American Society for Public Information p243.
[26] Genesis 41:38–45.
[27] Esther 3:6–14.
[28] 1 Kings 12:10–20.
[29] See for example 1 Kings 15:27–29, 2 Kings 8:14–15, 2 Kings 9:14–10:17.
[30] He renounced his divinity in 1945.
[31] 1 Samuel 9:16,17, 1 Samuel 16:12.
[32] Psalm 2:12.
[33] Catherine the Great was not Russian-born, and thus not strictly a tyrant of the same race as her subjects, although she had lived in Russia for many years before seizing the throne, and had converted to the Russian Orthodox faith, so could hardly be regarded as a foreign invader.
[34] Henry, M A Commentary on the Whole Bible Volume 1 p76 (Genesis 9:6–14) World Bible Publishers Iowa (originally published 1710).
[35] 1 Samuel 13:14.
[36] 2 Samuel 23:3, 5.
[37] Deuteronomy 16:18.
[38] Genesis 4:21.
[39] Readers wishing to pursue this subject should consult David Held's

Models of Democracy, (Third edition: Polity Press, Cambridge 2006) which traces the development of democracy from ancient Athens to the present day.

[40] http://ukpollingreport.co.uk/blog/archives/3802 Accessed 01/02/ 2012.

[41] Booker C and North, R *The Great Deception*, p443 Continuum Books, London 2003.

[42] Genesis 3:4

[43] Deuteronomy 17:14–20.

[44] Deuteronomy 22:21.

[45] Leviticus 25:35, Deuteronomy 15: 7–11.

[46] Deuteronomy 16:18–20.

[47] Deuteronomy 15:1–3.

[48] Exodus 18:18, Deuteronomy 1:15.

[49] Numbers 5:11–31.

[50] See, for example, Leviticus 13–15.

[51] Deuteronomy 4:9, 6:7.

[52] See, for example, Nehemiah 13:16–22.

[53] Ruth 2:15–16.

[54] Ruth 4:1–12.

[55] Judges 21:25.

[56] 1 Samuel 8:5.

[57] 1 Samuel 8:11,13,16.

[58] 1 Samuel 8:15,17.

[59] 1 Samuel 8:1–20.

[60] 1 Samuel 8:22.

[61] Deuteronomy 17:14–20.

[62] See, for example, 2 Chronicles 24:20–22; 27:16–20.

[63] See, for example, 1 Kings 14:10–11 or 1 Kings 16:1–4.

[64] See, for example, 1 Kings 18:17 or 1 Kings 22:3.

Chapter 2:

Jesus, Politics and the beginnings of a Christian Worldview

My kingdom is not of this world.[1]

Gospel, Church and Kingdom

Jesus was born into a highly politicised world. At the time of His birth, the Roman Empire dominated the Mediterranean region – one of the largest and most powerful empires the world had seen up to this time. The land of Israel had been under Roman rule since 63BC, although since 40BC that rule had been exercised via the Edomite puppet king Herod the Great. The Jews resented their subjection to Rome, and were looking for a warrior king to deliver them – a second King David who would drive out the occupiers and bring back the glory days of the Jewish state. A number of would-be Messiahs arose during Jesus' life, all of which were quickly and ruthlessly dealt with by the Romans. After He miraculously fed five thousand people, the crowd briefly entertained hopes that Jesus might be their liberator. The apostle John states that following this miracle "Jesus... perceived that they would come and take him by force to make him a king.[2]" Someone able to do such an amazing feat looked just the man to lead an insurrection. If he could supernaturally feed five thousand people, he might also be able to call down fire from Heaven like Elijah and deal the occupying army a devastating blow.

Jesus declined the offer of kingship. He had come not to deliver the Jewish nation from the bondage of Rome, but to deliver men's souls from the bondage of sin. He deliberately kept out of the political debates, even though His enemies tried to embroil Him. Matthew 22:15–22 tells of one particular trap sprung on Him by the Pharisees – "Is it lawful to give tribute unto Caesar or not?" To say these taxes were lawful would have enabled His enemies to paint Him as a toady for the oppressors, but to deny their legality would have enabled them to denounce Him to these very oppressors as an insurrectionist. Jesus' masterful reply, "Render….unto Caesar the things which are Caesar's and unto God the things that are God's" completely took the wind out of their sails and ensured His mission did not become entangled in the burning political issues of the time. Jesus talked frequently about a kingdom – called either the Kingdom of Heaven or the Kingdom of God by the different Gospel writers – and made it clear that His ministry marked the inauguration of this kingdom. However, although in reply to a question from the sceptical Roman procurator Pontius Pilate He admitted that He was a king[3], He stressed that His kingdom was not of this world.

There is an "already" and a "not yet" to Jesus' kingdom. One day, as the Bible informs us in numerous passages, Jesus will return to this earth, bring history as we know it to an end and set up His everlasting kingdom[4] in all its glory. Every knee will then bow before Him and every tongue confess Him as Lord[5]. Even now, the exalted, risen Jesus is "crowned with glory and honour[6]" in Heaven, in preparation, among other things, for the day when all men and women – including all rulers – will be judged by Him. Of the three models of government studied in the previous chapter, two will be merged in Jesus' kingdom – it will be both an absolute monarchy and a theocracy. There will be no democratic element at all, for unlike any earthly model of government, the need for restraint and sense of accountability which democracy engenders better than any other mode of government will not be needed, as the ruler will be sinless and so will His

42

subjects, for they will bear His image[7] – in other words, in our resurrection bodies we will be completely devoid of any contamination by sin, any desire to sin, and there will be no tempter present to incite us into sin, Such will be Christ's kingdom in all its glory – the "not yet" aspect.

At the present time "we see not yet all things put under him.[8]" The world in which we live is still fallen and sinful, even though Jesus' kingdom has been inaugurated and people have been "pressing into it[9]" for nearly two thousand years. Anyone who becomes a Christian becomes a citizen of this kingdom – in other words, they acknowledge Jesus as their Lord[10], and seek to obey His commands.[11] The motive for this obedience, which sadly, even in the holiest of men, will always be a very imperfect obedience, is loving gratitude for what Jesus has done in saving us, rather than any attempt at salvation through works, which besides being impossible, is completely unnecessary – as the penalty for the sin for all believers has already been fully paid by Jesus Christ on the cross.

The community of Christian believers is known as the church, which is related to the Kingdom of God, but not identical to it. The Kingdom is the rule of God; the church is a society of men[12]. When Jesus taught about the Kingdom, He was usually emphasising the individual believer's relation to God, whereas when He talked about the church, he was focusing on the community of believers. Theologians make a further distinction between the so-called "visible" and "invisible" church. Wayne Grudem defines the visible church as "the church as Christians on earth see it" while the invisible church is "the church as God sees it.[13]" The invisible church is a community consisting of every individual throughout all ages who has been chosen from before the foundation of the world for salvation,[14] and has professed faith in Jesus Christ as saviour. The visible church, which will be the focus of this and subsequent chapters, consists of local congregations at any one point in time, the greater majority of whom will be also part of the invisible church (and thus subjects of the kingdom), but there may be some members of local congregations who are not true believers, even if they appear to be so for a while on the surface[15]. Some of these spurious believers reveal their true colours after a while, but others do not, especially if their sins remain secret and do not involve any public scandal. Ultimately, only God knows the hearts of individual men and women.

Any community of fallible, sinful human beings – even a community the vast majority of whose members are Christians – requires both leadership and ethical guidelines. When considering the leadership of the early church, it is striking how many parallels can be made between the church and the Old Testament theocracy. In the first century, it appears that local churches were led not by one man but a team of elders, who were chosen democratically by the church members, just as the village elders in the Old Testament. Jesus made it clear that church leaders were not to behave like despots, and stressed their accountability to their congregations: "Ye know that the princes of the Gentiles exercise dominion over them, and they that are great exercise authority upon them. But it shall not be so among you; but whosoever will be great among you, let him be your minister; and whosoever will be chief among you, let him be your servant, even as the Son of man came not to be ministered unto but to minister.[16]" The Apostle Paul adds the requirement that church leaders were not to be covetous or violent men[17]. Church leaders were to imitate the supreme Head of the Church in His gentleness and restraint. The decentralised nature of the early church, where individual congregations had a considerable degree of autonomy, did not totally prevent the rise of ambitious, unsuitable leaders[18], but the lack of any elaborate hierarchy limited their scope for empire building. The only men in the early church who functioned at an authority level higher than the local church eldership were the apostles – men chosen by Jesus Himself, and given an unique authority to establish churches, which manifested itself, among other things, in their power to work remarkable miracles[19]. By the beginning of the second century, only a few years after the death of St. John, the last survivor of the apostles, leadership by a plurality of elders began to be replaced by a single "bishop.[20]" However, the new bishops did not claim to be successors to the apostles. "I do not enjoin you, as Peter and Paul did," wrote Ignatius, bishop of Antioch, to the Romans, as he travelled to Rome in 107AD to be put to death for his faith. "They were apostles, I am a convict.[21]"

Another parallel between the Israelite theocracy and the early church was the strong emphasis on compassion. In the Gospels, Jesus is described as being moved with compassion[22], and from the earliest days of the church, ordinary men and women and individual churches followed in their master's footsteps as they displayed the love of Christ to those around them. Dorcas, commended in Acts 9 for her practical care, was the first of many Christians to be remembered by posterity for having left a legacy of good works. Christian compassion was characterised by its bottom-up nature and by the voluntary principle. Christians were strongly encouraged and expected to care for one another, but were allowed, for instance, the discretion to give as they felt able[23]. Unsurprisingly in such circumstances, the administration of that charity was also handled carefully and not dished out willy-nilly. The Apostle Paul, writing to his young assistant Timothy, instructs him to make sure that receipt of charity was confined the deserving poor – those with no means of support. The undeserving poor, who "live in pleasure" and "learn to be idle, wandering about from house to house" were not to receive financial aid[24]. Christians also gave willingly to support needy believers further afield. The New Testament tells of Paul's appeal on behalf of the believers in Judaea, who were suffering from a famine at the time,[25] to which the Gentile churches responded generously[26].

As with the Israelite theocracy, there were, sadly, disciplinary issues to be addressed in the church. Jesus urged that disputes between church members should be settled by the parties in question if possible, and only involve the whole church as a last resort[27]. However, on some occasions, some formal sanctions were necessary, including the removal of the believer from church membership[28].

This study of the early church is not a digression from the main theme of the book, for having brought out the parallels between the early church and the Old Testament Israelite theocracy, it is logical to suppose that God's guidelines for government of the nations should follow a similar pattern. There will be in every nation a need to protect and provide for the vulnerable, a need to administer justice in the event of wrongdoing, and a need to restrain tyrannical leadership. Jesus had taught His disciples to pray "Thy will be done on Earth as it is in Heaven[29]" so when it came to determining how they were to bring to pass God's will on this earth, the guidelines provided by His dealing with Israel and the church – God's special people in the Old and New Testament periods respectively – must surely be the starting point. The challenge Christians have encountered in developing their political thought will be considered in this and the two following following chapters, along with the obstacles they faced.

The components of a Christian political worldview (1) Compassion

The care shown by the Christian community to each other has already been pointed out. However, as was noted in the previous chapter, Christians are encouraged to do good to all men[30]. For the first 300 years of church history, intermittent persecution by the Roman empire limited the opportunities for Christians to care for individuals outside their immediate community, but when this came to an end, a wider sphere was opened up for Christian compassion. So extensive, for instance was the Christians' care for the poor in the 4th Century that the emperor Julian (361–363), remembered for his belated and futile attempt to revive paganism, bemoaned the fact that the "godless Galileans," as he contemptuously referred to Christians, "supplied not only their own but even the heathen poor.[31]" St. Basil of Caesarea (328–379) founded one of the world's first hospitals in the city in which he was bishop. It also contained a poorhouse and a hospice. Care for the poor and needy continued to be a feature of the church even in the spiritually degenerate Middle Ages. St Bartholomew's Hospital in London, the oldest hospital in Britain, was founded in 1123 by the monk Rahere (d. 1144), as an act of obedience to St Bartholomew whom he believed had appeared to him in a vision while on a pilgrimage to Rome.

These examples further underline the voluntary and bottom-up nature of Christian compassion. There were instances, however, where concern for the vulnerable by individual Christians did ultimately require the involvement of the state, for in certain instances, the only effective way of addressing certain injustices is through legislation. One individual Christian whose actions led to a change in the law was Telemachus (d404) who was so appalled at the inhumanity of gladiatorial combats, where slaves fought each other to death for public entertainment, that he travelled from the Eastern Mediterranean to Rome to make a protest. Leaping into the arena of the amphitheatre to disrupt the show, he was stoned to death by an angry mob. On hearing of his tragic death, the emperor Honorius banned these grisly spectacles shortly afterwards.

With church leaders now being consulted by emperors rather than persecuted by them, it was inevitable that the compassionate spirit of Christianity would result in the passing of legislation that restrained exploitation and protected the weak. In 321AD, Sunday was declared a day of rest by the emperor Constantine (306–337). The courts were not to sit and no secular labour was to be undertaken, apart from essential agricultural work. This law would have provided a welcome day of rest particularly for the slave population of the empire. Constantine also granted women the same rights as men to control their property except in the area of selling their landed estates. In 315, he banned the practise of branding criminals on the forehead on the grounds that "the human countenance formed after the image of heavenly beauty should not be defaced.[32]" The poor

47

were protected by law from extortion by judges, and although there was no move to abolish slavery during this period, marriages of slaves achieved legal recognition for the first time. In 374, infanticide was made a capital offence. This is the Biblical pattern for Christian compassion – the passing of legislation to protect the vulnerable in society is the responsibility of the state, but the actual caring process – feeding the hungry, nursing the sick and dying – is the responsibility of individuals and communities.

Christian involvement in social action is viewed by some in our own day as a distraction from the preaching of the Gospel. However, our 4th Century counterparts rightly saw that Jesus' command to love our neighbour was not in any way opposed to the call to proclaim the good news of salvation. Sometimes, of course, it actually complements it, for Christian compassion can be a factor in bringing someone to faith in Jesus, although not always. In the Gospels there are several accounts of individuals being healed or blessed by Him, but who did not respond to His call. We likewise are called to care for our fellow men, whether they are Christians or not.

The components of a Christian political worldview (2) – Liberty

Whenever Christians have had any influence in a country's government, the result has been an increase in liberty for the citizens of the nation in question. There are several reasons for this. Firstly, any rulers or legislator steeped in the knowledge of the Scriptures cannot fail to notice either the emphasis on servant leadership, or divine condemnation of cruel and oppressive regimes[33]. Furthermore, aware of the sufferings of many believers over the years, Christians, as compassionate people, do not want to see their fellow human beings groaning under the yoke of harsh tyranny.

It took until after the period covered in this chapter for all the components essential for true Christian liberty to be developed, but one important element – the need to limit the size and scope of government – was discussed as early as the 5th Century by one of the most profound Christian thinkers of all time. Indeed, Augustine of Hippo (354–430) was one of the first theologians to look at the whole area of government through Christian eyes. He made the point that the need for government arose only as a consequence of the fall. God "did not intend that His rational creature, who was made in His image, should have dominion over anything but the irrational creation – not man over man, but man over the beasts.[34]" It was Augustine who first recognised that restraint was one of the most important roles of government, and that some degree of coercion is an unfortunate necessity brought about by the sin of man.

However, although Augustine grants the state this important role, he allows it only the level of authority which consensus allows, and in a world made up of believers and unbelievers, the degree of consensus is not likely to be very large. On a few basic issues everyone will agree:– "Whoever gives even moderate attention to human affairs and to our common nature will recognise that if there is no man who does not wish to be joyful, neither is there anyone who does not wish to have peace.[35]" But how can there be any large-scale agreement between the believer and the unbeliever beyond such elementary desires? Best therefore to restrict government to "the things necessary for the maintenance of this mortal life[36]" rather than look to it to solve all man's problems. This argument was centuries in advance of its time, and is particularly relevant to the religious and ideological pluralism of our present age.

Augustine also emphasises servant leadership: "Even those who rule serve those whom they seem to command, for they rule not from a love of power, but from a sense of duty they owe to others – not because they are proud of authority but because they love mercy[37]." Although such sentiment seems somewhat idealistic, countries like the UK and the USA have produced some fine examples of men and women going into politics to serve rather than to rule:– "As I would not be a slave, so I would not be a master" said the

American president Abraham Lincoln (1809–1865).

Augustine's teaching, especially the idea that government was a necessity only brought about by man's sin, demoted the state from the elevated position it enjoyed in Greek thought, which still dominated the ancient world at the time. In Plato's *The Republic*, for instance, the state "secures the basis for the citizen to fulfil his calling[38]" – a far more exalted view of government than Augustine's. Servant leadership accountable to the people and committed to doing the bare minimum – the maintenance of order, the provision of peace and the enforcement of legal contracts – will of necessity be government modest both in scale and ambition.

At the root of Augustine's support for limited government was his emphasis on the importance of the individual. Plato taught that there was a perfect world beyond this earth, and this earth was an imperfect copy of the "real" world above. He thus regarded individualism as a trait of this imperfect world, and thus something to be overcome. Augustine, while also recognising the imperfection of this present world, took a very different view of the individual. Of all the early Christian writers, Augustine was the most comprehensive in his treatment of the subject of divine grace – that Christian salvation is a free and unmerited work of God in accordance with His eternal decrees. However, he held this teaching in balance with an emphasis on human responsibility – that every individual is responsible for their sin, and cannot plead ignorance about God's existence and His requirements[39]. However, Augustine's focus on the individual also had a positive angle. The individual was an eternal being, created with a soul and spirit as well as a body, and therefore of value. "A man cannot hope to find God unless he find himself," wrote Augustine in his autobiographical *Confessions*. While Augustine had much to say in his writings about the Fall and its consequences for man, he did not regard individualism as having originated as the result of the Fall, seeing rather it as a God-given uniqueness to be cherished and not, like Plato, a defect to be eliminated.

The components of a Christian political worldview (3) Moral Restraint

Although Augustine argued in favour of small government to ensure that the coercive element should be as small as possible, he made the point that some form of restraint of evil will always be necessary in a fallen world, or else nations will slide into lawless anarchy. This in turn requires some definition of evil that will be acceptable to believer and unbeliever alike. For a Christian ruler, the obvious place to look for such a definition would be the Bible, for there in His Word, God sets out certain standards for all men.

One of the most notable attempts prior to 1500 to grant any sort of prominent role to the Bible in the compilation of a nation's law code can be found in the *Liber Justicialis* or *Domboc* of England's King Alfred the Great (871–899). Alfred inherited a legal system that cannot be said to be Biblical in origin – the Saxon and Viking invaders who occupied Britain in the centuries after the Roman legions withdrew in 410AD were probably responsible for much of what was later known as Common Law, but for all its pagan origins, this system recognised that there was a higher source of right and wrong than the decrees of kings and emperors – indeed, the king himself was subject to the law. Discovering what this higher source was actually saying, which in Britain has often involved the laborious process of case law (judicial decisions that are derived from the application of particular areas of law to the facts of individual cases) requires humility on man's part, along with much patience.

Nonetheless, English Common Law, like democracy, can be regarded as another example of a providential blessing which originated among pagans, but which has been widely appreciated by Christians. The American legal scholar J. Reuben Clark Jr (1871–1961) highlighted its virtues: "The sovereign power in a Common Law system rests exclusively with the people. Individual rights, by extension, become a fact of daily life that cannot be breached by an aspiring tyrant without bloody consequences. Over time, this system of judge-made law allows for the gradual development of an organic legal framework whilst minimising encroachments upon individual rights.[40"] As a Christian, Alfred would naturally have identified God as the ultimate source of law, and thus gave English Common Law a more pronouncedly Biblical character than it had exhibited previously. His law code begins by quoting the Ten Commandments and contains many other quotations verbatim from the Bible. Its 120 chapters, although devoid of any logical arrangement, are believed to be so numbered because Moses died at the age of 120, thus making a very clear statement that this law code was meant to be a reflection of God's laws adapted to suit Anglo-Saxon Wessex.

A godly king looking to the Scriptures for the basis of his laws will inevitably leave a legacy of greater liberty for his subjects, as has been noted above. Indeed, Alfred laid a foundation which resulted in Englishmen, even in the Middle Ages, valuing their freedom more than their contemporaries on mainland Europe. However, he was very much a man of action rather than a theologian. His quotation of the Bible was a step in the right direction, but there was no detailed exegesis of Biblical texts to work out in any great detail how to apply the Scriptures to the nation's life. Indeed, Alfred's law code hardly began to scratch the surface of the most important issue facing any ruler desiring to build his nation's laws on God's laws – the relevance of the Old Testament in the New Testament era. The teaching of Jesus – in fact, most of the New Testament – dealt more with how the individual Christian or the church as a whole was to relate to the world than about how the nations were to be governed. Christians are told that government is a good thing[41], that they are to be good citizens[42] and to pray for their rulers[43], but the New Testament does not go into anything like the level of detail found in the Old. One of the most common mistakes made by Christians throughout the ages has been to ignore the fact that the greater part of Jesus' teachings – and the Sermon on the Mount in particular – were addressed to Christians but rather to treat them as if they were addressing rulers and lawmakers in their capacity as governors of nations, which they clearly are not. Alfred did not go into sufficient detail to fall into this trap, but Dr Martyn Lloyd-Jones illustrates the fallacy of this approach in his study of Matthew 5:38–42, quoting the example of the Russian writer Leo Tolstoy, who, when talking about not resisting evil and turning the other cheek, "did not hesitate to say that these words of our Lord are to be taken at their face value. He said that to have soldiers or police or even magistrates is unchristian.[44]" Tolstoy's proposals, if adopted, would have led to anarchy, with criminals being unpunished. They ignore the fundamental truth that God has decreed that certain evils are to be punished in this world, and this task has been delegated to magistrates and rulers. Christian meekness and forgiveness do not negate the need to maintain law and order in society. As a general rule those who erroneously apply to rulers and nations those teachings of Jesus which were aimed at the church tend to ignore the Old Testament, and the Mosaic law in particular.

This is a grave mistake, for Jesus Himself emphasised the ongoing relevance of the Old Testament when He stated quite specifically that he had no quarrel with the Mosaic law. He came not to destroy it, but to fulfil it. Furthermore, He added that "till heaven and earth pass, one jot or one tittle shall in no wise pass from the law till all be fulfilled.[45]". The issue that needs to be addressed, therefore, is not whether the Old Testament has an on-going application in the New Testament age, but how it is to be applied.

A different approach was inevitably going to be required compared to its application under the unique Israelite theocracy. Returning to Jesus' confrontation with the Pharisees over the question of paying taxes to Caesar mentioned briefly at the start of this chapter, Jesus' reply to their loaded question indicated God and Caesar, and therefore church and state, were separate. This was in contrast to the time of Moses where "church" (or rather, "the earthly manifestation of covenant people of God") and "state" were one. This explains, to take just one example, why the punishment for the person found guilty of sacrificing their children to Molech was to be carried out by "the people of the land" and not by a magistrate or any other agent of the state[46]. Even the Roman Catholic Church of the Middle ages, which had departed drastically from the essentials of the Gospel, still maintained this distinction. The Bull "Unam Sanctam" of Pope Boniface VIII (1294–1303), one of the most extreme statements of papal power prior to the 19th Century, took the reference to the two swords by Jesus in Luke 22:38 to imply that the sacred and secular realms – church and state – had both been committed by Jesus to the Papacy. Unquestionably poor exegesis, but still an important statement from a spiritually degenerate age that church and state were two separate entities, or "spheres" as Abraham Kuyper was later to call them. Adherence to this principle lay behind the pantomime of committing condemned heretics to the secular authorities for execution rather than the death penalty being carried out representatives of the church. "Ecclesia non sitit sanguinem" (The church does not thirst for blood).

Well before the time of the Reformation, a consensus had emerged among the majority of Christian commentators of a threefold division of the Mosaic law. Indeed, Jonathan Bayes, in a well-researched article, argues that the concept of a division in the law can be found in the Scriptures themselves[47]. The first division comprised the rules relating to the sacrificial system, which were a type of acted prophecy pointing to the one sacrifice of Jesus on the cross of Calvary. Being thus fulfilled there was no need for the church to continue with a priesthood or sacrifices. Secondly, there were the civil or "badge" laws, designed to mark the Jews out as a particular people, but not to be enforced on the Gentile believers in the church – the prohibition of the use of two different types of material in clothing being an example of this sort[48]. Finally came the moral law, such as the Ten Commandments, which were to be regarded as God's standards for all times and all nations. Even if, as the Apostle Paul frequently points out in his epistles, the keeping of the Law is impossible in its totality for fallen human beings[49], and that as a result of our failures with regards the law, no-one can be regarded as righteous in God's eyes[50], this section of law still sets out God's moral restraints. Every nation where Christianity has taken root has rightly looked to a greater or lesser extent to the Pentateuch for guidance when framing their laws.

However, there have always been two problems facing every Christian ruler. Firstly, there is the issue of how exactly the moral law passages should be understood and applied. Even taking such important and well-know injunctions as the second table of the Ten Commandments, any Christian legislator needs to consider that if the state must punish thieves and murderers – issues upon which there is almost universal consent – should it likewise punish liars and adulterers? – after all, lying and adultery are condemned as strongly as theft and murder in the Ten Commandments. Secondly, for all the strong arguments in support of a threefold division of the Law, the Pentateuch is not conveniently divided into three, and there are a few grey areas where it is not completely clear whether some individual verses fall into the "civil" or "moral" category.

It was to be many centuries after Alfred's death before these questions were tackled in any great detail for reasons that will be considered below. Nonetheless, in looking to the Bible as the source of law, he laid the third foundation of a Christian political worldview alongside compassion and liberty.

Restrictions to the development of a Christian political worldview (i) Most Governments don't like being limited.

While the three basic components of a Christian political worldview had all slowly crystallised by the time of Alfred's death, a number of changes had already taken place within the church which acted as stumbling blocks towards any further progress. In fact, even before Augustine propounded his argument for limited government, rulers who professed the Christian name were exhibiting the same love of the trappings of power as their pagan predecessors. This unfortunate trait is illustrated by the life of Constantine the Great and his immediate successors. Constantine was the emperor who finally brought the persecution of Christians by the Roman Empire to an end. After receiving what he believed to be a vision of a shining cross in the sky and the words, "by this conquer," he vowed in 312AD to follow the God of the Christians if he gained a victory over his rival Maxentius (306–312) in the battle of Milvian Bridge. This military triumph started a process that ended with Christianity becoming the official religion of the Roman Empire by the end of the 4th Century.

Constantine is a classic example of the concept of restraint discussed in the previous chapter. The influence of Christianity on the laws passed during his reign has already been noted, but of his actual conversion there is much doubt. Certainly neither he nor his successors would have supported as limited a view of government as Augustine was shortly to expound nor would they have looked to the Bible to play such a prominent role in their legislative processes as Alfred. Following the removal of the nerve centre of the Roman Empire from Rome to Byzantium, which he re-named Constantinople, Constantine and his successors began to adopt a most extravagant lifestyle which was meant to proclaim their greatness to all and sundry. According to a contemporary account the court of Constantine's son Constantius (337–360) included a thousand barbers, a thousand cup bearers and a thousand cooks[51]. Arcadius (395–408) rode in a chariot set with precious stones, seated on a snow-white cushion drawn by white mules with gilded trappings[52].

By the time of Justinian (527–565), Christianity had become very much a tool of subjection. The emperors were using the Christian faith to bind their empire together, much as their predecessors in the first centuries AD had used the old paganism as a test of loyalty. Constantine's precedent of imperial interference in church affairs, which began when he called the council of Nicaea in 325AD to resolve the Arian heresy, which denied the divinity of Christ, proved a double-edged sword, for he and his successors used that same authority to keep the church firmly under their control. Justinian is a good illustration of the uncomfortable consequences of too close an alliance between church and state. While being a man of great outward piety, he kept a determined grip on power that showed itself distinctly intolerant of dissent, either political or theological. It is perhaps ironic that while it was Justinian who finally outlawed paganism and closed the neoplatonic philosophy school in Athens, his model of kingship owed far more to the exalted view of the state derived from pagan philosophers whose teaching he sought to outlaw than to the Christian faith he supposedly professed. Certainly, for all the talk of Byzantium being a new theocracy and the emperors being likened to David or even Melchizedek, Augustine's ideal of servant leadership found little echo in the Byzantine Empire.

Justinian was responsible for the compilation of the most celebrated collections of law from the ancient world, the *Codex*, also known as *Corpus Juris Civilis*. While including much Christian-inspired legislation initiated by Constantine and his successors, it also retained much from Rome's pagan past – for example, in its reaffirmation of the ancient distinction between freemen and slaves. The most important feature of Justinian's Codex was that law was essentially what had been decided over the years by legal experts, and since the third century in particular, what the emperors had decreed. Consequently, while reflecting the influence of Christianity, the Codex concentrated too much power in the hands of the authorities, making them, rather than God, the ultimate arbiters of what is right and wrong. Unlike English Common Law therefore, under Roman law (and Justinian's *Codex*) "The sovereign power rested in the head of the state, who granted to the people, his subjects, the rights he decided they should have, reserving any other rights in himself, as likewise the right to extend, alter, add to, or withdraw these rights already granted.[53]" Such an environment is not conducive to the development of Christian liberty.

Justinian's *Codex* was adopted in parts of Italy within his own lifetime, and spread to much of Western Europe in the 12th Century. It formed the basis of Napoleon's legal reforms in early 19th Century France and even today forms the basis of the legislation of most countries in the European Union. Obviously, no country uses all Justinian's Codex verbatim 1500 years later, but the top-down "law is what we say it is" Roman influence remains. It is for this reason that virtually all recent authors addressing the renewal of their nation's laws on the basis of the Bible tend to be citizens of countries such as Britain and the USA, whose legal systems are derived not from Roman law but from Common Law with its greater openness to a higher authority than man.

The tradition of interference by the state in the affairs of the church established by Constantine and Justinian lasted in what became known as the Orthodox churches right through to the 20th Century, when the Soviet Union ensured that the leaders of the Russian Orthodox Church were suitably compliant individuals who would not openly criticise the Marxist-Leninist régime. In the West, the reverse happened as the bishops of Rome gradually became more powerful. Constantine's relocation of the imperial capital to Constantinople resulted in the decline of the political importance of Rome. The government of the western, Latin-speaking part of the empire moved firstly to Milan and then to Ravenna, and the line of emperors in this area came to an end in 476AD following the capture of Rome by the barbarian Visigoth Odoacer. The Roman bishops stepped into the political vacuum, and in due time began to acquire the trappings of the imperial power which they, in effect, superseded. The title *Pontifex Maximus* (literally, the greatest bridge-builder), which was one of the historic titles of the Roman emperor, and which had been used in connection with the official state religion, was appropriated by the Roman bishops at some stage between the 4th and 6th centuries, and is used by their successors to the present day. They also adopted another most inappropriate title in view of their increasing power – Servant of the Servants of God (*Servus servorum Dei*). The term was first used by Gregory I, bishop of Rome from 590 to 604, a man with a very exalted view of his position, but of genuine personal humility. He had not wanted this office, and only reluctantly agreed to abide by the will of the people who had elected him unanimously following pressure from the Byzantine emperor. Few of Gregory's successors shared much of his humility, yet held an even more exalted view of the office of bishop of Rome, which by the 8th Century included both spiritual and temporal rule – taking over the government of an area of Italy that included the city of Rome.

The papacy, as it had become by this time, was the very antithesis not only of Augustine's teaching on limited government, but also – in spite of the adoption of Gregory's title – of Jesus' teaching on servant leadership. The papacy adopted instead the absolutism of Roman imperialism, paying scant regard to any concept of accountability. In the late 11th century, the popes, not content with their own little kingdom, began to flex their muscles in the rest of Western Europe, claiming not only spiritual but political oversight here too. Limited government – indeed any real advance in liberty – was never going to be on the agenda in any country owing allegiance to men claiming such extensive power as the mediaeval popes.

Hand in hand with the growth of papal power came an increasing departure from the Gospel. The great doctrine of Justification by faith alone had largely been obscured centuries before the rise of the papacy, and in its place had evolved a religion emphasising salvation by works, prayers to Mary and the saints, a belief that the bread and wine at the Communion table turned miraculously into the actual body and blood of Jesus, along with a host of other teachings not found in the Bible. Any person with access to a Bible could not fail to notice the growing contradiction between the teachings of the mediaeval church and the scriptures. To circumvent this scenario, the laity were banned from owning a Bible, especially in any language other than Latin. The first known prohibition took place in 1229 at the Council of Toulouse, where Canon 14 stated, "We prohibit also that the laity should be permitted to have the books of the Old or New Testament; unless anyone from motive of devotion should wish to have the Psalter or the Breviary for divine offices or the hours of the blessed Virgin; but we most strictly forbid their having any translation of these books[54]" Further decrees banning Bible ownership followed in other parts of Europe.

The Bible was now to be interpreted as the church decreed. Traditions were granted equal weight to its teachings. In such circumstances, God's Word was neither going to have the chance to bring liberty nor be treated by kings and rulers as the basis of moral restraint.

Restrictions to the development of a Christian political worldview (ii) Monasticism.

By the 5th Century, the compassionate spirit of Christianity had left its benign mark on the government of nations where Christianity had taken root. This process slowed down, indeed ground to a halt, by a movement that encouraged keen Christians to turn their backs on the world instead of seeking its further renewal.

The origins of monasticism can be traced back to the end of official persecution by the Roman Empire in the early 4th Century when some Christians began to feel uncomfortable with the worldliness which was becoming more prevalent in the church. Imperial support for Christianity led to many people now attending churches for other reasons than because they had become Christians. The first Christians to retreat into contemplative isolation had already departed into the wilderness before the fires of persecution had died down. Paul of Thebes (228–340) was a young man when he fled into the Egyptian desert to escape the persecution instigated by the emperor Decius (249–251). The Decian persecution was the first systematic empire-wide persecution, and although especially vicious, was mercifully brief. However, when the emperor's death brought in less pressured times for the church, Paul decided he liked life in his cave, and remained there even though it was safe to return.

His isolation ended when he was befriended by Antony (251–356), who likewise settled in the Egyptian desert. Antony, regarded as the father of monasticism, lived to see the end of Roman imperial persecution. Seeking the martyr's crown, he left his solitude on numerous occasions during the final great persecution of Diocletian (284–305) and Maxentius (306–312), appearing in Alexandria to encourage those already condemned to death. Although the authorities declined to arrest him, his bravery gained him a reputation as a holy man, and his return to the solitude of the desert after the persecution set a trend whereby the more zealous Christians, unable to seal their faith in blood, chose instead to withdraw from society into a remote spot to live a life of self-denial and contemplation.

Monasticism in its early days attracted all manner of eccentrics who indulged in the most bizarre feats of self-denial in the name of Christianity. The extraordinary "pillar saints" lived for years on end at the top of high, unsheltered pillars, exposed to the elements and sometimes only eating once a week. Other hermits declined to wash or comb their hair, regarding poor personal hygiene as a sign of holiness! Such extremes never caught on in Western Europe, as much due to the unfavourable climate as anything else, but even the more organised communal monasticism of Benedict of Nursia (480–547) shared the same trait of renunciation of the world, including marriage.

While the single life has scriptural support[55], there is no justification for the exaltation of celibacy and monasticism to the point whereby the married Christian in a secular occupation is viewed as a second-class believer. Nor is there any justification for the setting up of dysfunctional communities which withdrew Christians from the more natural communities of church, family and neighbourhood. Indeed, by the 11th and 12th centuries, the monastic life was sometimes forced on young men against their will thanks to the widespread custom of the eldest son being the sole heir of his parents' estate (the right of primogeniture.) Monasteries became convenient dumping grounds for younger sons of the nobility, who may not necessarily have felt the slightest call to the contemplative life – or to celibacy for that matter. While the first monks retreated to the wilderness out of a genuine desire to seek God, the austerities that monasticism demanded of its adherents further encouraged the decline from Biblical Christianity towards works-based religion. By the Middle Ages, legalistic penances had superseded repentance as the recommended pathway to finding forgiveness with God. Penances were a form of works that were meant to pay the price of sin. The mediaeval bishops often imposed penances after wars. For example, after the battle of Soissons in 923, the Frankish bishops imposed a three-year penance on all who had taken part. Every participant had to fast on bread, salt and water for three 40-day periods each year[56]. Rather than endure this privation themselves, the members of the respective armies paid monks to undergo this penance on their behalf. In an age where warfare and violence were endemic, a strange symbiosis thus developed between the warriors and the monasteries, and ultimately resulted in the monasteries ending up as extremely wealthy landowners, as the nobility were happy to pay out money in various ways not just for the monks to undertake these penances, but also in the hope that founding and maintaining these institutions would save their souls. This hope was sadly misguided, as was the abdication of personal responsibility for sin which resulted from the idea of transferable penances. The treatment of the individual as a responsible, albeit fallen human being, is an essential component of Christian liberty that the Middle Ages chose to ignore, and much of the blame for this has to be laid at the door of the monasteries.

To be fair to monasticism, it did carry on the tradition of practical Christian care. Alms were distributed to the poor, and the old and infirm were cared for. These institutions "provided a kind of mediaeval nursing home plan. If you lived – rather unusually – to a good old age, you could pay a sum of money to the monastery which would then look after you until you died.[57]" Furthermore, monasticism throughout the mediaeval period attracted to its ranks men who, while unquestionably misguided in their enthusiasm for what was an unbiblical institution, exhibited genuine piety and faith. For example, Columba (c521–597) often referred to as the apostle of Scotland, founded the monastery of Iona and preached the gospel most effectively to the surrounding neighbourhood. Several hundred years later, Bernard of Clairvaux (1091–1153), a man highly regarded by Luther and Calvin particularly for his adherence to the doctrine of justification by faith in an age when it was largely unknown, was a Cistercian, one of the most austere of all monastic orders. Such illustrious and godly men as these cannot, however, excuse monasticism's shortcomings. Benedict had stressed the importance of work in his celebrated rule, but to what end? To avoid idleness, certainly, but was this all? So many of the "good works" undertaken by monks, such as vicarious fasting or praying for the souls of the dead, were hardly the type of good works enjoined by Jesus. If the supposed spiritual élite were living such an unbalanced impersonal and unbiblical life, what example was being set to the rest of the population? Furthermore, how could the government of nations ever be remodelled on Christian lines when those regarded as being in the vanguard of the church had withdrawn from society?

Restrictions to the development of a Christian political worldview (iii) Lukewarm attitudes to private property and trade.

Another vital component of Christian liberty is the right to private property. If the state's role is to be limited as Augustine had argued, so should be its demands on its citizens. The scriptures offer strong support for the right of individuals to own property. Mosaic law placed a strong emphasis on inheritance, with tribal and family lands regarded as inalienable, albeit ultimately belonging to God and held on trust. Jesus, although unwilling to act as an arbiter in a dispute about inheritance[58], never challenged the right of individuals to own property and to pass it down from generation to generation. Furthermore, the New Testament uses the concept of inheritance on several occasions to illustrate the future awaiting the Christian in glory[59] – a strange analogy to use if God is opposed to private property

There were two reasons why support for private property was so limited in the period under consideration. Firstly, the monks and friars did not own any property. They were required to take vows of poverty and live with all things in common. Such a lifestyle, it was claimed, was true to the apostolic ideal, for the earliest church of all, in Jerusalem, had "all things common[60]". The fact that this communal living was unique to the Jerusalem church and not a feature of life in the Gentile churches subsequently planted by the Apostle Paul and others did not appear to enter into the thinking of the early monastic enthusiasts, especially as monasticism was able to build on an earlier tradition of hostility to private property. The most extreme statement on this subject comes from the pseudo-Clementine homilies, a Christian romance written probably in the 2nd or 3rd century, which stated that "For all men, possessions are sins." St. John Chrysostom (354–407) argued that ownership of private property was a cause of strife. "When one attempts to possess himself of anything, to make it his own, then contention is introduced, as if nature herself were indignant, that when God brings us together in every way, we are eager to divide and separate ourselves by appropriating things, and by using those cold words 'mine' and 'thine'.[61]"

In the Middle Ages, hostility to private property was more muted. Thomas Aquinas (1225–1274) whose *Summa Theologica* is one of the most important and influential writings of the entire Middle Ages, only allowed private property as an unfortunate necessity. Community of goods was part of "natural law" – the participation of rational creatures in God's eternal law, but "The ownership of possessions is not contrary to the natural law, but an addition thereunto devised by human reason[62]". He called these additions "positive laws" to which he assigned a subordinate position compared with natural law. To allow Christians to own private property was a step forward from the hostility of the Patristic age, but it was a somewhat grudging concession on a par with the supposed need for the institution of slavery[63]. The belief that the earliest men lived in a supposedly ideal society where all goods were held in common was a concept that was to surface again many years after the mediaeval theologians had largely lost their influence.

Free trade and commerce were fiercely debated issues in the Middle Ages. Certain theologians, notably Henry of Langenstein (1325–1383), argued that there should be a "just price" determined by the state, based on the cost of production. Duns Scotus (d1308) allowed for a certain element of profit on top of the production costs[64] but disapproved of the price of articles being determined by market forces. Lurking behind the mediaeval theologians is the shadow of Aristotle (384–322BC), whose works became popular in the universities of Western Europe during the 13th Century and which profoundly influenced Aquinas in particular. Aristotle regarded any form of production for material gain as wrong, only giving his approval to commercial activities that aimed to bring a perceived benefit to others[65]. This is hardly the teaching of the Bible, which in no way condemns profit, as long as it is not the result of exploitation or in violation of the Sabbath[66].

The views of Aquinas on the subject of a just price have been hotly debated in recent years, but at the very end of the period under consideration, a more enlightened view of the market economy – in other words, freedom to trade for a profit without the state (or church) determining the price – began to develop in Spain in the writings of several theologians who were influenced by his writings. Luis Saravía de la Calle (c. 1544) of Salamanca taught that the just price for an object was market price, determined by the forces of supply and demand. He also pointed out that the price of a thing will change in accordance with its abundance or scarcity[67]. A just price, therefore, could include a profit margin. Another Spanish theologian, Diego de Covarrubias y Leiva (1512– 1577), taught that an object's value was determined by supply and demand, with demand including both scarcity and the subjective opinions of men in different parts of the world[68].

Spain was isolated from the developments to be considered in the next two chapters, and thus, these men and their writings had no influence on the development of Evangelical political thought, but their ideas were to be resurrected and developed in the 20th Century by men who were to play an important part in influencing, among others, the greatest British Prime Minister of the last half century, and the one most influenced by the Bible's teaching.

The challenges of the Renaissance.

The mediaeval church of 1300 presented an image of great power and magnificence, epitomised by its splendid cathedrals, elaborate liturgies, patronage of great artists and the voluminous writings of its theologians. However, behind the outward splendour was an organisation whose departure from the essentials of Biblical Christianity was actually hindering the renewal of society on Christian lines.

Although not apparent at the time, its long period of dominance was about to come to an end. The change can be dated to a quarrel between the arrogant pope Boniface VIII and the French king Philip the Fair (1285–1314). The conflict began with Boniface's anger over Philip's taxation of the French clergy. It escalated to the point where Philip was excommunicated. Papal sanctions had brought many a king into submission during the previous 250 years, but Philip's defiant response was to send an army to Rome, sack the city and take the pope prisoner. Five years after Boniface's death, his successor Clement V, a Frenchman and very much under Philip's influence, moved the Papal court to Avignon in France. All the subsequent popes until 1378 were Frenchmen. When an Italian pope was elected in 1378 and moved back to Rome, the French cardinals decided to choose a rival pope who stayed in Avignon. For nearly 40 years, the western church found itself with two, sometimes three men, all claiming to be its true spiritual leader. The papacy suffered a loss of prestige from these events from which it has never recovered.

These developments were symptomatic of wider changes. Although some examples of genuine piety can be found as late as the 15th Century, notably the celebrated *Imitation of Christ* by Thomas à Kempis (1380–1471), the papacy's loss of prestige was part of a wider disaffection with the mediaeval Roman Catholic Church. It was failing to address men's needs in a changing world, and few of its leading representatives commanded much respect, being widely regarded as hypocrites or worse[69]. The disciples of John Wycliffe (c1330–1384) in England and of Jan Hus (d1415) in Bohemia actually broke away on doctrinal grounds, challenging many elements of Roman Catholic teaching. Wycliffe encouraged his followers to look not to the teachings of popes and councils but to the Bible as their authority. With such "heresy" punishable by a painful death, few others went this far, but gone were the days when wealthy princes or noblemen would found a monastery or nunnery in the belief that it would earn them a place in Heaven. As the discovery of new trade routes and inventions such as the printing press brought growing prosperity to Europe in the fifteenth century, its principal beneficiaries were quite happy to conform outwardly to the ordinances of the church, but preferred to use their wealth to patronise artists and musicians, set up a library or build a fine new house to dwell in. Venice, Florence and other Italian cities openly flaunted their increasing wealth in the late 15th Century, and even in England, the court of the flamboyant king Edward IV (1461–1483) was thoroughly worldly.

Furthermore, the church of the late Middle Ages was totally unable to offer any real guidance to the rising generation of merchants and tradesmen seeking to live a life in a secular profession for the glory of God, nor to the far more important question of how to find peace with God. There were answers, of course, in the Bible, and circumstances providentially conspired to raise its profile in the late 15th and early 16th Centuries. The fall of Constantinople to the Turks in 1453 brought the Byzantine Empire to an end and resulted in an exodus of scholars to Western Europe. These Greek-speakers carried with them their Greek New Testaments, and their arrival heralded a revival of interest in the study of the New Testament in its original language. The term "Renaissance" (Literally "Rebirth") often used of this period, refers to the desire of the nobility, the merchants and bankers both for a greater level of education and a broader base for that education. No longer merely content with Aquinas and other mediaeval theologians, this new generation of scholars revived the study of the ancient civilisations of Greece and Rome. Studying the New Testament in Greek fitted perfectly into this broader quest for knowledge and the renewed interest in the classics, but it was to develop into something far beyond anything that could have been imagined – a move of God that was to reshape the face of Europe.

Notes

1 John 18:36.
2 John 6:15.
3 John 18:36–37.
4 Daniel 7:14.
5 Philippians 2:10–11.
6 Hebrews 2:9.
7 1 Corintians 15:49.
8 Hebrews 2:8.
9 Luke 16:16.
10 Romans 10:9,1 Corinthains 12:3.
11 Luke 6:46–49, John 14:21.
12 G.E. Ladd, as quoted in Grudem, W, *Systematic Theology*, p863 IVP Leicester/ Zondervan Grand Rapids, 1994.
13 Grudem, W, *Systematic Theology*, p855–6, IVP Leicester/ Zondervan Grand Rapids, 1994.
14 Ephesians 1:3–5.
15 Matthew 13:24–30, 36–43, Acts 20:30, Philippians 3:18–19.
16 Matthew 20:25–28.

[17] 1 Timothy 3:3, Titus 1:7.
[18] See, for example, Diotrephes, mentioned in 3 John 9–10.
[19] 2 Corinthians 12:12, Acts 3:1–10, 5:13, 10:36–40, 14:8–10, 19:11, 20:7–12.
[20] The word "bishop" (*episkopos*) was used interchangeably with "elder" (*presbuteros*) in the Apostolic period – see Philippans 1:1.
[21] http://www.earlychristianwritings.com/text/ignatius-romans-lightfoot.html. Accessed 24/01/2012.
[22] See,for example, Matthew 9:36, Mark 1:41, 6:34, 8:2.
[23] 2 Corinthians 9:2,7.
[24] 1 Timothy 5:3–16..
[25] Acts 11: 27–30, Romans 15:25–26,1 Corinthians 16:1.
[26] 2 Corinthians 9:1–3.
[27] Matthew 18:15–17.
[28] 1 Corinthians 5:2.
[29] Matthew 6:10.
[30] Galatians 6:10.
[31] Schaff, P. *History of the Christian Church*, Volume 3, p50. Scribner 1910/Eerdmans Grand Rapids 1989.
[32] *ibid*, p121.
[33] See, for example, 2 Kings 24:3–4 Jeremiah 22:1–7, Ezekiel 34:1–10, Micah 3:1–4.
[34] Augustine, *City of God* Book XIX Chapter 15 translated by Marcus Dods, Eerdmans, Grand Rapids, 1988.
[35] *ibid*, Book XIX Chapter 12.
[36] *ibid*, Book XIX, Chapter 17.
[37] *ibid*, Book XIX Chapter 14.
[38] Held, D *Models of Democracy* (Third Edition), p26 Polity Press Cambridge 2006.
[39] Augustine is developing the argument made by the Apostle Paul in Romans 1:18–32.
[40] http://www.tfa.net/2012/03/26/a-new-old-legal-settlement/
[41] Romans 13:1–4.
[42] Romans 13:5–7, 1 Peter 2:13–17.
[43] 1 Tim 2:1–3.
[44] Lloyd-Jones, M *Studies in the Sermon on the Mount*, Volume 1 P275 Eerdmans, Grand Rapids 1959–1960.
[45] Matthew 5:18.
[46] Leviticus 20:2.
[47] See http://www.christian.org.uk/html-publications/theology/three-fold.pdf Accessed 09/03/2012.
[48] Leviticus 19:19.
[49] Romans 7:15–23.

[50] Romans 3:10,23.

[51] Schaff, *op cit*, p129.

[52] *ibid.*. p129.

[53] http://www.tfa.net/2012/03/26/a-new-old-legal-settlement/

[54] http://www.aloha.net/~mikesch/banned.htm Accessed -09/03/2012.

[55] See, for example, 1 Corinthians 7.

[56] Southern, R.W. *Western Society and the Church in the Middle Ages*, p226, Penguin Books, Harmondsworth 1970.

[57] Bartholomew, J. *The Welfare State we're in*, p27, Politico's London, 2004.

[58] Luke 12:13–14.

[59] See, for example, Ephesians 1:14, 18; 1 Peter 1:4.

[60] Acts 2:44.

[61] Quoted in Robbins, J *Ecclesiastical Megalomania*, p31 The Trinity Foundation 1999, USA.

[62] Thomas Aquinas, *Summa Theologica* ii-ii, 2nd article, as quoted in Robbins, J *Ecclesiastical Megalomania*, p31 The Trinity Foundation 1999, USA.

[63] Robbins, *Op cit* p31.

[64] http://mises.org/daily/2357 Accessed 25/02/2012.

[65] Hayek, FA, *The Fatal Conceit*, p46. University of Chicago Press, Chicago, 1988.

[66] Amos 8:5–6, Nehemiah 13:15–18, Micah 6:10–11, Leviticus 19:35–36.

[67] http://mises.org/daily/2357 Accessed 25/01/2012.

[68] *idem.*

[69] See, for example, Chaucer's treatment of the monk, the friar or the pardoner in his *Canterbury Tales*, or Dante's *Inferno* where several popes are placed in the second lowest circle of Hell.

Chapter 3:

The development of a Christian worldview (1) – Calvin and the Reformation

Thus, when dealing with all the concrete problems such as money, wages, property, etc, instead of seeking out norms based on natural morality, which would be applicable for everyone regardless of their spiritual state, the reformer aims to bring man back before his living Lord.

André Bieler, *La Pensée Economique et Social de Calvin, p516.*

When a German monk with a troubled conscience opened his Bible and found peace with God through faith in Jesus Christ, he had no intention of starting a revolution The ninety-five theses which Martin Luther (1483–1546) nailed to the door of the Castle Church in Wittenberg were a challenge to the Roman Catholic Church to debate the precious truths he had discovered, not a call for separation. However, the popes, bishops and cardinals did not wish to reform the church's teaching according to the Word of God and fought Luther and his teachings tooth and nail. Luther was a man with a conservative temperament, but faced with such intransigent opposition, he was left with no choice but to withdraw from a church whose leader he had come to regard as the Antichrist and "the most hellish father of Christendom[1]".

In reality, the Roman Catholic authorities were fighting someone far greater than Luther, someone against whom they could not possibly prevail. God began a work in the early 16ᵗʰ Century that grew into the most remarkable and widespread revival that the church had experienced since the days of the apostles. This powerful movement of the Holy Spirit, known as the Reformation, was centred on the Bible and its message that man must be reconciled with God through faith in Jesus Christ alone. What began in a monk's cell ended up shaking the entire continent of Europe, with only Portugal remaining completely untouched. In Scotland, during the second part of the 16ᵗʰ Century, the scale of the Holy Spirit's work was quite extraordinary – "Whereas in other nations the Lord thought it enough to convert a few in a city, village or family to himself, in Scotland the whole nation was converted by lump[2]" wrote one historian. Even though few, if any, other nations could talk of revival on quite this scale, across Europe many thousands of men and women were converted. Even some kings, queens and princes professed the great truths of the Gospel.

The rediscovery of the doctrine of justification by faith was Luther's great contribution to the Reformation, but he was not the man to progress the work any further. In the words of André Bieler, "In the Bible, Luther had rediscovered the primitive faith of the church – direct communion with the living God; but he stopped there; preoccupied with so many urgent problems, and not able to find in it a concern for the 'temporal city' which it inspires.[3]" This is not to say Luther ignored political issues in his writings. In his exposition of 1 Peter, published in 1523, he wrote, "Civil government is confined to external and temporal affairs...If an emperor or prince asks me about my faith, I would give an answer, not because of his command, but because of my duty to confess my faith before everybody. But if he should go further and command me to believe this or that, I would say, 'Dear sir, mind your secular business; you have no right to interfere with God's reign and therefore I shall not obey you at all.'[4]" In his later years, Luther no longer supported such a degree of freedom of belief nor the separation church and state. He was dependent on the support of successive electors of Saxony throughout the rest of his life, and largely for reasons of expediency, accepted their leading role in sustaining the Reformation even at the expense of the independence of the church. However, by allowing the "godly prince" essentially to step into the shoes of the bishops, Luther had shut the door to building any sort of coherent Christian worldview. The limitations of his thinking were graphically illustrated in 1525 when the German peasantry rose up in revolt against their masters. Luther started off as a peacemaker, travelling around at the risk of his life to preach against the use of violence, but when violence did break out, he totally and unequivocally supported the authorities, sometimes using quite extreme language against the peasant army. "You cannot meet a rebel with reason. Your best answer is punch him in the face until he has a bloody nose", he wrote. Such sentiments prove that Luther was not looking to the Scriptures for guidance in temporal matters in the same way he had done in spiritual. This was the weakness of the Lutheran reformation.

Calvin's work in Geneva

The Reformation in Switzerland pursued a different course, notably in Geneva under John Calvin (1509–1564) who arrived in the city in 1536 only intending to stay for one single night before moving on to Basel or Strasbourg. Providence determined otherwise, and apart from three years in Strasbourg (1538–41), he remained in Geneva for the rest of his life. Even before persecution had forced Calvin to flee his native France in 1535, he was putting the finishing touches to the first edition of his great systematic theology, the *Institutes of the Christian Religion*. At the heart of Calvin's theology was the sovereignty of God. Calvin is associated in popular thinking with the doctrine of predestination – in other words, certain people end up becoming Christians because God decreed it before they were born. However, this is only one facet of God's sovereignty. Besides ruling over the individual, He is sovereign over the affairs of nations and indeed over the whole universe.

So while Calvin was in total agreement with Luther that man is saved by faith in Christ alone and not by works, he went far beyond Luther in applying the Bible to every area of social and political life as well, constructing from the scriptures a comprehensive Christian worldview based on God's sovereignty. A number of factors combined to magnify his influence. Firstly, his legal training equipped his naturally tidy mind to tackle the issues involved in a well-structured manner. Secondly, he lived in an age where there was something of an ideological vacuum, with mediaeval theology being widely discredited and as yet no influential secular worldview capable of competing with his thought. Thirdly, the city state of Geneva, with its elected assemblies, had a type of government that could readily put Calvin's teachings into practice. His success in this area is all the more remarkable considering that for much of his time in Geneva he faced strong opposition from a highly influential group of citizens known as the Libertines. Only when a failed coup d'etat in 1555 led to the flight of his opponents could Calvin's teaching take root unopposed in the life of the city. It must be emphasised at this point that Calvin was a pastor and theologian, not a politician. He never held civic office and did not even become a citizen of Geneva until 1559. However, those of his supporters involved in the government of Geneva inevitably sought his opinions on political matters, and usually followed his advice. When the lawyer Germain Colladon (1510–1594) began a revision of the city's code of laws in 1560, Calvin was naturally consulted.

The fourth factor that magnified his influence was the rapidly changing social, political and religious scene in Europe at the time which compelled Calvin to address a number of contemporary issues in great detail in order to refute opposing views. This point is particularly significant. Christian truth, while existing in the Bible from the beginning, has most frequently been systematised and developed when

confronted with serious error. The denial of the divinity of
Christ by Arius in the beginning of the 4th Century led to the
compiling of the Nicene Creed and other historic statements
of faith that fully affirm the deity of Father, Son and Holy
Spirit and the doctrine of the Trinity. In the same way, the
teachings and practises both of Roman Catholicism and some
groups on the fringe of the Reformation provided the stimulus for Calvin to forge his teachings from the scriptures in
order to refute their errors. There is, however, one important difference as far as the issues relevant to this book are
concerned. The Arian controversy revolved around finding
the right answer to a single yes/no question – was Jesus God
or not? When looking at the development of a Christian
worldview, rather than seeking to define truth, the issues
concern the application of truth. There are so many subjects
to tackle, and so many passages of the Bible to weigh and
interpret. When it comes to the finer points of how God's
will is to be put into practise in the life of a nation, it is unreasonable – indeed impossible – to expect total consensus in
every area. Some aspects of Calvin's work in Geneva have
been rightly criticised by subsequent generations, but he
nevertheless built a firm and solid structure based on the
same threefold foundation mentioned in the previous
chapter – compassion, liberty and Christian restraint. His
immense labours were built upon by others in the 17th
Century, with certain emphases changed and most of the
excesses eventually corrected. However, the debt that Christian political thinking owes him cannot be overstated.

Compassion

Calvin's concern for the poor and oppressed will strike any
reader of his writings. There were plenty of poor people in
Geneva during Calvin's time, including a large number of religious refugees fleeing persecution elsewhere, some arriving
penniless. "If these people are rejected by us and we allow
them to die of poverty", said Calvin,, "what a crime this will
be considering that God commends the poor stranger to

us.[5]" God "gives us the poor, which are in our midst," he adds, "so that they may be helped." Calvin displayed this same concern for the poor through the practical measures he instituted to organise their relief. In the Genevan *Ecclesiastical Ordinances* of 1541, which was largely his work, four "ordinary offices" were defined – pastors, teachers, lay elders and deacons. The deacons were subdivided into two groups – those who administered alms and those who devoted themselves to the poor and the sick[6]. "Scripture specifically designates as deacons those whom the church has appointed to distribute alms and take care of the poor, and serve as stewards of the common chest of the poor,[7]" he wrote in the *Institutes.*

Relief for the poor was a particular problem for any city or country which rejected the teachings of Roman Catholicism. For all the faults of monasticism, the monasteries had at least offered a facility to care for the destitute and elderly. Wherever the Reformation triumphed, the monasteries disappeared. This was not only due to the Reformers' teaching that monastic vows were unscriptural. Those monks and friars who wished to continue in their profession tended to be fierce opponents of the Reformation and thus were forced to migrate to another city or country where Roman Catholicism still held sway. Geneva had taken steps to address this problem before Calvin's arrival in the city. The city had declared for the Reformation in 1535 and only a few months after the inevitable departure of the monks and nuns, a hospital had been established to provide assistance for the sick, the poor, orphans, and the elderly.[8] Although this hospital had been established by the city rather than the church, the actual relief and care of the poor was entrusted to officers of the church – i.e. the deacons – under Calvin's ordinances. This emphasis on church participation in the relief of the poor alongside the state makes an interesting comparison with the approach taken in England following Henry VIII's dissolution of the monasteries in 1536–1540. In the Elizabethan Poor Laws of 1563–1601 care of the poor was entrusted to the parish (the "local government" of the time) with the people of the parish legally obliged to provide the necessary finance after an attempt to finance care for the poor through voluntary means, with the threat of dragging reluctant givers before the bishop, proved inadequate[9]. While this was, in a sense, state intervention, responsibility was at least decentralised to the local community, who would have had the discretion to judge who were the truly deserving poor. In a tight-knit city state like Geneva, the entire population could be counted as a single community, and thus it would have likewise been reasonably easy to discern the genuine poor from the indolent.

It is in connection with compassion for the poor that Calvin's teaching on charging interest should be considered. The mediaeval church had taken the ban of Deuteronomy 23:19 regarding the charging of interest absolutely literally, although there were ways of circumventing it. Calvin was prepared to take a softer line: "Reason does not suffer us to admit that all usury is to be condemned without exception.[10]" He argued that a total ban on lending money at interest was only applicable in the context of lending to the poor, but "if we have to do with the rich, usury is freely permitted.[11]" Calvin's reasoning is that money can beget money, and if a person makes a considerable profit by borrowing some money for a project, should not the lender be entitled to a share in that profit? "If any rich and monied man, wishing to buy a piece of land, should borrow some part of the sum required of another, may not he who lends the money receive some part of the revenues of the farm until the principal shall be repaid?[12]" Commenting on Psalm 15:5, he adopts a similar line, saying that although at first glance, all usury appears to be condemned, "it follows that the gain which he who lends his money upon interest acquires, without doing injury to anyone, is not to be included under the heading of unlawful usury.[13]" "The end for which the law was framed was that men should not cruelly oppress the poor, who ought rather to receive sympathy and compassion.[14]" Calvin's support for lending money at interest, which he openly acknowledges to be based on reason, has been questioned in recent years,

although the influence of his writings led to the rapid abandonment of the prohibition of usury in countries where the
Reformed doctrines prevailed. However, he was no friend of
bankers: "It is scarcely possible to find in the world a usurer
who is not at the same time an extortioner, and addicted to
unlawful and dishonourable gain....It is also a very strange and
shameful thing that while all other men obtain the means of
their subsistence with much toil...that moneymongers should
sit at their ease without doing anything and receive tribute
from the labour of all other people.[15]" Calvin speaks approvingly of the year of Jubilee (Leviticus 25) as a God-ordained
method of redressing the extremes of wealth and poverty. It
"gave relief to the poor that their liberty should not be
destroyed....it was a kind of imposing memorial of the sacred
rest, to see slaves emancipated and suddenly become free;
houses and lands returned to their former possessors who
sold them; and.....all things assuming a new face.[16]" In his
comments on the earlier verses in the chapter, which discuss
the seventh year Sabbath, where the land was left fallow, he
stated that God's purposes here were "to remind them that
(the land's) fruits were nevertheless common to all during the
Sabbatical year.[17]" He did not argue from these verses, as
some have subsequently attempted to do, that the state
should compulsorily redistribute goods from the rich to the
poor. On the contrary, he emphasised that although
landowners had to share the produce of their land every
seventh year, in the other six years, "the possessor might
boast that the property was its own, and consequently that
the harvest should be left entirely to himself.[18]"

In the light of Calvin's emphasis on compassion, it is no
surprise that he was a strong opponent of slavery. There
were no slaves in Geneva, but following the discovery of the
New World by Columbus and the voyages of the Portuguese
round the west coast of Africa, the transatlantic slave trade
had come into existence before Calvin arrived in Geneva,
having been sanctioned by Charles V, King of Spain (and later
Holy Roman Emperor) in 1517[19]. Calvin would have been
aware of this insidious traffic, and his comments on Genesis

12:5 should be viewed in this context: "It appears that not long after the deluge, the wickedness of man caused liberty, which by nature, was common to all, to perish with respect to a greater part of mankind.[20]" Elsewhere, in discussing the death penalty prescribed for kidnappers in Deuteronomy 24:7, he adds, "The same punishment is here deservedly denounced against man-stealers as against murderers, for so wretched was the condition of slaves that liberty was more than half of life, and hence to deprive a man of such a blessing was almost to destroy him.[21]" Slavery is "contrary to every order of nature,[22]" he added in a sermon on Ephesians 6:5–9. As mentioned in the previous chapter, the coming of Christianity had not led to the abolition of slavery in the lands where it took root. One reason for this is that slavery was not condemned outright in the Old Testament, being permitted in certain circumstances in Ancient Israel. While no Israelite was to retain a fellow countryman as a slave for more than seven years, unless the individual in question chose to remain a slave[23], there were no such restrictions on non-Hebrew slaves, who were often enslaved after being carried away captive in war[24]. The Mosaic law required slaves to be treated in a humane fashion, and in particular, if their owner injured them deliberately, they were to be set free[25]. Such compassion formed a stark contrast with later Roman law, which treated slaves as property with no rights whatsoever. However, the lack of any unequivocal condemnation of slavery in the Old Testament resulted in it being as late as the 19th Century before Evangelical Christianity arrived at any sort of consensus that slavery was wrong. Calvin's arguments were thus many years in advance of his time, as will be noted in the following chapter.

Regrettably, Calvin did not show the same humane spirit in opposing torture. Writing to his friend and fellow-reformer Guillaume Farel (1489–1565) about one of the conspirators in the failed 1555 coup, who had been captured and imprisoned, he wrote, "Before ten days, we shall see, I hope, what the rack will wring from him.[26]" All that can be said in Calvin's defence is that, in this instance, he failed to rise above the spirit of the age. Torture was widely sanctioned in 16th century Europe, regardless of the religious persuasion of the government.

A more positive side of Calvin's compassion was his insistence on measures to improve the cleanliness and health of the citizens. The magistrates were to supervise the markets in Geneva to prevent unhealthy food being sold, and refuse was to be cleared from the narrow streets of the city[27]. He was also concerned to ensure that the refugees who settled in Geneva were able to make a living, and encouraged the Council to support the silk-weaving trade to boost employment. He thus can be accredited with laying the foundations for the later prosperity of Geneva by the practical measures he proposed to relieve poverty.

Another weapon against poverty is education, and by the time of Calvin's death, besides having a hospital, Geneva also boasted one of the world's first free schools. To be exact, the Academy of Geneva was a composite institution comprising a "private school" (*schola privata*) offering elementary instruction, and a "public school" (*schola publica*) for older students which was more akin to a theological college. Founded in 1558, the Academy was teaching 1,200 junior and 300 senior students by the time of Calvin's death six years later[28]. Calvin had looked to the civic authorities to fund this project, but there was not sufficient money available, so finance had to come from gifts and legacies[29]. Support for new schools was a characteristic of many of the Reformers. A number of towns and cities in England still boast a "King Edward VI Grammar School" – testimonies of a similar concern for education of the poor by the young Christian king whose tragic death aged only fifteen was a great loss to the Reformation.

Liberty – (1) Private property

The suppression of monasticism was part and parcel of the Reformation's emphasis that marriage and family life – as opposed to living in unnatural celibate communities – should be the norm for Christians, even those engaged in Christian ministry. However, a Protestant version of community living – albeit comprised of family units rather than celibate individuals – sprang up among some of the Anabaptist groups that emerged in the 16th century in opposition not only to Roman Catholicism but to the principal reformers such as Luther and Calvin.

We shall return in more detail to the Anabaptists in the following chapter. However, Calvin's support for private property must be considered in the light of his vehement opposition to the views of the Anabaptists, including the community of property practised by the Hutterites and radicals of Münster. His comments on Acts 2:44, which was used as a proof text by these Anabaptists groups, are particularly significant. "This place has need of a sound exposition because of fanatical spirits," he writes. "In this age the Anabaptists have raged because they thought there was no Church unless all men's goods were put and gathered together, as it were, in one heap, that they might all with one another take thereof.[30]" He points out that in Acts 4, Luke "names two alone which sold their possessions of so many thousands.[31]" The community of goods in Jerusalem, in other words, was voluntary, and came about as a result of a particular situation – "that the poor might be relieved as every man had need.[32]" Calvin's teachings on private property and compassion were closely linked. Hence while strongly refuting any talk of Biblical insistence on community of goods, Calvin did not teach the unconditional absolute right to property as defined in Roman law, for example, which went as far as giving a male property owner the right of life and death over his wife, children and slaves. God gives us goods as stewards – in other words they are ours on trust. Riches are to be used to relieve the needs of the poor. Commenting on Jesus' challenge to the rich young ruler to sell all that he had and give to the poor, Calvin says, "Christ applauds not simply the selling but liberality in assisting the poor....To keep what God has put in our power, providing that, by maintaining ourselves and our family in a sober and frugal manner, we bestow some portion on the poor is a greater virtue than to squander all.[33]" As for the rich, he states that they "have greater abundance given them on the condition that they may be ministers of the poor in the dispensation committed to them by God.[34]" but significantly, he offers no divine mandate for compulsory wealth redistribution. "No sacrifice is pleasing to God if it is not voluntary,[35]" he writes.

Liberty (2) The size of the State

Government is a good thing, said Calvin, as it is God's ordained method of restraining evil. The preservation of peace had already been identified by Augustine as one of the most important functions of government, and Calvin vigorously rejected the teaching of certain Anabaptist groups who taught that government was "a thing polluted which has nothing to do with Christian men", and that the church could reach such perfection that no civil government was required.[36] "Since the insolence of evil men is so great, their wickedness so stubborn, that it can scarcely be restrained by extremely severe laws, what do we expect them to do if they see that their depravity can go scot-free – when no power can force them to cease from doing evil?[37]"

The state is also the only authority able to regulate commerce to ensure it is conducted in an honest manner. God is strongly opposed to dishonest trade practises, for "if the laws of buying and selling are corrupted, human society is in a manner dissolved.[38]" Calvin thundered out against deceitful weights and measures like an Old Testament prophet: "If the weights and measures are false, there will not be any more commerce. No one will be able to buy or sell. Men will be like wild animals....[39]"

Action by the state to ensure honesty in commerce was all the more important in a society supporting the right to private property and inheritance. "It is necessary for the preservation of human society that some should acquire property by purchase, that to others it should come by hereditary right, to others by the title of presentation, that each should increase his means in proportion to his diligence, or bodily strength, or other qualifications. In fine, political government requires that each should enjoy what belongs to him.[40]" In subsequent comments on this verse, Calvin expresses no objection to riches as long as it is accompanied by generosity rather than greed. However when commenting on Joseph's proposal to Pharaoh to store up grain in the years of abundance in order to prepare for a famine, he is prepared to make an exception when affluence leads to frivolous waste, saying that "because luxury generally prevails in prosperity and wastes the blessings of God, the bridle of authority was necessary.[41]" Likewise, he is supportive of "laws by means of which a rage for superfluous expenditure shall be in some measure restrained.[42]"

This support for state intervention to restrain luxury may seem controversial, but less so than Calvin's teaching on the state as the guardian of true religion. Commenting on 1 Timothy 2:2, he defines the preservation of 'godliness' in this context as being "when magistrates give themselves to promote religion, to maintain the worship of God, and to take care that sacred ordinances be observed with due reverence.[43]" But is it the role of the state to go this far? – especially bearing in mind that Geneva had replaced the uniformity of Roman Catholicism with a new uniform Reformed Protestantism. Refugees from other countries were welcome and free to worship in their mother tongue, but no doctrinal dissent was allowed. Calvin was nonetheless quite unequivocal in affirming the church/state distinction. Commenting on one of the most important passages to address this subject, Jesus' statement in Matthew 22 about rendering to Caesar the things that are Caesar's and to God the things that are God's, he writes, "There is a clear distinction made between spiritual government and the political or civil government,[44]" and in the section in the *Institutes* dealing with church discipline, he states that it "depends for the most part...upon spiritual jurisdiction.[45]" In Geneva, however, the dividing line between the responsibilities of church and state was not as clear in practise as it appeared to be in theory. It was the punishment by the state of one particular individual for a spiritual offence (doctrinal dissent) that has generated more criticism of Calvin than any other aspect of his work in Geneva, a subject to which we shall return shortly.

In order to function, governments need funds, and Calvin, in accord with Romans 13:6, affirms the legitimacy of taxation. "Tributes and taxes are the lawful revenue of princes,[46]" he states, but with the important proviso that taxes must be modest in scope and not squandered by rulers on extravagances. "Let them consider that their imposts and levies, and other kinds of tributes are nothing but supports of public necessity, but that to impose them upon the common folk without cause is tyrannical extortion.[47]"

It is significant that many of the extracts from Calvin's commentaries that relate to government are taken from the Old Testament and the Pentateuch in particular. However, in applying these texts to the contemporary situation, he recognised that the unique nature of the Israelite theocracy, where in many cases "the people" acted as God's agents rather than "the state[48]", could not be recreated in the New Testament era. While any Christian must surely agree that the state must assume responsibility for such areas as the punishment of offenders, the prominent role given by Calvin to the state in the area of compassion was not repeated – and with good reason – by the Christian thinkers who will be considered in the next chapter. Nonetheless, Calvin may still be reckoned an unequivocal supporter of small government. "How highly pleasing to God is a mild administration of affairs among men.[49]" he wrote. Calvin taught that rulers are accountable both to their people and to God. There are few better ways of limiting the size of the state than this two-way accountability, which is an elaboration of Augustine's concept of servant leadership. The accountability of all rulers before God is set forth in a number of passages in the Old Testament, including sections of the books of Amos, Isaiah and Jeremiah where God pronounces judgement on a number of states surrounding Israel, and also Psalm 2. Commenting on the latter, Calvin writes, "The beginning of true wisdom is when a man lays aside his pride and submits himself to the authority of Christ. Accordingly, however good an opinion the princes of the world may have of their own shrewdness, we may be sure they are arrant fools until they become humble scholars at the feet of Christ[50]." After all, as he writes elsewhere, "all magistrates...rule by command of God and are sent by him.[51]"

But there is a second accountability too. Rulers "are not to rule for their own interest, but for the public good; nor are they endued with unbridled power, but what is restricted to the well-being of their subjects; in short they are responsible to God and to men in the exercise of their power. For as they are deputed by God and do his business, they must give an account to him; and as the ministration which God has committed to them has a regard to the subjects, they are therefore debtors also to them.[52]"

One practical example of accountability to the people has already been mentioned. When Calvin sought funding for the Geneva Academy he had to rely on donations and legacies because the Council did not have sufficient money. A modern administration in a similar situation would probably have decided unilaterally to impose additional taxation to address the shortfall or to take a loan (a government bond in other words), which the people would have had to pay back with interest at a later date. Small, accountable government may be more modest in what it aims to achieve, but at least it is more likely to live within its means.

The accountability of government was more important to Calvin than the mode. He had no objections to the principle of monarchy as long as kings were compassionate and godly. He had a sufficiently high regard for England's godly young king Edward VI as to dedicate several Bible commentaries to him. As already noted, the Geneva where Calvin resided from 1536–8 and from 1541 to his death was ruled in a very different way – a self-governing republic under the protection of neighbouring Berne and the Swiss Confederation. The government (which combined the roles of executive and judiciary) consisted of three councils: the Small Council of twenty five members, the Council of Sixty, the least important of the three, and the Council of Two Hundred (the Great Council) The Small Council included four syndics (or chiefs of state), two secretaries and a treasurer, and maintained ultimate jurisdiction in all affairs of state. It supervised the conduct of all public officials. It also acted as the court of final appeal in any disputes. The primary role of the Great Council was to vote on legislation presented by the Small Council and, each February, to elect members to that Council. It could also grant pardons to convicted criminals[53]. The officers of the Great Council were chosen democratically, although the franchise was limited to male citizens.

It was noted in Chapter 1 that democracy is not mandated by the Bible and actually originated among pagans. Genevan democracy nonetheless created not only the means of putting Calvin's political theory into practise by the election of his adherents and supporters to civic office, but also ensured their relative durability. Had Edward VI outlived the Protectorate to reign in his own right, it is not unreasonable to imagine England being governed in an equally godly way as Geneva under Calvin. However, on Edward's death in 1553, his Roman Catholic half-sister Mary put paid to any chance of Britain's government being reformed according to the Word of God. Genevan democracy ensured that Calvin's reforms did not die with him.

It has been argued that the very idea of "the State" only emerged in the 16th Century. There is some justification for this view. Mediaeval Roman Catholicism taught that both church and state were separate entities under the control of the pope, but treated the state as subordinate to the church, comparing the two to the moon and the sun respectively. David Held therefore correctly claims that "the idea of an impersonal and sovereign political order, i.e. a legally circumscribed structure of powers separate from ruler and ruled, with supreme jurisdiction over a territory, could not predominate while political rights, obligations and duties were closely tied to religious tradition, monarchical powers and the feudal system of property rights.[54]" In Geneva, although religion was the obvious driving force behind the Calvinistic Reformation, Held's comments are otherwise apposite to the city's political development, and in particular the continuation of that reform after 1564 when death removed its greatest citizen, pastor and thinker.

Liberty (3) The Individual and their calling

Held also credits the Reformation with the development of the idea of the person as an individual, with "a right to be citizens of their state[55]". The claim of some Marxist critics that the individual was a 16th century invention aimed at sustaining economic productivity is manifestly false. True, support for the right of private property implies recognition of the individual, but the Reformation emphasis on the individual derives not from private property but from the doctrine of justification by faith alone. Emphasising the Bible's teaching that "there is one mediator between God and man, the Man Christ Jesus,[56]" (the priesthood of all believers) the reformers stripped away the human mediators – the Roman Catholic clergy who claimed power to forgive sins and impose "penances" which could be performed at a price by another person – and left the individual alone before God and responsible for their actions.

The individualism engendered by the Reformation was very different from that of the early monks who retreated into the wilderness to seek solitude with God, for it was balanced by the strong emphasis both on family life and on communal as well as personal responsibility. However, personal responsibility is the key to understanding an apparent paradox in Reformed teaching. Calvin, like Augustine before him, strongly emphasised the Fall and the resultant inherent sinful nature of all the offspring of Adam. Being dead in trespasses and sins, we are unable to save ourselves. Salvation comes by grace through faith – that is, by receiving a free unmerited gift of God, who firstly regenerates those He has predestined for salvation:– "When we were dead in sins, (he) hath quickened us together with Christ.[57]" Although salvation is seen as God's work from first to last, this does not mean, however, that men bear no responsibility for their actions. "God's foreknowledge does not hinder man from being accounted a sinner, inasmuch as the evils God foresees are man's, not his own.[58]"

On the other hand, even if fallen man is unable to save himself, the image of God is not totally erased. Following Augustine, whose influence he openly acknowledges, Calvin says that while the "supernatural gifts" – in other words the "qualities belonging to the blessed life of the soul" are "extinguished," the "natural gifts" are only "corrupted.[59]" In brief, human ability in reasoning, in leadership, in practical skills and in the arts, along with a sense of compassion for one's fellow human beings, may be greatly diminished and soiled with sin, but are still present in fallen man. As these gifts are endowments from God, they should be used responsibly.

The Christian seeks to use these natural gifts for God's glory. One of the principal means of so doing is through his work. Reformed teaching, by investing a dignity to the "secular" calling, took a huge leap forward from mediaeval theology, which treated anyone who was not ordained or a member of a religious order as a second-class Christian. The English poet George Herbert (1593–1633) expressed this doctrine of the sacredness of even the most menial tasks in a particularly delightful way in his well-known hymn:–

Teach me, my God and King,
In all things Thee to see;
And what I do in anything
To do it as for Thee...

All may of Thee partake;
Nothing can be so mean,
Which, with this tincture, "For Thy sake",
Will not grow bright and clean.

A servant with this clause
Makes drudgery divine;
Who sweeps a room as for Thy laws,
Makes this and the action fine.

It was as a consequence of the Fall that work had become drudgery:– "Cursed is the ground , for thy sake. In sorrow shalt thou eat of it all the days of thy life...In the sweat of thy face shalt thou eat bread till thou return unto the ground.[60]" Nonetheless, it was not total drudgery, for Calvin notes in commenting on this passage, "something of enjoyment is blended with the labours of men[61]" and as for believers, "those who submit meekly to their work and sufferings present to God an acceptable obedience.[62]" The later prosperity of Geneva and the prominence of Calvinists among the leaders in commerce and science in the next century was a by-product of his teaching about living life to the glory of God. Indeed, wherever Calvin's teachings took root, the result was the emergence of "austere, fearless, hard-working, devout men of the Bible. They knew what they believed, they knew what they must do and they knew by what authority they must do it.[63]" This strong sense of personal responsibility before God brings liberty because it produces restraint. Edmund Burke understood this link well over 200 years later when he said, "Society cannot exist unless a controlling power upon will and appetite be placed somewhere, and the less of it there is within, the more there is without."

Moral Restraint

This being said, Geneva in Calvin's time saw plenty of restraint from without as well as from within. Of all the changes that he inspired, it has been the strict application of moral restraint, the third component of a Christian worldview, which has been subject to the most debate and criticism, to the point where his commitment to compassion and liberty has been questioned. Many commentators, even Christians sympathetic to the reformer's ideals, claim that he went too far, and Genevan moral discipline resulted in an unacceptable degree of scrutiny over the lives of individual men and women. Less sympathetic voices have used quite extreme terms to denounce "Calvin's prurient, repressive influence" and the "theocratic reign of terror" he allegedly inspired. However, bearing in mind that Geneva was a democracy, albeit a limited one, if the Genevans themselves had been so unhappy with the degree of moral restraint in the city, there was no reason why, as in 1538, they could not at a later date have again elected new syndics and a new council who would have ended the strict discipline and expelled the reformers. As far as can be ascertained, it appears that after 1555, a city composed largely of converted people was content with its government.

Calvin's contemporaries were certainly fulsome in their praise. John Knox (c1510–1572) the Scottish reformer, spent several years in exile in Geneva during the 1550's and famously described it as "the most perfect school of Christ that ever was in the earth since the days of the apostles." Calvin's friend and colleague Guillaume Farel wrote in 1557 that "he would rather be the last in Geneva than the first anywhere else.[64]" The Lutheran Valentin Andrae (1586–1654) who was less likely to be sympathetic to Calvin than Knox or Farel, visited Geneva in 1610, nearly 50 years after Calvin's death and was most impressed with what he saw: "All cursing, swearing, gambling, luxury, strife, hatred, fraud, etc are forbidden, while greater sins are hardly heard of. What a glorious ornament of the Christian religion is such purity of morals![65]"

In the early 21st Century, such comments are worth bearing in mind. When confronted with the petty crime, swearing, immorality, drunkenness and antisocial behaviour that is all too common in many towns and cities to-day, what Christian would not prefer to live in a peaceful, well-ordered society where such behaviour would be rare in the extreme and regarded as unacceptable when it occurred? It is easy with the benefit of hindsight to criticise certain aspects of the way Calvin's teaching on moral restraint was put into practise in Geneva, but it must be remembered that he was a pioneer. No-one had ever attempted to reform society according to the Word of God before. In such circumstances, it is hardly surprising if there were some excesses. It was opposition to his insistence on strict discipline that brought Calvin's first stay in Geneva to an end. The *Confession of Faith* he wrote shortly after his arrival in 1536 was a theological document, but as the fledgling Reformed Church had been established by edict of the Council, it also had to approve this document, including the disciplinary measures demanded. It duly did so, but when the 1538 elections returned four syndics and a majority on the council opposed to the reformers, Calvin, along with his fellow pastors Farel and Courault (d1538), were expelled from the city. He spent the next three years in Strasbourg, and when new elections in 1541 saw the supporters of reform in power again, Calvin only very reluctantly agreed to their pressing requests to return to Geneva, and insisted that if he returned, strict ecclesiastical discipline must be enforced.

With church and state so closely linked, it was inevitable that discipline should go beyond the ecclesiastical censure of excommunication, and that an element of moral restraint would find its way into Geneva's civic laws. What is so remarkable, especially considering the opposition Calvin faced until 1555, is the degree to which moral restraint was enforced, even in the early years of his return. Punishments were meted out not just for obvious offences like murder and theft, but also for gambling and drunkenness – the latter being punished by a fine, while habitual gamblers were exposed in the pillory with cords around their neck[66]. Adultery was punishable by death on the second offence. Any form of sexual deviancy was punished. Two male Genevans were brought before the magistrates in 1551 for engaging in a bout of nude wrestling. One was banished from the city, while the other was chained to a large stone for a year and a day[67]. As for homosexuality itself, one of the great hot potatoes of our own age, Calvin makes clear his utter revulsion with the practice and unashamedly supports harsh punishment of offenders. "The most abominable (crime) of all –

that monstrous pollution which was but too prevalent in Greece,[68]" he calls it, and adds, "It ought to be more severely punished than other crimes.[69]" Freedom of the press was restricted by a law in 1560. All books were to be scrutinised by a team of three men appointed by the government to prevent unsuitable material being circulated.[70]

Punishments were meted out for lesser offences too. In the *Minutes Book* of Geneva City Council can be found details of a man who was imprisoned for three days for smiling while attending a baptism, while a man who fell asleep in a sermon likewise found himself in jail.[71] Excess and extravagance in dress were forbidden too. Calvin's determination to create a godly society meant that any sin, however trivial, could not be ignored, as it was an offence against God.

The Inconsistencies in Calvin's political thinking

There is one obvious criticism that can be made not only about this policy on moral restraint, but also of Calvin's political thinking as a whole. It can be most clearly understood by looking at the one criminal punishment for which Calvin has been criticised more than any other – the execution of Michael Servetus (1511–1553). Servetus, a Spaniard who practised medicine in France, rejected the orthodox Christian view of the Trinity, and claimed, like Arius in the 4th Century, that Jesus was a created being and thus not fully God. He began a correspondence with Calvin whom he tried to win over to his views, but Calvin, who for his part tried to convince him of the error of his ways, broke off contact when it became apparent that this obstinate man was quite incorrigible. Servetus had used a pseudonym when writing his many heretical books, but when the Roman Catholic authorities in Vienne in France discovered his identity, he was arrested and charged with heresy. He managed to escape from prison, and arrived at Geneva, only intending to stay for a few weeks before moving on, either to Zürich or Italy. Attending church one Sunday, he was recognised and arrested. Calvin worked hard in the ensuing trial to secure either his recantation or his condemnation on a charge of heresy. Servetus for his part refused to recant, calling Calvin a liar, an impostor and a miserable wretch. Although Calvin at this time still had powerful opponents on the Council, Servetus' ranting and abusive conduct won him few friends, and he was condemned to death by burning. Calvin was not opposed to his execution, only its severity, appealing in vain to the Council that Servetus be beheaded instead.

If Calvin's role in the affair of Servetus appals the 21st Century Christian, it must be said that in the 16th Century, Servetus would have met exactly the same fate under a Roman Catholic, Lutheran or Anglican regime. However, Calvin's support for the execution of heretics highlights one of the biggest weaknesses of his otherwise well-thought out political teaching. Calvin's belief that church and state had different realms of jurisdiction has already been noted, so why did he support the execution of Servetus by the state for a "spiritual" offence? Calvin published a defence of his actions in February 1554 relying extensively on the Mosaic Law. "Why is so implacable a severity extracted but that we may know that God is defrauded of his honour, unless the piety that is due to him is to be preferred to all human duties, and that when his glory is to be asserted, humanity must be almost obliterated from our memories?[72]" he asks. God's honour, in other words, is so important that when such pernicious and incorrigible teachers of error as Servetus emerge, we must suspend both our compassionate instincts (as well as the church/state distinction) in deference to His glory. Such an argument did not convince his contemporaries and sounds even less convincing today.

The banishment of a man from Geneva for commenting in jest on hearing an ass bray, "He prays a beautiful psalm", or the fining and putting in the stocks a man who swore "by the body and blood of Christ[73]" are equally indefensible. Once again, the authority of the state was being invoked for an offence requiring ecclesiastical rather than civil sanction. The reason for Calvin's usually clear thinking confusing the boundaries of jurisdiction was that the Reformed Church of

Geneva had been established by the government. That government, like all governments of the period, required all the population to attend a place of worship, so everyone found themselves *de facto* subject to ecclesiastical as well as civil jurisdiction, whether they were true Christians or not. Calvin would not have disputed that believers and unbelievers were sitting side by side in the church, but state-enforced compulsory church attendance inevitably results in more chaff than necessary remaining among the wheat. It is true that in Old Testament times the entire nation of Israel was subject to the totality of God's law, whether they were true worshippers or not, but their theocracy was unique. Even in a place like Geneva where a good deal of the population appear to have been genuinely converted, no state has a mandate to punish its citizens for offences relating solely to their Christian conduct – or lack of it. You cannot compel religion, and the state must not do so. Only when a different understanding of the church as a voluntary society of converted individuals helped provoke a re-thinking of the relationship between church and state could Christian liberty move forward from this throwback to the Middle Ages which Calvin and others perpetuated. Subsequent Christian thinkers attempting to apply the Bible to the life of a nation have largely proposed a smaller role for the state. This is hardly surprising bearing in mind how many of these men who, unlike Calvin, were addressing the subject of reforming nations according to the Bible produced their works under the shadow of a hostile government, and were thus only too aware of the threat to liberty posed by the big state.

Another inconsistency in Calvin's thinking was to argue on the one hand for a less than literal interpretation of the Old Testament texts on usury while retaining a literal interpretation in some areas of discipline on the other. A girl was actually beheaded for striking her parents,[74] and while the death penalty was the appropriate punishment for such an offence under Mosaic law[75], there is surely a case to be made for applying its principles as the basis for Christian restraint without going as far as inflicting such an exact replication of the punishments decreed.

Nonetheless, for all these criticisms, there was much in Calvin's teaching that was to inspire his own and later generations. A truly great man raised up and gifted by God, his influence was immense, thanks in particular to the force of his biblical theology and the widespread circulation of his writings. No other city or country ever replicated his approach in Geneva, but wherever Evangelical Christianity stressing the sovereignty and glory of God in every area of life has taken root, the same threefold foundation of compassion, liberty and moral restraint has brought transformation and blessing in its wake.

Notes

[1] Schaff P. *History of the Christian Church*, Volime 7 p251. Eerdmans, Grand Rapids (Originally puhlished 1910).

[2] Kirkton, J, *The Secret and True History of the Church of Scotland* (1817), as quoted in Murray, I *The Puritan Hope*, p5, Banner of Truth Trust, Edinbugh, 1971.

[3] Bieler, A *La Penseé Economique et Sociale de Calvin*, p23 Librarie de l'Université Georg & Cte S.A. Geneva, 1959.

[4] Quoted in Schaff, P, *History of the Christian Church,* Volume 7, p545, Eerdmans, Grand Rapids (Originally puhlished 1910).

[5] Bieler, A *op cit*, p350.

[6] Schaff, P. *History of the Christian Church*, Volume 8, *The Swiss Reformation* p479–480. Eerdmans, Grand Rapids (Originally puhlished 1910).

[7] Calvin, J, *Institutes of the Christian Religion* IV:3:9. Translated by F. L. Battles. *The Library of Christian classics* Volume XX. The Westminster Press, Philadelphia 1960 (Based on Calvin's 1560 French edition)

[8] Bieler, A *op cit*, p153.

[9] Bartholomew, J, *The Welfare state we're in*, p 29, Politico's London, 2004.

[10] Calvin's commentaries, Exodus 22:25/Leviticus 25:35–38/Deuteronomy 23:19–20 Baker Book House, Grand Rapids 1998 reprint.

[11] *idem.*

[12] *idem.*

[13] Calvin's commentaries, Psalm 15:5.

[14] *idem.*

[15] *idem.*

[16] Calvin's commentaries, Leviticus 25:8–13,
[17] Calvin's commentaries, Leviticus 25:1–7/Exodus 23:10–11.
[18] *idem.*
[19] Bieler, A, *op cit*, p171.
[20] Calvin's commentaries, Genesis 12:5.
[21] Calvin's commentaries, Deuteronomy 24:7.
[22] Bieler, A *op cit*, p173.
[23] Exodus 21:1–6
[24] See, for example, Numbers 31:7–31,
[25] Exodus 21:26–27
[26] http://socrates58.blogspot.com/2010/03/john-calvins-sanction-of-torture-of.html Accessed 04/02/2011.
[27] Schaff, P, *op cit*, p516.
[28] Beeke, Joel R, *365 days with Calvin*, preface, Day One publications, Leominster, 2008.
[29] Bieler A, *op cit*, p135.
[30] Calvin's commentaries, Acts 2:44.
[31] *idem.*
[32] *idem.*
[33] Calvin's commentaries, Matthew 19:20.
[34] Calvin's commentaries, Acts 10:29.
[35] Calvin's commentaries, 2 Corinthians 8:7.
[36] Calvin's *Institutes* 4:20:2.
[37] *idem.*
[38] Calvin's commentaries, Leviticus 19:35.
[39] Sermon 114 Deuterronomy 19:14–15 as quoted in Bieler A , *op.cit*, p384,
[40] Calvin's commentaries, Exodus 16:17.
[41] Calvin's commentaries, Genesis 41:35.
[42] Calvin's commentaries, 1 Timothy 2:9.
[43] Calvin's commentaries, 1 Timothy 2:2.
[44] Calvin's commentaries, Matthew 22:1.
[45] Calvin's *Institutes*, IV.12:1
[46] Calvin's *Institutes*, 4:20:13.
[47] *idem.*
[48] See for example, the comments on Leviticus 20:2 in chapter 2 of this book.
[49] Calvin's commentaries, Genesis 11:8.
[50] Calvin's commentaries, Psalm 2:10–11.
[51] Calvin's commentaries, 1 Peter 2:14.
[52] Calvin's commentaries, Romans 13:4.
[53] http://anduril.ca/bible/essays/ce_his290.html Accessed 09/03/2012.
[54] Held, D, *Models of Democracy*, (third edition) p58, Polity Press,

Cambridge, 2006.

[55] *idem.*

[56] 1 Timothy 2:5i.

[57] Ephesians 2:5.

[58] Calvin's *Institutes*, 3.23.6.

[59] Calvin's *Institutes*, 2:2.12.

[60] Genesis 3:17 (ii), 19 (i)

[61] Calvin's commentaries, Genesis 3:17.

[62] Calvin's commentaries, Genesis 3:19.

[63] Chadwick, O *The Reformation, Pelican History of the Church* Volume 3. p96. Penguin books, Harmondsworth, 1964

[64] Schaff, P, *op cit*, Volume 8 p518.

[65] Schaff, P, *op cit*, Volume 8 p519.

[66] Schaff, P. *op cit*, Volume 6 p490.

[67] Naphy, W, *Sex Crimes from Renaissance to Enlightenment*, Tempus Publsihing, Stroud 2002 as reviewed in http://www.guardian.co.uk/books/2002/nov/23/history.highereducation Accessed 09/03/2012.

[68] Calvin's commentaries, 1 Corinthains 6:10.

[69] Calvin's commentaries, Leviticus 20:13.

[70] Schaff, P *op cit*, Volume 8 p465.

[71] http://www.a-voice.org/tidbits/calvinp.htm Accessed 09/03/2012.

[72] Schaff, P, *op cit*, Volume VIII, p791–792.

[73] *ibid,* p491.

[74] ibid, p491–2

[75] Exodus 21:15

Chapter 4:

The Development of a Christian Worldview (2) The Netherlands, Puritanism and the American colonies

Rightousness exalteth a nation,
but sin is a reproach to any people[1]

Thanks to the translation and circulation of his commentaries and the *Institutes,* Calvin's influence permeated widely throughout Europe. The transformation of Geneva under his ministry likewise proved an inspiration for other reformers who visited the city. However, nowhere else in Europe provided the same combination of favourable circumstances for such a work to be replicated. Support for such a thoroughgoing reform, particularly the disciplinary measures, requires both the support of the civil authorities and a significant number of the population to be converted people all content to be members of churches holding to the same doctrinal position and the same form of church government. While both Scotland and the Netherlands saw large numbers of conversions, and the Scottish reformation featured a strong doctrinal consensus, thanks to the powerful influence of its principal reformer John Knox, the political conditions were not satisfied in either country. The great truths of the Gospel were preached in Scotland and the Netherlands against a background of opposition, or indeed persecution, and even when the worst of the hostility was over, in neither land were the political powers sympathetic to a replication of the state-enforced moral restraint of Geneva.

It was the related question of whether secular powers should intrude into the spiritual realm which became the most significant issue in Christian political thinking during the late 16th and 17th centuries. To put it another way, what balance should be struck regarding freedom – in particular freedom of worship – and the desire for a Godly society? By 1700, the eventual consensus in favour of freedom of worship has been regarded as far more convincing from the Biblical perspective by subsequent generations. However, the views of Calvin and other godly men who supported a state-enforced uniformity of religion with civil sanctions for dissent should not be lightly dismissed, even if their zeal now seems abhorrent.

While other aspects of Christian political thinking will be discussed, it is the battle for freedom of worship that runs like a thread through this chapter, and at this point, a slight back-track is required to consider its earliest Protestant advocates.

The Anabapists and freedom of worship

As far back as the 1520's, in the early days of the Reformation under Luther in Germany and Zwingli (1484–1531) in German-speaking Switzerland, some of those who embraced their teachings began to feel uncomfortable about the close link between church and state that characterised the Reformation in both these lands. Was not the church the *ekklesia* – a society of individuals called out of the world? If church and state were separate entities, as all the reformers were teaching, was it right for the state to enforce church attendance or one particular form of religious belief? Should not this recovery of apostolic doctrine also lead to the recovery of the concept of local, autonomous Christian communities free from control by the state or ecclesiastical hierarchies? Furthermore, if one is not a Christian until trusting in Jesus Christ for salvation, should not initiation into the church be deferred until an individual has made a clear profession of faith? The leaders of this radical movement began to baptise their followers and indeed, each other on public profession of faith, and it was from this act that they acquired the name Anabaptists – literally re-baptisers.

Nowadays, the doctrine of believer's baptism is perfectly acceptable in mainstream Evangelicalism. In most Baptist and Pentecostal churches, among others, it is a requirement for membership. Attitudes in the 16th century were very different. The rejection of infant baptism and denial of the right of civil authorities to interfere in the area of religion horrified not only the Roman Catholic hierarchy, but also the reformers. Zwingli took a strong stand against the Zürich Anabaptists, and when the city council decided to execute one of the Anabaptist leaders, Felix Manz (1498–1527) by drowning him in the river, there is no record of the reformer objecting. During the 1520's and 1530's suffering was to be their lot wherever their scattered congregations were established, regardless of the religious persuasion of the authorities.

It would be wrong to treat the Anabaptists as a cohesive body. Belief in a pure church separate from the world is the only common factor. Some adopted communal living with all possessions in common, as was noted in the previous chapter. A few adopted heretical views, denying the divinity of Christ. Some were sure that the return of Christ was imminent, and this conviction led the Anabaptists of Münster in North-West Germany down the road of wild excess, swinging to the very opposite extreme with regard to toleration. The city expelled its bishop and all Roman Catholic priests in 1533, and declared itself Lutheran. One of the Lutheran preachers Bernhard Rothmann (d?1535) who had studied at Wittenburg and had been friendly with Luther's colleague Philip Melanchthon (1495–1560), adopted Anabaptist views in 1533–4 and ended up the most influential Christian minister in the city. He was joined by two radical Dutch Anabaptists Jan Matthys (d1534) and Jan Beuckelszoon, or John of Leyden (d 1536), who were both convinced that they were to turn Münster into the new Jerusalem in preparation for the Second Coming. Matthys, believing he was a second Gideon sent to destroy the wicked, was killed fighting the army raised by the deposed bishop to recapture the city. Beuckelszoon then married Matthys' widow and no less than 15 other women, while Rothmann took 9 wives. Community of goods was decreed. It became an offence not to be married, and death was decreed as a punishment for all manner of offences. including complaining. To top it all, Beuckelszoon had himself crowned "King of the people of God in the New Temple." His regime did not last long. The bishop's army recaptured the city in 1535, and the leaders were executed after being barbarously tortured.

The Münster debacle made the very name Anabaptist odious for well over a century, but the movement did not die out. It continued to flourish albeit illegally in the Netherlands, under the leadership of Menno Simons (1496–1561), a man of moderation and peace who was a strong advocate of religious liberty. It is no coincidence that the loudest cries for freedom of worship usually come from those who are persecuted for their faith. In the early days of the German Reformation when its survival was by no means secure, Luther had been an advocate for freedom of worship, as was noted in the previous chapter. When the threats receded thanks to the support of the prince, he changed his mind on this issue. With the Anabaptists' refusal to turn to the state for support, their stance on freedom did not alter. Church and state must be separate in reality as well as theory, which means no government may compel religion and individuals must be free to worship according to their conscience. It was in the Netherlands first where after much suffering, this aspiration was finally to become reality.

The Reformation in the Netherlands

The prosperous cities of the Low Countries proved fertile ground for the Reformation from the very start. Copies of Luther's writings were being sold in Antwerp as early as

1518[2] although Calvin's theological influence had become dominant by the second half of the 16th century. Evangelical congregations sprang up widely right across the areas corresponding to the modern countries of Belgium and Holland, but meeting in secret. This area was under the rule of the Hapsburg Charles V (1500–1558), who was also king of Spain and Holy Roman Emperor. One of the most powerful men in Europe, he opposed the Reformation across all his domains, appointing an inquisitor-general for the Netherlands as early as 1523, with the death penalty being authorised for anyone professing the Evangelical faith in 1529. These repressive measures failed to stop the spread of the Gospel. By 1566, reformed congregations numbered 15,000 in Amsterdam, 7,000 in Ghent and 10,000 in Tournai,[3] all without any legal sanction. Unfortunately, in August of that year some over-zealous Christians began a campaign of destruction of statues and religious paintings, believing that they should address these violations of the Second Commandment. In response, Philip II, who had succeeded his father Charles V as king of Spain in 1556, appointed the ruthless Fernando Alvarez de Toledo, Duke of Alba (1507–1582) as governor, giving him a mandate to exterminate Protestantism by whatever means necessary. A petition against the Inquisition had been sent to Alba's predecessor, signed by 400 leading men, including both Calvinist and Roman Catholic noblemen. On Alba's arrival, two leading Roman Catholic signatories, the Counts of Egmont and Hoorn, were arrested, accused of treason, tried and executed. Alba put 12,000 believers to death in 1567 and over 100,000 fled the country. The following year, in response to this reign of terror, the fight for independence began. Although Calvin had strongly advised the Huguenots (the French Evangelicals) against taking up arms to defend the Reformation, the Netherlands were different. With Spain treating the country like a distant province of its empire, and ruling it in a brutal and unsympathetic manner, the desire to regain national sovereignty transcended religious loyalties.

Space does not permit a detailed study of the heroic and lengthy battle against the most powerful army in Europe, which eventually won the Dutch their independence, but the leader of the independence movement, William the Silent (1533–1584) is worthy of mention for his insistence on religious toleration. In 1577, freedom of worship was granted to the Anabaptists in the Union of Utrecht in 1579, whereby the seven northern provinces of the Netherlands pledged to drive out the Spanish, and left each province free to order its religious affairs as it saw fit, provided no-one was persecuted for their faith. William had declared himself a Calvinist in 1573. Whether he was a "political protestant" or whether he had been truly converted cannot be ascertained. He had a genuine horror of Alba's brutality, but also recognised the need of the support from those Roman Catholics who may have shared the Spaniards' religion but who disliked their cruelty and were thus equally keen to seek independence.

William was not the first leader supportive of freedom of worship. The king of Hungary, John II Sigismund, had issued an edict at Torda in Transylvania several years earlier, which allowed total freedom of worship for Roman Catholics, Lutherans, Calvinists and the Trinity-denying Unitarians, with other groups including Eastern Orthodox, Jews and Moslems being given toleration although not the same degree of freedom. The prime movers in this accord were the heretical Unitarians, who had gained the support of the king. The freedom of worship granted in the Netherlands is more significant in that the moving spirit was a member of an Evangelical church rather than a heretic. This toleration did not go down well with the Calvinist (Reformed) Church, and William had had to intervene personally to prevent their persecuting the Anabaptists[4] but although the Reformed Church enjoyed privileged status and all state officials had to be communicant members[5] it never became formally the religion of the state. Toleration was never revoked and different religions learnt to settle down in peaceful coexistence. For the next 100 years, Protestant refugees of all persuasions fleeing intolerance were glad to find a place of refuge in The Netherlands. In 1581, the seven provinces that signed the Union of Utrecht formally declared their independence. William wrote a work the same year defending the right to remove an ungodly ruler. This was a subject that was greatly to exercise Christian leaders in England and Scotland in the following century. Although the Dutch state never enforced moral discipline after the manner of Geneva, the churches, both Reformed and the Mennonite Anabaptists, insisted on a godly lifestyle among their own members. The outstanding Reformed theologian Gijsbert Voet, or Voetius, (c1588–1676) emerged as one of the leaders of what was known as the Further or Second Reformation (*Nadere Reformatie*) which sought, very much in the tradition of Calvin, to apply the Word of God to every area of life, including the family and society as a whole, as well as to the life of the church.

Once again, the inner restraint engendered by the influence of the Bible on personal and family life acted as a catalyst for limited government, for Holland developed as a society permeated with God's Word, but applied in a "bottom up" way rather than enforced by the state. One of its most distinctive features was the application of the principle of the all-embracing nature of God's Word to the arts. Perhaps the greatest masterpiece of Dutch painting, *de Nachtwacht* (the Night Watch) by Rembrandt (1606–1669) is a particularly beautiful illustration of this. While any visitor to the Rijksmuseum in Amsterdam where the painting is exhibited cannot fail to notice how Rembrandt has infused a real personality into the characters depicted, of greater significance is the choice of subject matter. No Italian Renaissance artist would have produced a huge, detailed canvas depicting these ordinary militiamen engaged in a very mundane activity. Here is a visual expression of the significance of the individual and the dignity of ordinary work – one of the hallmarks of the Christian political worldview.

The Dutch were unique among those nations most touched by the Reformation in their policy of free trade. While evidence suggests that their approach was driven more by pragmatism than theology, it is more consistent with the Bible than mercantilism, which was the norm during the

16th and 17th centuries. Mercantilism is the name given to the regulation of foreign trade by the state with a view to using it for competitive advantage – in other words, exports were to be encouraged but imports discouraged. It would be hard to find any Biblical justification for state interference in this particular field.

Opinion in the Netherlands remained divided throughout the 17th Century as to whether the country should be a republic or a constitutional monarchy ruled by the House of Orange, the family of William the Silent. Both the two factions, in spite of sometimes coming to blows over this issue, were nonetheless agreed on the idea of limited government. This is hardly surprising considering the history of the area. Until the dukes of Burgundy, Charles V and Philip II had tightened their grip, the main cities in the Low Countries had enjoyed a considerable degree of independence, with the magistrates being elected by the tradesmen of the city. The Reformation reaffirmed this tradition of small government and clothed it with a Christian ethos. The combination of limited government and freedom of worship within a society permeated by God's Word remained a strong characteristic of the Netherlands throughout the 17th Century and for many years afterwards. Indeed, after years of decline, this distinctive approach found an articulate spokesman as late as the early 20th Century in the person of Abraham Kuyper (1838–1920), Prime Minister from 1901–1905, who frequently extolled the link between Calvinism and liberty[6]. That he was able to present such a persuasive case is a measure of how much his own countrymen, perhaps sometimes against their better judgment, had ended up with a religious settlement which had corrected the worst excess of Calvin's political thinking.

Scotland – the land of the Covenant

Another country where Calvin's theology had a profound impact on the course of the Reformation was Scotland. The leader of the Scottish reformation, John Knox (d1572), was a man of great piety and bravery of whom it was said that he feared God so much that he never feared the face of any man. Knox had spent several years in exile in Geneva after the inevitable opposition from the Scottish Roman Catholic hierarchy to the preaching of the gospel became so intense that he felt that his presence in his home country could achieve nothing. His enthusiasm for what he saw in Geneva has already been noted, and when he returned to his home country following a change in the political situation, he preached with great power to his fellow Scots those same doctrines exalting the work of Christ and the sovereignty of God.

Politically, Scotland was very different to Geneva or the Netherlands. The monarchy was weak and allied to France while the nobles were powerful, and many of them were growing increasingly uncomfortable about French influence in Scotland's affairs. The work of the Holy Spirit, which had begun before Knox's exile, had continued unabated during his absence, and some nobles came to profess the Evangelical faith. Five of these men, known as the Lords of the Congregation, signed a covenant in December 1557, 'to establish the most blessed word of God and his congregation" and to renounce "all the superstitions, abominations and idolatry" of the Roman Catholic Church[7]. Knox's return emboldened them to further action, and in 1559, the French Queen Mother, Mary of Guise, was deposed as regent, while the following year, the Treaty of Edinburgh saw French troops withdrawn from Scotland. Later that year, the Scottish parliament met and, under Knox's guidance, finally gave the Reformation a legal basis. The authority of the pope was repudiated, the Roman Catholic mass was declared illegal, and persecution of Evangelical believers ceased forthwith. The Parliament authorised a Confession of Faith, which was drawn up by Knox and others, and the following year, a book of discipline was introduced, although it never had legal force.

At this point, the course of events in Scotland began to diverge significantly from those in Geneva a quarter of a century earlier. The year after the Reformation was established, Mary Queen of Scots, newly widowed after the death of her sickly husband Francis II, King of France (1559–1560), returned to her kingdom after a long stay in France, where she had been brought up since the age of six. Mary was determined to oppose Knox and to restore Roman Catholicism, but Knox refused to be intimidated by her, even though he was convinced of her "hardened heart against God and his truth[8]". Her supporters were encouraged to take up arms, while one of her leading opponents, the Earl of Moray, plotted armed rebellion against her.

Mary's own conduct saved Scotland from civil war. She made two disastrous marriages in quick succession. The first in 1565 to the disreputable Lord Darnley (1545–1567) was bad enough, but when his arrogant behaviour resulted in his murder less than two years later, Mary then married James Hepburn, Earl of Bothwell (1535–1578), who was widely believed to be complicit in the murder. This act lost her such remaining public support as she enjoyed. Her abdication in 1567 in favour of her infant son James VI (1567–1625) removed the last serious obstacle to the progress of the Reformation, although there were plots to restore her to the throne and re-establish Roman Catholicism at periodic intervals right up to her death in 1587.

The established Scottish church was structured very much along the lines of Geneva, with councils of elders responsible for church government. The pastors were regarded as teaching elders, and although the congregation issued the call to the pastor, it had to be approved by the council of elders. Regional councils, known as synods, would meet periodically. In Scotland, and throughout the Anglophone world, such churches have been known as Presbyterian, from the Greek word *presbuteros,* meaning an elder. In the period of Knox and his immediate successors, the many Scots who professed faith in Jesus as saviour seemed happy with this arrangement, and such was the degree of consensus that in 1581 a National Covenant was written, a pledge to God that people of Scotland will be faithful to true religion, founded on the Word of God, which essentially meant support for the Presbyterian church. This covenant was to be signed by all ranks and classes from the king downwards. A second subscription to the Covenant took place in 1590. The most polemic sections of the Covenant deal with the errors of Roman Catholicism, which it denounces in no uncertain terms as the principal threat to true Christianity. However, it left no room for the possibility of any alternative expression of Evangelical truth. This was to pose a major problem in the following century. Meanwhile, the royal House of Stuart remained aloof from the great work of God among their subjects. As James VI grew to maturity, he increasingly resented the power of the Presbyterian preachers, taking great exception to being called "God's silly vassal" by Andrew Melville (1545–1622), who was reminding him of his duties before God. In 1603, he became James I of England, which brought him far more power and prestige than he had enjoyed in Scotland. The arrival of the Stuarts in London was also to result in significant ramifications for the development of Christian political thought in both lands.

The English Reformation and the origins of Puritanism

England was unique in separating from Rome for political rather than theological reasons. Henry VIII (1509–1547) sought a divorce from his first wife Katherine of Aragon, who had produced a daughter, Mary, in 1516 but no male heir. His requests to Pope Clement VII (1523–1534) fell on deaf ears. Henry, with the support of Parliament, then separated the English church from Rome and promptly divorced Katherine to marry Anne Boleyn. The 1534 Act of Supremacy declared that the King was the supreme head of the Church of England. This did not imply any theological reformation. True, Henry suppressed the monasteries and executed the most outspoken critics of the breach with Rome, including his former chancellor, Sir Thomas More (1478–1535), but the statute of Six Articles, published in 1539, were essentially an affirmation of Roman Catholic doctrine without the pope. Henry was not totally consistent. He stuck by Thomas Cranmer (1489–1556), whom he had appointed Archbishop of Canterbury in 1532, because he was known to support royal supremacy, even though he was becoming increasingly sympathetic to the Reformation. His last queen, Katherine Parr (d1548), was a firm Evangelical, who managed to survive attempts by her enemies to destroy her. Others, however, fared less well. Persecution continued throughout Henry's reign.

On his death in 1547, the Reformation advanced under his nine-year-old son Edward VI (1547–1553), the child of his third wife Jane Seymour (d 1537). Katherine Parr had proved a good stepmother to Henry's two younger children, providing them with tutors of an evangelical persuasion, and Edward shows every sign of having possessed real faith and trust in Jesus. However, when he died aged only 15, his half-sister Mary (1553–1558) reversed all these changes, bringing back Roman Catholicism, including submission to the papacy, and marrying Philip II of Spain. No less than 300 Evangelical believers were put to death in her reign. Many were ordinary men and women, but five were bishops, including Archbishop Cranmer, burnt at Oxford in 1556. Mercifully, England only had to endure five years of her reign. Across the country news of her death in November 1558 was greeted by the lighting of bonfires and the ringing of church bells.

Her half-sister Elizabeth I (1558–1603), Henry's daughter by Anne Boleyn, then came to the throne aged 25, and found herself ruling over a divided people. Disgust at the persecutions of Mary's reign had alienated many Englishmen from Rome, but there were still strongholds of Roman Catholicism, particularly in the North West. At the other end of the scale, some Evangelicals who had fled to Geneva during Mary's reign returned full of zeal to see the English church reformed on similar lines. The Elizabethan settlement of 1559, which has shaped the Church of England to the present day, was an attempt to hold everyone together. Elizabeth assumed the title "Supreme Governor" of the church, and the authority of the pope was repudiated. The Thirty Nine Articles, which are still the church's statement of faith, were firmly protestant, but the worship services of the Elizabethan church incorporated much that harked back to the days before the Reformation, as did the retention of bishops.

Puritanism began as a reform movement within the Church of England, seeking not separation but a furtherance of a work which was regarded as only half complete. The term "Puritan" was originally a term of abuse, meaning over-strict or severe. Puritans honoured the Bible and most of them held to the same theology as Calvin, with its emphasis on the sovereignty of God in every area of life. Such men and women were therefore bound to feel uncomfortable with the compromise of the Elizabethan settlement. Elizabeth was unsympathetic to their call for reform, although she avoided violent persecution for most of her reign. She rebuked Archibishop Grindal (d1583) who refused to discourage them, and ensured on his death that a man who would take a more anti-Puritan line was appointed to succeed him in the see of Canterbury. Only when independent churches started to meet in secret, led by men who regarded the Church of England as corrupted beyond redemption, was it felt necessary to resort to the scaffold. Henry Barrow, John Penry and John Greenwood, three of the leaders of this movement, were all put to death in 1593. Subsequently, similar offenders were banished rather than martyred, with The Netherlands the most favoured destination for their exile.

Opposition did not stamp out Puritanism, even within the Church of England, notably thanks to the system of patronage – the right of a local magnate to appoint the minister of a church. Although a throwback to the pre-Reformation era, Puritan squires made good use of it to support a like-minded man in the pulpit. Wealthy Puritans also founded educational establishments, such as Emmanuel College, Cambridge, in order to provide an appropriate training for Puritan preachers.

Besides seeking a reform of the church itself, Puritanism also sought to apply the principle of the sovereignty of God to the life of the nation. With no support from the monarch for Genevan-style moral discipline, the only methods available were protest, the preaching of the Word and encouraging those eligible to vote in parliamentary elections to support godly candidates. Puritans protested among other things against the playing of sport on the Lord's day, excessive drunkenness and the theatre – both on the grounds of such places being a rendezvous for prostitutes and also because of men taking the part of women, in contravention of Deuteronomy 22:5. The playwrights responded by caricaturing Puritans in their plays as over-strict and distorted their willingness to face unpopularity for the sake of truth into a mania for persecution. However, the Puritans were not deterred. By the 1620's, such was their concern for the nation's morality that they were convinced that God's patience was running thin with the nation and moral reform was therefore imperative if judgement was to be averted.[9]

If popular dislike of the Puritans among the unconverted was a manifestation of the time-honoured English love of liberty and individualism, Puritanism ironically developed into a theological outlook with a particular emphasis on the individual, although not to the point of denigrating the importance of marriage, family life and the local church community. It is significant that the Reformation in England produced no Luther, Calvin or Knox. The study of the Bible in small groups or in private houses played a particularly significant role in the spread of the Gospel truths in England during the 16th Century, and as the 17th Century began to unfold, the individual English Christian, jealous of his right to read and study the scriptures for himself, would turn out equally individualistic when applying them to the political realm.

The Stuart Kings and the Civil War

With James I having been educated under Calvinistic tutors in Scotland and a signatory to the Covenant, hopes were high among English Puritans that he might prove more sympathetic to a reform of the Church of England along Presbyterian lines. These hopes were soon to be dashed. A conference was convened by James in 1604 at Hampton Court, where he and a number of bishops met with some leading Puritan divines. Although agreeing to modify several points of detail in the services deemed as "popish", James and the bishops declined to promote widespread reform. James had never felt comfortable with the searching preaching of great pastors of the Scottish Presbyterian Church, so he had understandably no desire to see a similar church established in England, which would lessen his power. James believed that he ruled by divine right. In 1599, shortly before coming to England, he had written a book to instruct his young son Prince Henry in the art of kingship. Entitled *Basilikon Doron*, the book set out James' vision of monarchy. He tells Henry that as king, God "made you a little GOD to sit on his Throne, and rule over other men.[10]" There are some positive features to the book. It quotes frequently from the Scriptures and advises Henry to live a godly life and to show favour to the poor and oppressed: "Embrace the quarrell of the poore and distressed, as your owne particular, thinking it your greatest honour to represse the oppressours.[11]" However, James makes it clear who should be boss. He speaks disparagingly of people who "fantasie to themselues a Democraticke forme of gouernment[12]" and states in no uncertain terms his dislike of "Puritanes, and rash-headie Preachers, that thinke it their honour to contend with Kings, and perturbe whole kingdoms.[13]" The biggest fault in James' opinion, and one that he felt to be all too common was "to judge and speake rashly of their Prince.[14]" Accountability to his subjects was never going to be high on his agenda.

So the tensions continued under James much as they had done under Elizabeth. Some Puritans seeking an independent church free of state control migrated to Holland, although Puritan preaching within the established church continued wherever the patron was supportive. Had Henry succeeded his father, he may have been more accommodating of Puritan demands, but he died aged only 18 in 1612, and on James' death in 1625, Henry's younger brother

Charles came to the throne. Charles, not content with promoting anti-Puritan clergy in England, decided to impose bishops on Scotland and abolish the Presbyterian system. It was this act of insensitivity that produced one of the most well-known Puritan political writings of the period, *Lex, Rex, or The Law and the Prince*, by Samuel Rutherford (1600–1661), which will be considered in more detail below. Charles' actions had provoked the Scots into two rebellions in 1639–40, known as the Bishops' Wars. Rutherford's work, published in 1644, was an attempt to justify the rebellion, but its 470 pages go far deeper, setting out in some detail his vision of government.

Charles did not learn the lesson from the Bishops' wars, and having alienated Parliament and much of the nobility as well as Scottish Presbyterians and English Puritans, he plunged the country into civil war in 1642, which was eventually to lead to his execution in 1649, being declared guilty of being a "tyrant, murderer and a public and implacable enemy of the Commonwealth of England.[15]" However, his removal did not see the establishment of a Presbyterian Church in England. The emergence of Oliver Cromwell (1599–1658) as the most powerful figure among the king's opponents resulted in an unprecedented situation – the effective disestablishment of the church and granting of freedom of worship, except for Roman Catholics and supporters of episcopacy who were too politically dangerous to be tolerated. Cromwell had come to faith probably in his 20s or 30s, but only moved towards Independency in the 1640s. When the Scots insisted that the English should sign their covenant in 1643 as a condition of their support in the war, the English parliament with its Presbyterian sympathies had signed willingly. However, not only Cromwell but also many of the soldiers in his New Model Army were more of an Independent persuasion. "New Presbyter is but old priest writ large" wrote the poet John Milton in 1646. The clash of opinions over church government led to a second civil war in 1648, with the Scots and Cromwell now on opposing sides. Cromwell's victory at Worcester in 1651 marked the end of any hope of establishing a Presbyterian Church in England. Puritanism embraced both Presbyterians and Independents with their different views on the relationship between church and state and the model of church government, and also Baptists, who differed from both the other denominations over the mode of baptism. A number of fringe groups also emerged during this period, most of which have since disappeared from history. These included the Fifth Monarchists, who believed that the Second Coming was likely in 1666, the Ranters, who believed that God's grace had made them incapable of sinning, or the Muggletonians, led by two London tailors convinced they were the two witnesses mentioned in Revelation 11. The Quakers, who are still very much in existence today, also came into being around this time. A hundred years earlier, such groups would have faced severe persecution, but Cromwell initially felt that people agreed on the fundamentals of the Christian faith but differing in their interpretation of the scriptures in regard to church order or other secondary issues should be able to work together to produce a godly society. If Cromwell was perhaps a bit generous in his assessment of the orthodoxy of some of the more eccentric fringe groups, political thinking on these lines was remarkably enlightened and far more suited to the pluralism of more recent times. Cromwell's religious advisor, the Independent John Owen (1616–1683), enthused about his approach: "The reformation in England shall be more glorious than of any nation in the world, being carried on neither by might nor power, but only by the spirit of the Lord of Hosts.[16]" However, the eccentricities of some of the fringe groups, such as the habit of some early Quakers of interrupting church services in the middle of the sermon, forced a re-think. The *Humble Proposals* of 1652, co-authored by a number of Puritans, including Owen, included a recommendation that those who opposed the principles of Christian religion "should not be allowed to preach.[17]" The *Proposals* were never implemented, because, in 1653, Cromwell dissolved the Long Parliament, which had sat on and off since 1640, and replaced it with a nominated assembly of godly individuals of differing persuasions who were expected to rule England according to the Bible. Sadly, this assembly, known as Barebone's Parliament, after the nominee from the City of London, the Baptist preacher Praise-God Barebone, possessed little political acumen and spent a great deal of its time in heated arguments particularly over the issues of patronage and tithes. Greatly disappointed at its failure, Cromwell dissolved the assembly after only a few months, assuming personal rule himself under the title of "Lord Protector".

The debate about the limits of freedom of worship rumbled on, but for all the heated discussions and lack of an enduring answer on the subject, Cromwellian toleration was an enlightened and brave experiment. This cannot be said of Cromwell's resorting to the army to turn England into a "holy Republic" in 1655, a move thoroughly unpopular at the time. The predominantly Presbyterian Parliament had already introduced laws during the 1640s banning a number of activities they felt to be incompatible with the Word of God, such as theatre going, Morris dancing, the playing of sport on Sundays and even the celebration of Christmas. To this were added bans on, among other things, horseracing, bear baiting and cock fighting. Although the Presbyterian Richard Baxter (1615–1691) observed in 1656, "I do not believe that England had so able and faithful a ministry since it was a nation as it hath at this day,[18]" it does not appear, judging from contemporary accounts, that mid-17th Century England contained as high a percentage of truly converted men and women as 16th Century Geneva. Baxter's contemporary Thomas Watson (1620–1686) wrote, "Adultery is the reigning sin of the times....This may be called the unclean age, wherein whore-hunting is common.[19]" while another Puritan wrote in 1652, "This nation makes a god of its belly.[20]" In such circumstances, the enforcement of the strict laws of restraint by Cromwell's Major-Generals was inevitably going to cause resentment.

Cromwell's death in 1658 was followed by a period of

uncertainty which even many erstwhile opponents of Charles I eventually decided could only be resolved by the restoration of the monarchy in the person of his son Charles II, who returned to England by invitation in 1660. That same year, the Church of England was re-established and all ministers who would not conform to its articles were ejected two years later. Bishops were again imposed on the Scots and Presbyterianism was banned. Ironically, persecution was to breathe new life into Puritanism. The most enduring Puritan devotional work, John Bunyan's *Pilgrim's Progress*, was written when its author was a prisoner in Bedford during the 1670's. The Scots' reward for their loyalty to the House of Stuart was a far more ferocious persecution then their English counterparts had to endure, with martyrdom an all too frequent fate for the Covenanters – the members of the clandestine churches who met in secret during this period. Charles II was succeeded by his Roman Catholic brother James in 1685, who attempted to secure freedom of worship for Roman Catholics by offering it also to dissenters, as those refusing to conform to the Church of England were now known. For all the loathing of Puritanism that had been given free rein since 1660, the English loathing of Roman Catholicism was greater still, and James' high-handedness united the country against him. The Dutch prince William of Orange, who was married to James' daughter Mary, was invited to England, and James fled. William and Mary then ruled as joint sovereigns until Mary's death in 1694, and one of the first acts of their reign was the passing of the Toleration Act which finally granted the right of freedom of worship to dissenters, although not to Roman Catholics or Unitarians. Although the Act marked the end of state-enforced religious conformity, the degree of toleration granted to the dissenters had its limits. The Test and Corporation Acts, passed in the reign of Charles II to exclude all non-Anglicans from civil or military office, were not repealed until the early 19th Century, and dissenters were also excluded from the Universities of Oxford and Cambridge. Roman Catholics were debarred from the throne by the 1701 Act of Settlement, which remains in force to this day.

For all the shortcomings of the Toleration Act, it was a significant milestone in the development of liberty in Britain. The same year, the Bill of Rights established the sovereignty of Parliament and limited the power of the monarch. The concept of the accountability of rulers to the people had been enshrined in English law. England owes the Puritans a great debt. They may have quarrelled bitterly with each other over the limits of toleration and over the way a godly nation was to be governed, but their contribution to the cause of liberty, which will be considered in more detail below, cannot be underestimated. However, by 1689, the Puritan age was almost over, and with Puritanism died the detailed searching of the scriptures in an attempt to discover God's will regarding the government of the nation.

A Godly society – New England

Besides flight to the continent, a further option opened up in the early years of 17th Century for Puritans uncomfortable with the political situation in England. Exploration of North America by English sailors in Elizabeth's time was rapidly followed by colonisation. At first, trade was the prime motive, but the idea of establishing a godly community from scratch, free from the restraints of the mother country, became a particularly attractive option for Puritans of a Congregational persuasion. Congregationalists[21], like Baptists, believed in a democratic form of church government, which was never going to be adopted either by the Church of England as it stood, or by the proposed Presbyterianism favoured by other Puritans. The Pilgrim Fathers' exodus to the New World in 1620 paved the way for many others during the course of the century.

The democracy of Congregational church order naturally led to political democracy in the newly-established colony. The *Mayflower Compact*, signed by 41 of three ship's passengers, declared the signatories to be loyal subjects to the king, but also stated that they would "covenant and combine our selves together into a civil body politic, for our better

ordering and preservation and furtherance of the ends afore-
said; and by virtue hereof to enact, constitute, and frame
such just and equal laws, ordinances, acts, constitutions and
offices, from time to time, as shall be thought most meet and
convenient for the general good of the Colony.[22]" Government, in other words, was to be by the consent of the
governed.

It was not until the following decade that the form of
government was settled. The dismissal of Parliament by
Charles I in 1629 in order to rebuff Puritan demands for
reform of the church led to a more substantial exodus of Puritans to America. A fleet of seven vessels sailed the Atlantic in
1630 with 700 passengers on board, including John Winthrop
(1587–1648), a Suffolk Puritan squire who had obtained a
royal charter to establish the Massachusetts Bay Colony, and
who was to become their governor. The settlement they
established, Trimountaine, later known as Boston, grew
rapidly and soon became the largest town in British North
America.

The settlers were men and women of similar Christian
convictions, who hoped to create "a new Israel in America.[23]"
The Bible was to be their guide in all areas of life, so as with
their English counterparts, great importance was attached to
the character of all those elected to public office to ensure
that Biblical standards were maintained in the colony's life.
All adult male church members were eligible to vote, and
were expected to use their vote, although excommunicated
members had the vote withdrawn. On election days, a
minister would preach a sermon to the voters, encouraging
them to select pious leaders. This close link between church
members and their elected representatives meant that, even
among the fiercely democratic Congregationalists, church
and state, rigidly separate in theory, became blurred in practise, just as in Calvin's Geneva. For example, whenever there
were disagreements between the two legislative bodies, the
Court of Assistants and the House of Deputies, it was the
ministers of the churches who were called in to arbitrate[24].

Another parallel with Geneva was that no dissent from

Congregationalism was allowed. John Cotton, a minister who emigrated to Massachusetts in 1633, regarded religious dissenters as "weeds which attacked the Lord's pure garden in the wilderness." When errant seeds blew into that garden, the rulers were expected to root them out, "lest they choke 'the good herbs.[25]" Any dissenter was regarded automatically as a heretic, and Cotton and Winthrop both believed that the civil authorities had a duty to expel them. Church attendance was compulsory and strict moral restraint was also incorporated into the colony's laws. Adultery was declared a capital offence both in Massachusetts and neighbouring Connecticut, although the sentence was rarely carried out[26]. Bestiality and witchcraft likewise carried the death penalty. Over 100 alleged witches were executed during the 17th Century, the last following the notorious Salem witchcraft trials of 1692.

Roger Williams, one of the early settlers, begged to differ not only over the morality of state-enforced religious uniformity, but also over the state's right to interfere in spiritual matters. He argued that "the magistrate has nothing to do in matters of the first table, (i.e. the first five of the Ten Commandments) only in cases of disturbance to the civil peace[27]" Williams also argued "that a ruler could still be a good ruler even though he had never heard of Christ. There was no reason to assume that a person would perform better in his particular calling simply because he was a Christian.[28]" Although he then went on to proclaim his assent to the received wisdom that moral virtue and honesty were essential qualities for magistrates, he was expelled from the colony for his opinions, eventually to become the founder of Rhode Island, the first colony which from its inception permitted freedom of worship.

At the time, Williams was regarded as an aberration – good but wrongheaded. However, it was his stance on total separation of church and state which was ultimately adopted by the newly independent United States the following century, while his opinions on Christians not necessarily being the best rulers were endorsed by the many American

Christian voters in 1981 who threw their weight behind Ronald Reagan rather than the "born again" Baptist Jimmy Carter who had proved such a disappointment. The New England colonies enjoyed a considerable degree of autonomy until 1660, especially during the 11 years when England was without a king. Charles II made an attempt to impose a tighter control upon them. He insisted they implement the protectionist Navigation Acts, which demanded that English goods must be carried in English vessels, and insisted that the limit of the franchise to church members be dropped[29]. The Navigation Acts were a dead letter in Boston, but the colonists' resistance to Charles eventually precipitated a crisis in 1684, when the charter for Massachusetts Bay was revoked. This led to seven years of uncertainty when amongst other things, Edmund Andros, a governor directly appointed by the king, was locked up by the enraged colonists. A new charter was finally authorised in 1691. The significance of these tumultuous years lies in the political pronouncements of the ministers at the time. Puritanism in England was in its final years, and in New England, it was facing a very different world to that envisaged by Winthrop and the 1630 settlers. Not only Rhode Island to the south, but also the newly-founded and much larger colony of Pennsylvania some miles to the south west allowed full liberty of worship. Cracks in the Massachusetts religious uniformity had already begun to appear well before the crisis. A number of Quakers arrived in Boston in 1659 to find themselves apprehended and banished from the colony. Four of their number who returned in defiance of their banishment orders were executed between 1659 and 1661, but when an account of their death reached England, the Massachusetts General Court retracted its anti-Quaker measures out of fear that the colony's charter might be revoked[30]. When Baptists and Anglicans started to arrive in the colony in the 1670's, they received much less harassment from the authorities, and the state-enforced Congregational uniformity, already increasingly untenable by this period, was finally ended by the new 1691 charter, which removed membership of the

Congregational Church as a necessary requirement for the vote, and insisted that all citizens except Roman Catholics were to enjoy freedom of worship[31].

Freedom of worship had once again triumphed over state-enforced religious uniformity, although it has to be said, in spite of, rather than because of some religious leaders in the colony. However, without any change to their Calvinistic theology, they soon adapted to this new situation. Increase Mather (1639–1723), one of the leading ministers of the period, had gone over to England to attempt to persuade William III to restore the old charter, and when this proved fruitless, he had lobbied hard on the colony's behalf during the crafting of its replacement. He and his son Cotton (1663–1727) became the principal apologists for the new charter among their fellow colonists, and their line of defence was striking. Instead of viewing the preservation of a godly society as paramount, they argued that the charter was a good thing because of its support for liberty – freedom of worship, and significantly, freedom for the colonists to possess their own property. It had been Governor Andros' confiscation of the property of a number of leading colonists which, more than any other factor, had led to his imprisonment. The right to private property was viewed very much as God-given. Samuel Nowell (1634–1688) had argued in a 1678 election sermon, that liberty *and property* (emphasis mine) were given "both by the laws of God and man.[32]" In the final years of the 17th Century, the most desirable trait that the Christians of New England sought in their leaders was their commitment to the preservation of these rights.

This is not to say that in this new age, liberty was to mean licence. "Liberty of conscience", said Cotton Mather, "is not to be permitted as a cloak for the liberty of profaneness[33]" but he recognised that religious persecution was of little use, creating martyrs, rather than converts. It had taken a long time, but in this last remaining stronghold of Christian political activism, all debate about godliness and moral restraint was henceforth to be undertaken against a backdrop of religious liberty.

Puritan Political thought in detail

Taking the three headings of compassion, liberty and moral restraint, what strikes any student of Puritan political thought is that whenever the first of these categories is discussed, it is always in the context of the individual giving of his own free will out of his or her own resources. Article XXXVIII of the Church of England's Thirty Nine Articles, pre-dates the Puritan era, but very much anticipates its thought. After affirming the right to private property against the teaching of the Anabaptists it goes on say, "Notwithstanding every man ought, of such things as he possesseth, liberally to give alms to the poor according to his ability." Communal living in the manner of the Anabaptists never appealed to the Puritans. The Pilgrim Fathers had attempted it on their arrival in America in 1620, and had suffered famine and starvation. The abandonment of this arrangement in 1623 saw a marked improvement in their food supply. Individual land ownership had generated a sense of responsibility, which had proved itself economically superior to shared ownership.

John Winthrop, in his "Model of Christian Charity," written on board the *Arbella* as he sailed for America in 1630, addressed the possible hardship his colonists might face very much from the angle of individual responsibility. Christians must be self-sacrificially generous. "When there is no other means whereby our Christian brother may be relieved in his distress, we must help him beyond our ability rather than tempt God in putting him upon help by miraculous or extraordinary means. This duty of mercy is exercised in the kinds: giving, lending and forgiving *(of a debt)*[34]" he wrote. Even if "the time and occasion be ordinary" the Christian must "give out of his abundance.[35]" Richard Baxter took up the same theme in *The Saint's Everlasting Rest* (1650). Addressing "Men of wealth and authority", he reminds them "Have you not all your honor and riches from God? Doth not Christ say, 'Unto whomsoever much is given, of him much shall be required'?" Besides showing a concern for the souls of their neighbours, such men must "excel others in piety, *compassion*, (emphasis mine) and diligence in God's work, as (they) do in the riches and honors of the world.[36]" Thomas Lever, (1521–1577), an English precursor of the Puritans, emphasised that, "the rich man by liberality must dispose and comfort the poor[37]" while Matthew Henry said "one would not covet an estate for any thing so much as thereby to be put into a capacity of relieving the poor.[38]"

One of the main differences between Calvin and the Puritans was that Puritanism did not grant so prominent a role for the state in caring for the poor. It is interesting that James I's instruction book to his young son mentions compassion and the authority of kingship almost in the same breath. There is a profound and very contemporary lesson in this. Any government of whatever type that assumes responsibility for the areas of welfare and charity is unlikely to treat these issues in isolation, but rather as part of a strategy that will also make other, less acceptable, demands on its people. Significantly, the Puritan emphasis on compassion being the responsibility of individuals and churches rather than the state saw Christian compassion gaining somewhat of a higher profile in the 18th Century, by which time the debate over which models of government enjoyed the greatest Biblical support was long over. In the process, one of the worst deficiencies in the thinking of some Puritans, particularly in New England, was finally addressed – their support for slavery. John Milton, like Calvin before him, was opposed to slavery on Biblical grounds, but across the Atlantic, the first slaves had appeared in Massachusetts soon after the colony was founded and Boston was for a number of years the centre of the North American slave trade. Even Rhode Island and Pennsylvania, which stressed the importance of freedom of worship, did not see anything wrong in denying freedom to their fellow human beings. It does no credit to Christianity to read that Cotton Mather owned slaves himself. In *The Negro Christianised* (1706) he strongly urged their masters to pray for them and seek their salvation. He was dismissive of the idea that they had no rational souls, as some were arguing[39]. His statement that "the God who looks on the

Heart, is not moved by the colour of the skin; is not more propitious to one colour than another[40]" should be heartily endorsed by any Christian, and his encouragement to masters to treat their servants kindly, and make their lives comfortable as they would get better service from them, is a rather pragmatic application of Colossians 4:1, but when he adds "God has caused them to be servants[41]" he is slipping into bad biblical exegesis. The curse of Canaan in Genesis 9:24–27, where the son of Noah's youngest son Ham is condemned to slavery, was interpreted as condemning all the descendents of Ham to servitude. The Ethiopians, or Cushites, were descended from Ham (Genesis 10:6–7) and it was assumed that the other African peoples were as well. Stated in these bald terms, the idea that God foreordained all black people to slavery as a punishment for the sin of someone who may have been, but cannot definitely be proved to have been, their common ancestor, is ridiculous. Mather was neither the first nor, sadly, the last Christian to make this mistake.

Considering how Puritans on both sides of the Atlantic prized the idea of liberty, it is surprising and unfortunate that it was not until well after the Puritan era that Christians finally gave up any attempt to justify slavery from the Bible and instead led the fight for its abolition, and in North America, the theologically heterodox Quakers took up the gauntlet ahead of their more Evangelical brethren.

But of what does liberty consist? Liberty for the preaching of the Gospel certainly, but what about liberty for false religion? At the heart of the debate over religious toleration lay the question of the Law of Moses and its application. Only the extreme fringes of the Reformation proposed a reconstruction of Jewish theocracy. Bernhard Rothmann had stated in his *Restitution of Christian Teaching, Faith and Life* (1534) that the distinction between Old and New Testament had been abolished – in other words, church and state in Münster were one and the same. The Puritans, like Calvin, would all have strongly disagreed, but the very fact that subsequent writers have mistakenly described both Geneva and New England as theocracies is proof that the way they applied the Mosaic law muddied the waters of the Church/state divide. Rutherford in *Lex, Rex* reaffirmed the classic Scottish belief in the covenanted nation. He was strongly opposed to freedom of worship, arguing that "Magistrates....and judges are to maintain religion by their commandments" for "when the judges decline from God's way and corrupt the law, we find the people punished and rebuked for it.[42]" He argues from Old Testament examples that spiritual transgression will provoke God's wrath, and therefore must be punished by the state. Richard Baxter in *A Holy Commonwealth* (1659) takes a similar line, warning that freedom of worship "tendeth to the ruine of the commonwealth and therefore is no good cause." Citing the example of God's anger over Aaron's golden calf and the strange fire offered by his sons Nadab and Abihu, he warns that "Law and providence are quite changed if toleration of false religion and other abuses of worship tend not to the ruine of the Commonwealth.[43]" The Ten Commandments were "the vitall part of the Jews' political laws and every commandment of the first Table was seconded by a Penall Section. Therefore these things belong to the Magistrate.[44]"

Baxter was arguing against Sir Henry Vane (1613–1662), a long-term supporter of freedom of religion. Vane had emigrated to Massachusetts in 1635 because of his Puritan convictions, and being descended from a noble English family, made such an impact on the community that he was elected as governor while only in his mid-20s. However, once his support for liberty of conscience manifested itself, attitudes changed rapidly, and he returned to England after only a year. By the 1650s Vane's political thinking had matured, although his commitment to freedom of worship had not changed. He regarded Cromwell's assumption of power as an attack on liberty, and wrote a pamphlet called *A Healing Question Propounded* in 1656, which was a powerful defence of freedom of worship. It was Vane's work that Baxter was attempting to refute in *A Holy Commonwealth*, but he failed to trump Vane's central argument. As far as spiritual matters are concerned, Christ alone is king, "the Sole Lord and Ruler in and over the conscience.[45]" The magistrate is to be "a minister of terror and revenge to those that do evil in matters of outward practice,[46]" but thus far and no farther may he go. Magistrates must forbear "to put forth the power of rule and coercion in things that God hath exempted out of his commission.[47]" Four years later, John Milton (1608–1674), rightly fearing a return to tyranny with the impending return of Charles II, wrote a pamphlet entitled *"A Readie and Easie Way to Establish a Free Commonwealth,"* which proposed an alternative to monarchy. Milton was a long-standing supporter of liberty. In 1644, he had made a speech to Parliament in support of freedom of the press. In the *Readie and Easie Way*, he argues that, "The whole freedom of man consists either in spiritual or civil libertie. As for spiritual, who can be at rest, who can enjoy any thing in this world with contentment, who hath not libertie to serve God and to save his own soul, according to the best light which God hath planted in him to that purpose, by the reading of his reveal'd will and the guidance of his holy spirit? That this is best pleasing to God, and that the whole Protestant Church allows no supream judge or rule in matters of religion, but the scriptures, and these to be interpreted by the scriptures themselves, which necessarily inferrs liberty of conscience.[48]" He also argued for the separation of powers – in other words for the judiciary to be separate from the legislators.

The balance of argument comes down very much on the side of Vane and Milton. The work of Christ not only saves sinners, but under the New Covenant, writes the Law on their hearts by the Spirit, as Milton had argued in his 1651 treatise *de doctrina*. A professing church member who violates the law of Christ and commits a serious offence either of a civil or spiritual nature should face discipline by the church as the embodiment of Christ's kingdom on earth[49], but civil punishment is reserved only for offences that disturb society as a whole. The exact point at which sinful behaviour becomes a disturbance is hard to pinpoint, and Christians are likely to differ over this issue now as much as they did in the 17th

Century, but all would be agreed on the principle that Gordon Wenham sums up so well: "Unless the violent are punished, the earth may be swamped in violence as it was before the flood. There are many other offences that, left unpunished, will enrage the victim and lead to violence. The law thus has a vital role in the management of sinful humanity, to stop sin getting totally out of hand.[50]" The English Puritans' ban on the theatre or their New England counterparts' sanction of capital punishment for adultery may seem excessive to us, but one must not be too critical. Such laws were the product of men who genuinely viewed these sins as a disturbance to the stability of the godly society they desired. If God is pleased to send revival again to the West, just as Christians in such times develop an exceptional desire to live according to God's law, and thus hate any sin in their individual lives, so may we well find our thinking changed regarding the location of the boundary at which point sin becomes a threat to society.

Although the supporters of state punishment of spiritual offences hardly sound like advocates of small government, a close reading of their writings shows that in other aspects, they join the advocates of freedom of worship in seeking a government that is limited in scope. Rutherford reiterates the Augustinian line that government is only necessary because of the fall. It is natural for men to "join in a civil society" particularly to "defend themselves from violence[51]" and the role of the king is to be the servant of the people, preserving their safety. In other words, they are nothing more than "a means to an end.[52]" It was Charles I's failure to fulfil these obligations which in Rutherford's view justified the Bishops' Wars. He was accountable to his subjects and could not plead the unbiblical doctrine of the Divine Right of Kings to justify his actions. The Puritans repeatedly underlined how Romans 13:4 talked of the ruler as being a minister "for good". A ruler who was not "for good" was no ruler and need not be obeyed. Rutherford, however, was not against monarchy as such, and Richard Baxter actually supported the idea of a limited monarchy rather than a republic. Vane and

Milton disagreed. In the *Readie and Easie Way*, Milton takes 1 Samuel 8, one of the most important Biblical passages on the subject of limited government, and argues that just as the Israelites' demand for a king was sinful, so was his fellow countrymen's clamour for Charles II's return. England had been "once deliverd by (God) from a king, and not without wondrous acts of his providence" but was becoming "insensible and unworthie of those high mercies" and was about to return "precipitantly, if he withhold us not, back to the captivitie from whence he freed us.[53]" Milton also unusually regards Jesus' commands to the apostles in Matthew 20:20–28, which state that the church must not be organised along the lines of worldly government, as nothing less than a total condemnation of monarchy in the Christian age. "God in much displeasure gave a king to the Israelites, and imputed it a sin to them that they sought one: but Christ apparently forbids his disciples to admitt of any such heathenish government.[54]" It is interesting that neither Vane nor Milton advocated a New England-style democracy for their republic. Milton preferred the idea of a senate which would be elected for life, and Vane opted for a similar solution, placing particular emphasis on godliness as being a requisite qualification, believing that godly men would not pass laws that impinge on Christian liberty. The bottom line is that for all the divergences of opinion, on both sides of the Atlantic, Puritans were agreed in arguing for limited, accountable government which stuck to its task of preserving peace and order.

Some of the most radical thinking of this period was found among members of Cromwell's New Model Army in the 1640s. The debates held in the church of St Mary the Virgin, Putney, in 1647, between Cromwell and his son-in-law Henry Ireton on the one hand and certain members of the army on the other, were an attempt by Cromwell to take the sting out of some demands which, by the standards of the time, were considered quite extreme. The army radicals had drawn up a proposal entitled *The Agreement of the People*, which called for universal male suffrage, Parliamentary elections every alternate year, authority to be invested in the House of

Commons, rather than the Lords or the King, equality under the law and complete freedom of worship. Many of the more prominent spokesmen for the army were part of a movement known as the Levellers, although John Lilburne (d1657), one of the movement's leaders, preferred the name "agitators". They were not necessarily a united, cohesive group. Some of the movement's leaders argued that the democracy they proposed was Biblical, but others looked back to Magna Carta or indeed the Saxon days to justify their call for democracy and limited, accountable government. Before an agreement between the two parties could be finalised, Charles I, imprisoned at Hampton Court when the debates began, escaped from captivity, and with all elements of the army realising that this meant a renewal of the Civil War, no further discussions on the proposals took place. Cromwell's initial reaction to the Levellers' proposals is an indication of just how radical they were perceived to be at the time: "Truly this paper doth contain in it very great alterations of the very government of this Kingdom, that it has been under, I believe I may almost say since it was a nation...and what the consequences of such an alteration as this would be, if there were nothing else to be considered, wise men and Godly men ought to consider.[55]" The concept of such a limited and accountable government was a bit too radical, even for a man like Cromwell, whose views on liberty were in advance of his time.

Along with liberty of worship and small government, the other key component of liberty is respect for the individual. Individual rights carry individual responsibilities, hence the importance attached to voting in Massachusetts. The emphasis on individual property rights in New England in the latter part of the 17th Century has already been noted above, and the imprisonment of Governor Andros over his assault on private property can be readily understood considering the men who suffered loss had worked their land with "much prudence, payne and frugalitie[56]". The English Puritans were also hard-working and, like Calvin, attached great importance to the idea of a vocation – a calling that used the gifts which

God had given them. With these gifts went a sense of accountability. "We must give a strict account, (for) there is no calling so mean but a man shall find enough to give an account for" said Richard Sibbes (1577–1635)[57]. William Perkins (1558–1602), one of the earliest Puritan writers, emphasised that "The main end of our lives is to serve God in the serving of men in the works of our callings.[58]" The concepts of the sacredness of one's vocation and the stress on accountability fostered a diligent attitude among many Puritan workmen which not uncommonly raised their standard of living. With increased wealth came the danger of worldliness, against which Puritan ministers emphatically warned. "Remember that riches are no part of your felicity" wrote Richard Baxter in the *Christian Directory*. "Understand what it is to love and trust in worldly wealth. Many here deceive themselves to destruction.[59]" Significantly, Baxter places a greater emphasis on exhorting the rich to steer clear of temptation than to care for the poor, although elsewhere in the same work, he exhorts his reader to "love your poor brethren as yourselves, and delight in their welfare as if it were your own.[60]" Although riches were a source of temptation, the Puritans had no problems with wealth in and of itself, which they viewed, like everything else, as being part of God's providence and not to be despised as long as it was gained legitimately. Richard Sibbes wrote that "worldly things are good in themselves and given to sweeten our passage to Heaven[61]." The same applied to the right to private property, which William Ames (1576–1633) said was founded "not only on natural but on human and divine right.[62]". "Ownership and differences in the amount of possessions," he went on to say, "are ordinances of God and approved by him.[63]" In summary, as the Puritans studied their Bibles to guide their political thinking, liberty coupled with a strong sense of personal responsibility were the themes that leapt out at them, leaving little room for state intervention. The only exception is the absence of any Puritan support for free trade. The mercantilist Navigation Acts, which were a major cause of friction between England and its American colonies, were first put onto the statute books in 1651, thanks to lobbying from English traders unable to compete with the Dutch on equal terms. Although the Restoration parliament repealed all legislation from the "usurping powers" of Commonwealth period, it then passed a similar act which, like its predecessor, required English trade to be transported on English ships.

Little needs to be added under our third heading of moral restraint, as the debate about liberty and state-enforced religious uniformity which has been considered in detail above, was also a debate about where the boundaries of moral restraint were to be set. It is significant that although the more controversial Puritan restrictive acts, such as the bans on horseracing and theatregoing were speedily repealed by Charles II and his ministers, British laws retained a surprising element of moral restraint for a considerable period after the end of Puritanism. The Buggery Act of 1533, which treated homosexuality as a capital crime, remained in force until the 19th century. Witchcraft likewise was rigidly prohibited and remained a capital crime into the 18th century. Most surprisingly, the Blasphemy law, which deals with a "spiritual" rather than a moral offence, remained on the statute books until 2008, although it ceased to be a capital offence after 1676[64].

The Christian Worldview and its outworking – a summary

By the late 17th Century, the zenith of Bible-based political thinking had been reached. All the men whose political thought has been considered in this and the two previous chapters believed that the Bible was God's infallible Word, and it was to the Scriptures they looked for guidance in their writings. However, they were all fallible men seeking to apply God's word in an imperfect and fallen world, as they themselves readily acknowledged. In such circumstances, the lack of consensus in some areas is inevitable, as is the presence of occasional blind spots, with certain excesses being tolerated or even encouraged. Nonetheless, if the excesses are excluded, a reasonable summary of the Bible's teaching on

132

political matters, as interpreted by the best Christian thinking from Augustine to the Puritans, is as follows:

- Man was originally created free – accountable to God only. The need for some men to be subject to others only came about because of the Fall.
- Nonetheless, Government is a good thing – being part of God's providence, or common grace, which is a gift to all mankind, saint and sinner alike. Its main benefits are the restraint of evil, the enforcement of legal contracts and the preservation of order and peace. Rulers therefore rule by the delegated authority of God, and are accountable to Him.
- Although God Himself acted directly to put one restraint on the potential for large-scale tyranny by creating separate nations delineated by different languages at Babel, His other guidelines for restraining the size and scope of government are found in His Word, and it is for man to apply them.
- No government will be perfect in a fallen world, and the best rulers may not necessarily always be Christians. They should nonetheless have a reverence for God's laws, and be men with a servant heart who will not get carried away with their own importance and power. Christians should seek, wherever possible, to support and promote men who meet these criteria. Although citizens of the Kingdom of Heaven, Christians should take an active concern for the world around them, as it is ultimately under God's rule and Christians should therefore seek for His will to be done on Earth as in Heaven.
- Rulers and governments are accountable to those they rule. They have a duty to preserve their citizens' freedom, including their right to own property and pass it on to their heirs. Governments should not interfere with trading practises, unless they are unjust. The state is, however, entitled to take a modest amount in taxation to enable the process of government to function. Whether citizens have the authority forcefully to depose a ruler who ignores that accountability remains a debatable point. Property is on trust from God, to be used for His glory and the good of others. Christians should strive to honour God in their vocation, by performing it to the best

of their ability. Those who prosper should show a generous spirit towards the disadvantaged rather than living a life of extravagance and excess.

• The Bible does not mandate any one mode of government, but history and experience has shown that the governments that most consistently meet the Biblical criteria (particularly regarding accountability) are those where power is limited by the democratic process and/or the separation of the executive, the legislative and the judiciary – normally a constitutional monarchy or a republic.

• Church and state are two separate spheres or jurisdictions. The state should not interfere in the affairs of the church and neither should it inflict punishments for offences such as heresy that come under the jurisdiction of the church. God will punish unbelievers, heretics and hypocrites at the Last Judgement, but in this life, the state should uphold their freedom to believe (or not to believe) whatever they want, unless those beliefs involve practices seriously detrimental to the peace and order of society.

Although all men are born dead in trespasses and sins, the image of God is not completely obliterated in them. They are still endowed with abilities and able to act in a responsible way. The more a government honours, fosters and encourages that sense of individual responsibility, the less restraint it will need to apply to preserve peace and order.

Due to the tendency in fallen man to pursue gain by unlawful means, the freedoms which God allows and encourages must be tempered by laws endued with the spirit of justice to ensure that the poor and the disadvantaged are not treated badly, such as by enslavement or dishonest practises. The poor we will always have with us, but while profiteering by exploiting the poor is to be discouraged, the state has no scriptural mandate to redistribute wealth by compulsion.

Furthermore, for the peace and preservation of society, certain moral restraints must be applied by governments to curtail unacceptable and evil behaviour. Transgressors must be punished appropriately. The Bible, and the Old Testament

134

THE DEVELOPMENT OF A CHRISTIAN WORLDVIEW (2)

in particular, provides the best guidelines for moral restraint, although this does not imply an exact replication of the penalties prescribed by the Mosaic law. The degree to which moral restraint need be applied will vary according to the spiritual state of the nation.

Although few, if any governments have totally built their laws on the above synopsis, wherever men believing that God's sovereignty applies to every area of a nation's life have looked to the Bible to guide the process of law, blessing has followed.

It took a while for the separation of church and state into two separate jurisdictions to become reality in practise as well as theory, and for Christians to recognise the futility as well as the immorality of imposing "godliness" on a population the majority of which may not necessarily be converted individuals, but the toleration which eventually emerged in The Netherlands, Britain and North America is one of the best arguments that the Evangelical Christian worldview is superior not only to the mediaeval Roman Catholic view, but also to the essentially theocratic view of society in many Islamic states, which know no secular/religious distinctions and make life such a misery for many Christians even to-day. It is significant that as freedom advanced during the 17th Century in the nations considered in this chapter, it retreated among those nations that rejected the Reformation. In France, the limited toleration for Protestantism granted by the Edict of Nantes in 1598 was progressively eroded during the 17th Century and finally revoked by Louis XIV in 1685. In Spain, the dreaded Inquisition was not finally abolished until the Napoleonic wars, and the burning alive of Jews lasted well into the 18th Century. Freedom of worship for Spanish Evangelicals did not become a reality in practise until the death of General Franco in 1975. In Russia Peter the Great (1696–1727) turned the country into a police state and serfdom was not abolished until the 19th Century.

The economic balance in Europe also shifted significantly during this period, thanks in no small measure to the influence of Christian teaching on the sacredness and dignity of work, along with the Christian support for trade and limited government. Spain, rich with gold from the Americas in the early 16th Century was a poor and backward nation by 1700 whereas tiny Holland had become the most prosperous country in Europe. Napoleon may have ridiculed Britain as "a nation of shopkeepers," but notwithstanding the social stratification and the power of the landed gentry, his comments accurately reflected the significance of small family businesses in the nation's increasing prosperity. Such a development would not have been possible in the absolutism of 18th Century France.

And looking to more recent times, while the 19th German historian Leopold von Ranke was not totally accurate in calling Calvin the "virtual founder of America,[65]" it is no coincidence that the United States of America, the greatest nation of the present day and one of the most prosperous, owes more to the influence of Evangelical Christianity in the drafting of its Constitution than any other nation on earth. The "Deuteronomic principle" discussed in Chapter 1 – that the greater freedom and prosperity enjoyed by nations influenced by Evangelical political thought is proof of its divine origin – has been powerfully vindicated since the Reformation.

The beginnings of decline (1) Pietism

By the time of the death of the last of the Puritans, John Howe, in 1705, Evangelical Christianity had already slipped into a decline that was to last for some 30–40 years. Religious scepticism became widespread, particularly among the English aristocracy and intelligentsia. This decline was powerfully arrested by a revival, which has come to be known as the Great Awakening, and which affected the church on both sides of the Atlantic. Of the great preachers from this period, George Whitefield (1714–1770) and Jonathan Edwards (1703–1758) were both Calvinistic in their theology, although John Wesley, the founder of Methodism, was not – emphatically rejecting the idea of predestination. Regardless of doctrine, however, the Evangelicalism that emerged in the 18th Century revival showed some marked differences with Puritanism. It shared the Puritan emphases on the importance of personal piety, personal Bible study and a personal relationship with Jesus Christ, but withdrew to some considerable degree from the political arena. There were no treatises seeking to argue which form of government was mandated by the scriptures, nor how far rulers should go in the punishment of evildoers, for instance. It is hard to offer a satisfactory reason for the sudden disappearance of these considerations. In America, as was noted above, the idea of building a godly society around religious uniformity had been abandoned by 1691 and replaced by a fierce determination to uphold freedom and property rights. In Britain, the best explanation for the dramatic change may be that after the religious and political turmoil of the 17th Century, Christians were thankful to enjoy the freedoms enshrined in the Bill of Rights and the Act of Toleration. The toleration of dissent was briefly threatened during the final year of the reign of Queen Anne (1702–1714), but the Hanoverian monarchs who succeeded her showed no interest in either disturbing the religious peace or trying to reassert the absolutism of the Stuarts. A limited government and religious freedom may not have fully met the aspirations of the great Christian political thinkers of the 17th century, but their 18th Century successors were grateful for these mercies. Even in Scotland, with Presbyterianism now re-established after the brutality of Charles II's reign, there was no talk of state-enforced godliness. This is not to say that Christians took no interest in politics. The Dissenting ministers were only too aware that in spite of enjoying freedom to worship, they still suffered the restrictions imposed by the Test and Corporation Acts. Perhaps for this reason, many nonconformists, including the Baptist pastor J.C. Ryland (1723–1792), supported the American colonists during the War of Independence. Some ministers, however, took a very different line and condemned any Christian involvement in politics, viewing it as contrary to the will of God. The Baptist Andrew Fuller (1754–1815), for example, regarded "taking an eager and deep interest in political disputes" as "a sign of serious backsliding[66]".

Christian compassion nonetheless features prominently in both the words and deeds of the leading figures of the Great Awakening. Jonathan Edwards asked, "Where have we any command in the Bible laid down in stronger terms and in a more peremptory urgent manner than the command of giving to the poor?[67]" Whitefield and Wesley showed their compassion in the practical manner of opening orphanages while Robert Raikes of Gloucester (1736–1811) started the Sunday School movement. The compassion of concerned individual Christians also led to changes in the law, notably through the campaign of Elizabeth Fry (1780–1845) for improvement to the extremely harsh conditions found in prisons at the time, or the campaign to abolish the slave trade in which the Anglican hymn writer John Newton (1725–1807) and the Christian MP William Wilberforce (1759–1833) were prominent. Interestingly, one isolated example of a law with an element of moral restraint can also be found in this period – the Sunday Observance Act of 1781, which regulated and restricted Sunday trading in Britain until 1994. This act was passed thanks to the influence of Bishop Beilby Porteous (1731–1809), another anti-slavery campaigner and a rare example of an Evangelical Anglican minister raised to a bishopric.

Many Dissenters, granted freedom of worship but barred from public office by the Test and Corporation Acts, became tradesmen and merchants, in which professions they carried on the Calvinistic tradition of the sacredness of work, and not infrequently became prosperous in the process. The father of the hymn writer Anne Steele (1717–1778) was a timber merchant as well as pastor of the Baptist church in Broughton, Hampshire. The house in the village where he lived survives to this day, and testifies to a reasonable degree of prosperity. John Wesley's statement that "we must exhort on Christians to gain all they can and to save all they can, that is, in effect, to grow rich" in order that they can give all they can,[68] accords with the teaching of Calvin and Baxter that the right to private property must be balanced with generosity. Such words would have found echoes among the dissenting business community.

However, for all the sterling compassionate work, the residue of Puritan influence and the renewed influence of Christianity in British society thanks to the Great Awakening, the 18th Century presents a picture of decline as far as the idea of a Christian worldview is concerned. The new leaders of political thought in Britain were appreciative of its limited government and the accompanying freedoms, which were part of the Puritan political legacy, even if their Puritan origins were not widely acknowledged. Without a strong undergirding Christian element, however, there would inevitably be weaknesses and imbalances in their political thinking.

The beginnings of decline (2) Deism

The decline of Puritanism in the late 17th century marked the end of the period when leading thinkers in the fields of politics and science believed in the Bible as God's inspired Word and the supreme authority in all areas of life. The seeds of change had been sown earlier in the century, notably by the French philosopher René Descartes (1596–1650), often referred to as the father of modern philosophy. Descartes is best known for his little phrase *Cogito ergo Sum* – I think therefore I am. This short phrase, when understood in its context, was to usher in a revolution in thinking. Descartes "developed a philosophy in which his starting point was doubt of everything except his own consciousness and his ability to think[69]." Ironically, he was a firm believer in God, thinking that of all man's thoughts, "no idea is as clear as the idea of God. Since it is not derived from sense experience, and is not fashioned by our own act, it must be an innate idea, implemented in us by God himself.[70]" This view of God was nonetheless very different from that of Evangelical Christianity, for in order to discover what God is like, according to Descartes, the starting point should be human reason, rather than what had hitherto been believed to be divine revelation. Faith, in other words, was superfluous. For all his strong affirmations of the existence of God, the foundation of Descartes' philosophy was not, as in the Bible, "In the beginning, God….," but "in the beginning, Man."

Although Voetius in Holland vigorously attacked Descartes and effectively refuted his thinking, the late 17th and early 18th centuries favoured the rise of the cult of human reason. In 1650, things had been different. Both combatants in the second phase of the Civil War believed that their cause was righteous in God's eyes. The battle cry of the Cromwell's army at the battle of Dunbar was "The Lord of Hosts," while that of the vanquished Scots had been "The Covenant." Cromwell, to his credit, had recognised the absurdity of two nations so favoured by God coming to blows. "Since we came in Scotland, it hath been our desire and longing to have avoided blood in this business," he wrote. "God hath a people here fearing his name, though deceived.[71]" The Scots, for their part, did not lapse into unbelief following their defeat, concluding rather that, "their own fallibility must in some way be responsible for this rejection[72]." A year later, following the final defeat in Worcester, the Scottish writer John Nicoll stated that God's lack of support for their cause was due to his nation's religious hypocrisy. "The cloak of piety," he claimed, must have covered "much knavery[73]" Fast forward fifty years and a more cynical spirit began to prevail. At the end of a century which had seen so many people killed because of differences in religion, questions were being asked not merely about the morality of persecuting people for their religious beliefs, but whether Roman Catholicism or any of the different versions of Protestantism could possibly be divinely revealed truth considering the conflicts that had taken place in their name. Such scepticism very rarely degenerated into outright atheism. Even that most extreme cynic, the French philosopher Voltaire (1694–1778), who called Christianity *"la plus ridicule, la religion la plus absurde et sanglante qui ait jamais infecté le monde"* (the most ridiculous, the most absurd and bloody religion that ever infected the world.), retained at least a vague pantheistic[74] belief. Nonetheless, even among less radical thinkers, the god that developed from their reason was far removed from the Triune God of Biblical Christianity. For these men, known as deists, the divine authority of the scriptures, miracles, the atonement and Jesus being both God and man were too irrational to be acceptable. That the age of the deists has gone down in history under the name of the Enlightenment can only strike any Evangelical Christian as a sad example of the arrogance of man.

Such a radical departure from historic Christianity was bound to affect political thinking, although the most important deist political thinker of the period, John Locke (1632–1704), affirmed a surprising number of the key propositions of the Christian worldview as set out earlier in this chapter. Locke had been a student at Oxford during the Cromwell era when the Puritan theologian John Owen had been vice-chancellor of the university. However, besides being subject to the influence of Puritanism, he had also studied Descartes, and a book he published in 1695 epitomised in its very title how things had changed – *The reasonableness of Christianity as Delivered in the Scriptures*. In his political and philosophical works, Locke had argued for total freedom of religion as far back as 1667, when he wrote *An Essay upon Toleration*. He also argued for private property rights, limited government and Christian morality. While he rejected the Augustinian (and Biblical) view of man as fallen, his argument for the small state has a certain resonance with Augustine's writing – government must reflect the will of the governed, which in a diverse society will inevitably make it limited in scope. Criticising the teaching of Thomas Hobbes (1588–1679) that in the interests of security, individuals ought to surrender their rights of self-government to a powerful central government which will govern on their behalf, he wrote, "This is to think that men are so foolish that they take care to avoid what Mischiefs may be done to them by pole-cats or foxes, but are content, nay think it safety, to be devoured by lions.[75]" On the contrary, men have a right to "life, liberty and estate" which in his opinion the limited government provided by a constitutional monarchy would be the best guarantor.

It is significant that in Locke's opinion, the objectives of government all revolve around the individual. It is also significant that compassion is not prominent either. What was developing under Locke, which has since been given the name "liberal democracy", was a debasement of the Puritan tradition, which affirmed its emphasis on limited government and a broadly socially conservative outlook, while rejecting its fundamental *raison d'etre* – the sovereignty of God in every area of life. This was not to say liberal democracy despised Evangelical Christianity completely – it acknowledged the important and positive role played by tradition, including Christian traditions, in shaping society and preserving order, even if it regarded those traditions as founded on untenable or superstitious premises. The author of the *Wealth of Nations*, Adam Smith, (1723–1790) shared this same respect for tradition. He also reaffirmed the Puritan tradition of small government. In 1755, addressing a meeting in Glasgow, he said, "Little else is requisite to carry a state to the highest degree of opulence from the lowest barbarism but peace, easy taxes, and a tolerable administration of justice: All the rest being brought about by the natural course of things. All governments which thwart the natural course are unnatural, and to support themselves, are obliged to be oppressive and tyrannical.[76]" If compassion were to be included under the category of "little else," Smith's statement could well have been uttered by a Puritan, apart from the strong emphasis on material prosperity. Smith's writings turned the tables on mercantilism. The argument for free trade in the *Wealth of Nations* may have been based on the perceived material benefit for all parties concerned, rather than on the Scriptures, but nonetheless corrected one of the blind spots of Puritan political thought. It took until 1849 before the Navigation Acts were repealed, but from then onwards, Britain to this day has been one of the foremost enthusiasts for free trade, notwithstanding occasional lapses into protectionism.

Edmund Burke (1729–1797), regarded as the ideological mentor of the British Conservative Party, held similar views to Locke and Smith on the value of tradition and the need for limited government, and in more recent times, the same line was taken by FA Hayek (1899–1992), the economist who influenced the Thatcher revolution. Such men may not have been believers and may have scorned many of the essential doctrines of Evangelical Christianity, but, recognising the beneficial effects Christianity has produced, have never sought to attack those who profess its doctrines.

If Liberal Democracy is understood as a debasement of Christian political thinking that affirmed many of its principles without affirming its God, the still ongoing debate about whether America was founded as a Christian nation or on the principles of the Enlightenment loses some of its heat. Benjamin Franklin (1706–1790), who played such a pivotal role in the drafting of its constitution, epitomises the strange ambivalence of deism. His father held strong Calvinistic views, and in his mature years, he would go out of his way to listen to the preaching of George Whitefield whenever he visited America. When Whitefield died in 1770, Franklin paid a glowing tribute to him: "I knew him intimately upwards of 30 years. His integrity, disinterestedness and indefatigable zeal in prosecuting every good work, I have never seen equalled, I shall never see excelled.[77]" Yet he later added, "Mr Whitefield used to pray for my conversion, but never had the satisfaction of believing that his prayers were heard.[78]" Tolerant as such men might be of Christianity, it was obvious that Christians wishing to argue against unjust laws would henceforth increasingly have to use the language of reason; no longer would an argument based on the Bible being God's inspired and infallible Word hold water in the political realm.

For all the self-confidence of the Enlightenment, Descartes and Locke were actually making massive assumptions. Descartes believed it was reasonable to believe in God and Locke had maintained the reasonableness of the Christian faith – admittedly a Christian faith shorn of its Evangelical core – but on what basis? Suppose someone else maintained it was actually more reasonable not to believe in God at all, or that the religion demanded by human reason was Voltaire's pantheism? Human reason as the ultimate arbiter of truth could well decide that it would be more rational to be less sympathetic to tradition, and thus less willing to affirm, even in a debased form, the essentials of a Christian political worldview. By the time Burke and Adam Smith were laid in their graves, the seeds of this alternative reasoning had already been sown.

Notes

[1] Proverbs 14:34.
[2] Tudor Jones, R, *The Great Reformation*, p194, Inter-Varsity Press, Leicester, 1985.
[3] *ibid*, p203.
[4] *ibid*, p205.
[5] http://en.wikipedia.org/wiki/Dutch_Reformed_Church Accessed 20/01/11
[6] Kuyper, A, *Lectures on Calvinism*, p78. Eerdmans, Grand Rapids, 1987 (reprint).
[7] Jones, R.T. *op cit*, p188.
[8] *Lives of the British Reformers* (anonymous), p375, Religious Tract Society, London. Date of publication unknown.
[9] Breen, TH *The Character of the Good Ruler*, p22, Yale University Press New Haven, 1970.
[10] http://www.stoics.com/basilikon_doron.html#'OFFICE1 Accessed 01/02/2011.
[11] *idem.*
[12] *idem.*
[13] http://www.stoics.com/basilikon_doron.html#'ARGUMENT1 Accessed 01/02/2011.
[14] *idem.*
[15] Fraser, Lady A, *Cromwell, our Chief of Men*, p283 Mandarin Paperbacks, London 1993.
[16] Adair, A *Puritans – Religion and Politics in Seventeenth Century England and America*, p218 Sutton Publishing, Stroud 1998.
[17] http://dspacedev.stir.ac.uk/bitstream/1893/1400/1/Heresy%20rev.pdf Accessed 10/02/2011.
[18] Baxter, R *The Reformed Pastor*, p135, Banner of Truth, Edinburgh 1989 (Originally published in 1656).
[19] Watson, T *The Ten Commandments*, p155 Banner of Truth, Edinburgh 1995. Originally published posthumously in 1692 as part of *A*

Body of Practical Divinity.
[20] Adair, A *op cit,* p227.
[21] Congregationalists differed little from the Independents in their views of church order. Indeed, the two terms are to some degree synonymous.
[22] http://www.pilgrimhall.org/compact.htm accessed on 02/02/2011.
[23] Breen, T H *op cit*, p36.
[24] Breen, T.H *op cit*, p42.
[25] Breen, T.H *op cit*, p40.
[26] Clark, S (ed) *Tales of two cities – Christianity and Politics*, p281 IVP Leicester 2005.
[27] Brook, B, *Lives of the Puritans*, Volume 3, p478 Soli Deo Gloria Publications, Morgan Pennsylvania (reprint – original published in 1813).
[28] Breen, T H, *op cit*, p45.
[29] *ibid.* p90.
[30] *ibid,* p92.
[31] *ibid*, p184.
[32] *ibid,* p120.
[33] *ibid*, p201.
[34] http://religiousfreedom.lib.virginia.edu/sacred/charity.html Accessed 02/02/2011.
[35] *idem.*
[36] http://newdemonstration.com/files/books/richard-baxter/Richard%20Baxter%20-%20Saint's%20Everlasting%20Rest.pdf p85. Accessed 11/02/2011.
[37] http://www.apuritansmind.com/stewardship/rykenlelandpuritansandmoney.htm Accessed 11/02/2011.
[38] Henry, M *A Commentary on the Whole Bible* Volume 4 p901 (Proverbs 19:22) World Bible Publishers Iowa (originally published 1710).
[39] http://digitalcommons.unl.edu/cgi/viewcontent.cgi?article=1028&context=etas Accessed 03/02/2011.
[40] *idem.*
[41] *idem.*
[42] On-line version of *Lex, Rex* Question 14: http://www.lonang.com/exlibris/rutherford Accessed 11/02/2011.
[43] Baxter, R *A Holy Commonwealth*, p25 Edited by William Lamont, Cambridge University Press, Cambridge 1994.
[44] *ibid,* p26.
[45] http://www.bartleby.com/43/11.html Accessed 11/02/2011.
[46] *idem.*
[47] *idem.*
[48] http://oll.libertyfund.org/index.php?option=com_staticxt&static-

file=show.php%3Ftitle=272&layout=html Accessed 11/02/2011.
[49] See Matthew 18:15–17, Romans 16:17, 1 Corinthains 5, 2 Thessaloninas 3:6–14.
[50] Wenham, G *Biblical Ethics in a Multicultural Society*, in Clark, S (Ed) *Tales of Two Cities, Christianity and Politics*, p34. IVP, Leicester, 2005.
[51] On-line version of *Lex, Rex* Question 2: http://www.lonang.com/exlibris/rutherford Accessed 11/02/2011.
[52] Field, D *Put not your trust in Princes* in Clark, S (ed) *Tales of Two cities*, p93 IVP Leicetser 2005.
[53] http://oll.libertyfund.org/index.php?option=com_staticxt&staticfile=show.php%3Ftitle=272&layout=html Accessed 11/02/2011.
[54] *idem.*
[55] Fraser, Lady A, *Cromwell, Our Chief of Men*, p215, Mandarin Paperbacks, London 1973.
[56] Breen, T.H. *op cit*, p145.
[57] Breen, T.H. *op cit*, p7.
[58] http://www.ctlibrary.com/ch/2006/issue89/7.32.html Accessed 11/02/2011.
[59] http://www.ccel.org/ccel/baxter/practical.i.v.xxviii.html Accessed 11/02/2011.
[60] *idem.*
[61] http://www.apuritansmind.com/stewardship/rykenlelandpuritansandmoney.htm Accessed 11/02/2011.
[62] *idem.*
[63] *idem.*
[64] http://en.wikipedia.org/wiki/Blasphemy_law_in_the_United_Kingdom Accessed 11/02/2011.
[65] Robbins, J, *Ecclesiastical Megalomania*, p22 The Trinity Foundation, USA 2000.
[66] Ramsbottom, B A *William Gadsby*, p205 Gospel Standard Trust Publications, Harpenden, 2003.
[67] Dwight, S (ed) *The Works of Jonathan Edwards*, Vol 2, p164, Banner of Truth, Carlisle, Pa 1996.
[68] Quoted in Weber, M, *The Protestant Ethic and the Spirit of Capitalism* (1904–5). On line translation http://www.archive.org/stream/protestantethics00webe/protestantethics00webe_djvu.txt Accessed 11/02/2011.
[69] Cairns, Earle E, *Christianity through the Centuries*, p376, the Zondervan Corporation, Grtand Rapids 1954.
[70] Cragg, G R, *The Church in the Age of Reason 1648–1789*, p38 Penguin Books, Harmondsworth, M iddlesex, 1960.
[71] Fraser, Lady A, *op cit*, p363, Mandarin Paperbacks, London 1993.
[72] *ibid.* p374

[73] *ibid*, p374.

[74] Pantheism claims God and nature are synonymous – in other words, it goes beyond stating that God is everywhere but asserts that everything contains the divine and that there is no personal god distinct from creation. Hinduism and Buddhism are predominantly pantheistic, unlike the Abrahamic religions (Judaism, Christianity, Islam).

[75] Locke, J *Two Treatises of Government* p372 para 93 (1689) as quoted in Held, D *Models of Democracy*, p62, Polity Press, Cambridge 2006.

[76] http://www.facebook.com/AdamSmithInstitute?sk=info Accessed 09/03/2012.

[77] Dallimore, A *George Whitefield, Evangelist of the Eighteenth Century Revival*, p198, Wakeman Trust, London 1990.

[78] *idem.*

Chapter 5:

The origins and ideals of Socialism

The idea of Socialism is at once grandiose and simple. Even its most determined opponents will not be able to deny it a detailed examination. We may say, in fact, that it is one of the most ambitious creations of the human spirit. The attempt to erect society on a new basis while breaking with all traditional forms of social organization, to conceive a new world plan and foresee the form which all human affairs must assume in the future—this is so magnificent, so daring, that it has rightly aroused the greatest admiration. If we wish to save the world from barbarism we have to conquer Socialism, but we cannot thrust it carelessly aside.

Ludwig von Mises (1881–1973)
Austrian economist and philosopher

Having looked at the development of Christian political thinking in the previous three chapters and established some sort of yardstick with which to compare socialism, this chapter introduces some of the pioneers and key players in its development. However, before looking at these early socialists, we shall firstly consider one highly influential figure to whom they were indebted and one important event which should have served as a warning sign about the likely direction of socialism were it ever to gain power.

The Genevan-born philosopher Jean-Jacques Rousseau

(1712–1778) grew up, like Locke and Franklin, in an atmosphere where Calvin's thought exercised a powerful influence. Like them, he rejected the inspiration of the scriptures, the fall of man and the Atonement. Unlike them, he was less confident about the potential of unaided human reason to produce a vastly better world.

Rather than looking forward with hope, Rousseau looked backward with regret. In his *Discourse on Inequality* (1754), he stated that it was "cruel" that "every advance made by the human species removes it still farther from its primitive state.[1]" The primitive state Rousseau depicted was very different from the Bible's account of the early chapters of Genesis. "It appears, at first view, that men in a state of nature, having no moral relations or determinate obligations one with another, could not be either good or bad, virtuous or vicious.[2]" In other words, according to Rousseau, early man may have been a "savage", but he was morally neutral. Rousseau is not the inventor of the phrase "the noble savage," as has been claimed, but there is a wistfulness in his writings when he speaks so approvingly of the abstinence of "the Caribbeans, who have as yet least of all deviated from the state of nature, being in fact the most peaceable of people in their amours, and the least subject to jealousy, though they live in a hot climate which seems always to inflame the passions.[3]" What was responsible for creating the harsher conditions of the developed world? It all began, he went on to say, with private property:– "The first man who, having enclosed a piece of ground, bethought himself of saying 'This is mine', and found people simple enough to believe him, was the real founder of civil society. From how many crimes, wars and murders, from how many horrors and misfortunes might not any one have saved mankind, by pulling up the stakes, or filling up the ditch, and crying to his fellows, 'Beware of listening to this impostor; you are undone if you once forget that the fruits of the earth belong to us all.'[4]" It was the "establishment of laws and of the right of property" which began "the progress of inequality.[5]" In Rousseau's opinion, the concept of right and wrong only emerged as a result of the development of civil society – in other words. associations of people living together – towns and cities for example. Rousseau quotes frequently from ancient Greek and Roman authors in support of his thesis, but references to the Bible are few and far between, and when they do occur, tend to be somewhat confusing. Rousseau's brand of deism, like Voltaire's, was pantheistic, but he differed from his older contemporary in his love of nature, whose beauty, in his opinion, was a clear pointer to God.

Rousseau's other important political work is the *Social Contract* (1762), which after a brief introduction begins with the dramatic opening sentence, "Man is born free and everywhere he is in chains," – the most well-known quotation from all Rousseau's writings. He reiterates the theme that human beings were more content before the development of civil government, but that they began to realise that their survival depended on working together. Individualism therefore has to give way to the common good. He recognises the problem in arriving at an arrangement for a coexistence which would manage to preserve that liberty which the earliest men supposedly enjoyed. "The problem is to find a form of association which will defend and protect with the whole common force the person and goods of each associate, and in which each, while uniting himself with all, may still obey himself alone, and remain as free as before.[6]" His answer is that a social contract is required, the essence of which is that everyone has to agree that "each of us puts his person and all his power in common under the supreme direction of the general will, and, in our corporate capacity, we receive each member as an indivisible part of the whole.[7]" In practical terms, this pointed to a democratic republic where the citizens were involved in the creation of the laws by which they were governed. Such a government, "being formed wholly of the individuals who compose it, neither has nor can have any interest contrary to theirs; and consequently the sovereign power need give no guarantee to its subjects, because it is impossible for the body to wish to hurt all its members.[8]"

He is not advocating the direct democracy of ancient Athens. The "general will" of the people is to be exercised through its government, and Rousseau lists the different possible forms which government had taken over the centuries, although excluding any mention of the Old Testament Jewish theocracy – at least in this section. Without coming down in favour of one form of government as being the only suitable means of reflecting the "general will", he makes the point that "the larger the State, the less the liberty.[9]" If this suggests Rousseau is an advocate of small government, the surrender of individual freedom that he demands paints a very different picture, even if he attempts to sell it as a good thing. "It is seen to be so untrue that there is, in the social contract, any real renunciation on the part of the individuals, that the position in which they find themselves as a result of the contract is really preferable to that in which they were before. Instead of a renunciation, they have made an advantageous exchange: instead of an uncertain and precarious way of living they have got one that is better and more secure; instead of natural independence they have got liberty.[10]" When he mentions the individuals' lives "which they have devoted to the State", he is giving the state an authority which a Christian would question. Rousseau was aware of this, for he added that the "law of Christianity at bottom does more harm by weakening than good by strengthening the constitution of the State.[11]" On the other hand, having acknowledged the antagonism between Christian individualism and his vision of the state, he ironically accuses them of servility. True Christians, he maintains, "are made to be slaves, and they know it and do not much mind: this short life counts for too little in their eyes...... Christianity preaches only servitude and dependence.[12]" He also strongly criticised the Christian separation of church and state, believing that this would be unnecessary if people could return to the "holy, sublime, and real religion" where "all men, being children of one God, recognise one another as brothers.[13]"

Rousseau's vision of government could, by his own admission, most easily be brought into being in a small republic like Geneva. Bearing in mind how he looked back rather wistfully to a lost and mythical past, his political theorising appears merely to be an attempt to make the best of a bad job – indeed, he admitted the difficulty a large country like France would face in implementing his ideas. In many ways, he was an idealist, and his thinking contained weaknesses, even contradictions. The "general will," for instance, rather than being a guarantor of freedom, could develop into a tyranny of the majority. It could create a much more intrusive state than Augustine's ideal, which confined government to areas on which there would be virtual unanimity, such as the preservation of peace. Of particular significance, however, is his antagonism towards Christianity. The Liberal Democratic tradition of Locke, while rejecting the essential doctrines of Evangelical Christianity, acknowledged the benefits it had brought. Rousseau was less sympathetic, viewing Christianity as an obstacle to the creation of the type of state he outlines in the *Social Contract*.

Liberty, Equality and Fraternity in France

In 1789, barely a decade after Rousseau's death, King Louis XVI summoned the French Parliament, the States-General, for the first time since 1614. The country was facing a financial crisis as a result of several poor harvests, unpaid public debt incurred by earlier wars and a badly-run economy. The opportunity for the representatives of the "Third Estate" (everyone who was not a nobleman or clergyman), to have their say after years of absolute rule brought to the surface all manner of grievances relating to abuses in both church and state. Initially, however, for all their frustration, these representatives of the people desired reform, not revolution, unlike some of those they represented, who were less ready to wait for gradual change. On 14th July, the Bastille prison was stormed, setting in process a chain of events which saw France proclaimed a republic three years later. The moderate reformists lost power to a radical element which executed the king the following year and then began a "reign of terror" which sought to eliminate all enemies of the revolution. The author Madame Germaine de Staël famously described Rousseau as a man who "discovered perhaps nothing but set everything ablaze." Rousseau's thought was a significant influence on Maximilien Robespierre (1758–1794), the *de facto* leader of the Jacobins, the most radical of all the groupings that emerged at the time of the revolution and which came to hold almost complete power during the reign of terror. Robespierre's ideal was to create a "republic of virtue" based on Rousseau's idea of the general will. It cannot be said that he or his fellow-revolutionaries replicated the model of government Rousseau had set out in the Social Contract, nor did they share his pessimism about the possibility of human progress. Robespierre did, however, share Rousseau's deism, unlike his fellow-revolutionaries Jacques Hébert (1757–1794) and Pierre Chaumette (1763–1794) who were militant atheists. Under their auspices, a *Fête de la Raison* was held in November 1793 where a young woman was enthroned as the Goddess of Reason on the high altar of the Cathedral of Notre Dame in Paris. Such outright atheism outraged Robespierre, who repudiated the Cult of Reason, ordered the execution of the Hébertists and instituted instead the "Cult of the Supreme Being."

For all their violent disagreements deist and atheist alike were both committed to de-Christianising France and redesigning French society based on reason. One particularly eccentric manifestation of their idealism was the creation of a new calendar in 1793, which took as its starting point the establishment of a republic the previous year – in other words, 1793 became Year 2. The years were divided into twelve 30-day months, each of which consisted of three 10-day weeks[14]. Even time was decimalised – each day consisting of 10 hours of 100 minutes, each of which consisted of 100 seconds. The months and days of the week were given new names – the former based on the cycle of the year and likely weather in Paris, such as *Brumaire* (foggy) from late October-November or *Thermidor* (summer heat) from mid-July to mid-August. The metric system, also based on powers of 10, came in during the revolution, and unlike the decimal calendar, survived it. Bizarre as the calendar was, the abolition of the God-ordained seven-day week, including the Lord's Day, along with the abolition of Christmas, Easter and all festivals of the church underlined just how determined the revolutionaries were to eliminate the influence of Christianity. During the initial moderate phase of the revolution (1789–1792), the Evangelical minority had been supportive, hoping for greater freedom than they had enjoyed since their faith had been declared illegal by the staunchly Roman Catholic Louis XIV in 1685. One Evangelical pastor, Jean-Paul Rabaut-Saint-Etienne (1743–1793) was elected as a member of the new government, the National Assembly, and sought to ensure that the right for everyone "to observe the form of worship to which he is attached[15]" was incorporated in the Constitution which the assembly was drawing up. After the radicals seized power, all churches were closed, and Rabaut-Saint-Etienne was guillotined, along with many Roman Catholic clergy.

Along with this direct assault on the church, the revolutionaries relaxed the laws on marriage and divorce. Contemporary reports speak of the 1793 *Fête de la Raison* as a "lurid, licentious affair of scandalous depravities[16]" and while some later historians have questioned the accuracy of these accounts, such were the numbers of abandoned women and illegitimate births brought about by "free unions" in France that divorce was made harder to obtain after 1804 and banned completely in 1816[17] to restore some sort of order to society.

The chaos and carnage associated with the radical phase of the revolution ended with the execution of Robespierre in 1794. The revolution's objectives – to establish "Liberty, Equality and Fraternity" – had not been achieved, and had bequeathed France a legacy of economic and political instability, along with a war to fight. The man who restored some degree of normality was Napoleon Bonaparte (1769–1821) the French army commander who was eventually crowned emperor in 1804. He was forced to abdicate in 1814 after a series of military reverses led to the occupation of Paris by a combined army made up of of Austrian, Prussian and Russian troops, and the French monarchy was restored. Napoleon escaped from exile in 1815 only to suffer his final defeat at Waterloo later in the year, which finally brought peace to France. The real winners from this period of turmoil were the middle classes, who acquired much more political power in the post-Napoleonic era. The peasants and craftsmen who supported the more extreme revolutionaries in the hope of a more egalitarian society had gained little. It was out of a desire to improve these ongoing imbalances in French society without the extremes of the revolution that socialism was born.

As an ideology, the defining feature of socialism in its earliest phase was that, "land and capital, which are the requisites of labour and of all the sources of wealth and culture, should be placed under social ownership and control.[18]" Social ownership, according to most socialists, means state control, and the processes by which they proposed that the process should be accomplished included the state compulsorily taking over land or factories. Particularly in the early days of the development of socialism, a few significant thinkers took a different line, but by and large, one of the most important features of mature socialism was the increased role of the state. As was noted, some political theorists attribute the idea of the state as an entity in itself to the effects of the Reformation. However, both Christian political thinkers and deists like John Locke were keen to confine the state within narrow bounds. Peace, law and order had to be maintained and individual freedoms preserved, but thus far and no farther in lightly-governed Britain or newly-independent America was the state to intrude.

A young French nobleman, Comte Henri de Saint-Simon (1760–1825) enjoyed a taste of limited government when he volunteered to fight against the British in the American war of independence. He had been impressed by the relative classlessness of America, although the strong influence of

Christianity does not appear to have made any impression on him. After his American adventure, he withdrew from politics until he had turned forty years of age, by which time the excesses of the revolution had come and gone – indeed, he only became an influential figure in the last few years of his life. Saint-Simon's proposals for a more egalitarian society called for the country to be run by the chiefs of industry and the spiritual direction of society to be entrusted not to clergymen but to scientists[19]. Saint-Simon, like Rousseau, wanted to reduce religion to a bare minimum, and set out his views in a work called *The New Christianity*. Not surprisingly, there is very little of the Gospel to be found, just a belief that all men are brothers and that "the whole of society ought to strive towards the amelioration of the moral and physical existence of the poorest class; society ought to organise itself in the best way adapted for attaining this end.[20]" He gathered around himself a group of disciples, the most notable being Barthélemy Enfantin, (1796–1864), who travelled widely preaching Saint-Simon's new religion and who became the leader of the movement on Saint-Simon's death. Enfantin proposed that in this proposed new society, marriage should be replaced by free love. The French government, not wanting a repeat of the social anarchy that resulted from the immorality of the revolutionary years, quickly closed their meeting halls.

Charles Fourier (1772–1837) had developed a different version of socialism prior to Saint-Simon, in his *Théorie de Quatre Mouvements*, published in 1808. He advocated the setting up across the world of *phalannstères*, or *phalanxes*, groups of 1700–1800 individuals living as self-sustaining communities in one large, beautiful building with a communal dining area. These communities would be autonomous, electing their officials. Fourier allowed for individual capital, and also for different levels of remuneration for different tasks within the community although the distribution of produce was to be partly on a communal basis. He believed that such communities would provide the best guarantee of freedom. Like Enfantin, Fourier had very loose views on sexual relationships, believing that the best way of dealing with passions was to give them free rein, so sexual freedoms were therefore to be encouraged in his communities. He was a self-confessed optimist, believing that the world was to last for 80,000 years, the first 40,000 years of which would be a time of progress, to be followed by 40,000 years of decline. As he believed that the world had only been in existence for 7,000 years, there was plenty of scope for further improvement before decline set in[21].

Fourier's writings inspired one attempt at setting up a *phalannstère* in France, which proved a failure. They also influenced the setting up of the Paris *commune* in 1871 after France's defeat in a war against Prussia. By then, however, socialism had moved on from the naïve idealism that characterised its earliest advocates.

Following on from these "Utopian" socialists, French socialism took on a more pragmatic note under Pierre-Joseph Proudhon (1809–1865) and Louis Blanc (1811–1882). Proudhon published his first work in 1840, entitled *Qu'est-ce que la propriété?* (What is property?) to which he gave he answer *"La propriéte, c'est le vol."* (Property is theft.). Blanc established a reputation as a journalist in Paris during the 1830s with the founding of a magazine called *Revue du progres*, which included a scathing criticism of competition. These men were given a greater opportunity to promote their views by the frequent upheavals that engulfed France during the 19th century. Following an uprising in 1830, the reactionary king Charles X was forced to abdicate in 1830 in favour of his cousin Louis Philippe (1830–1848) who in turn abdicated eighteen years later in the wake of a further revolution. A provisional government was set up and a republic proclaimed. As in 1789, the February 1848 revolution was preceded by food shortages, which acted as a catalyst for popular discontent with a government which was widely seen to be indifferent to the needs of the poor. However, one of the differences with 1789 was the increased role of the working classes, who had been radicalised by the writings of Proudhon and Blanc. One of the first acts of the provisional government was to grant universal male suffrage. It also attempted to create "national workshops," state-run industrial enterprises that would provide employment for all. These workshops were very much the brainchild of Louis Blanc, who was a member of the provisional government. For some years before 1848, he had already been arguing for the creation of "social workshops", which he hoped would gradually supersede privately-run companies. The state would provide the funding and draw up the rules for these enterprises, while the workers would choose their own managers and directors. In other words, his vision was for self-governing industrial associations monitored by a benevolent state and not in competition with one another. Such a system, he believed, would bring freedom to all. When the provisional government attempted in a very half-hearted way to implement these ideas, the net result was failure. The government did not have sufficient funds to set up enough national workshops to provide work for all the unemployed workers in Paris, so it introduced a tax on both the landed gentry and small farmers to assist the urban unemployed, which proved highly unpopular in the rural areas. Four months after the February revolution, the national workshops were closed down, leading to riots in Paris in which the archbishop of Paris was killed. The army was called in to restore order, and a more conservative administration took charge, which blamed Blanc for the failure of the workshops. He left the country later in the year, and did not return to France until 1870. Four years later, Louis Napoleon, nephew of Napoleon I, was proclaimed emperor and a brief period of prosperity began, which took some of the heat out of any revolutionary movement for the time being.

Proudhon had been sceptical about the success of the national workshops, He was opposed to state ownership of factories and other means of production, preferring mutuality, where ownership belonged to the workers themselves. Proudhon's ultimate vision was of a society that needed no government at all. "Government of man by man in every form is oppression," he wrote. "The highest perfection of society is found in the union of order and anarchy.[22]" His insistence on individual liberty was rather at odds with his belief that all workers should be paid the same for a day's work regardless of the quality of their work.[23] Although inconsistent in his thought, he was realistic enough to recognise that no country could be transformed overnight and admitted he had no ready-made action plan. He did propose the setting up of a bank that would offer credit at no interest, but he was unable to raise the necessary capital and this scheme ended in failure[24].

After the events of 1848, France, having produced some of the first socialists, ceased to play a major role in the development of socialism, apart from one brief experiment in 1870–1, which will be considered below.

The industrial revolution and early socialism in Britain

England emerged straight from the Napoleonic wars into the Industrial Revolution. At this time, cotton mills were springing up all over Northern England, while the first steam locomotive had been built in 1804, and an entire district of London was first illuminated by gas-powered street lighting in 1825.

This period of great progress also saw great upheaval. Workers in both industry and agriculture were fearful of being made redundant by the new machinery. A few mills were burnt down, and there were riots in a number of areas. Although the worst of these disturbances were over by 1830, industrialisation continued apace, and with it a substantial exodus from the countryside into the rapidly growing towns and cities. Those who left the countryside hoping for a vastly better life in the towns and cities were to be disappointed. Factory hours were long, conditions at work could be quite dangerous, housing conditions left much to be desired, while pollution from the chimneys added to the unsavoury atmosphere. Sanitation was poor and disease rife.

The Church of England was ill-equipped to provide for the

spiritual needs of these urban incomers. The rigidity of the Parish system ensured that it was a very time-consuming process to erect new churches, and although a few were built in this period, the flexibility of the Nonconformists (as Dissenters were now usually known) enabled them to build places of worship more rapidly, many of which remain to this day as monuments to their concern for Britain's industrial population. A number of notable Christians continued the compassionate tradition of the 18th Century as they sought to minister to the urban poor in the growing towns and cities. The Baptist minister William Gadsby spoke at a meeting of the Anti-Corn Law league in Manchester in 1839, claiming that forbidding the import of foreign wheat until the price of English wheat reached a certain level caused suffering to the poor. "I consider the corn laws degrading to every principle of humanity and insulting to God and Man," he said. In stark contrast to the Puritan era, when Evangelical Christians were in the forefront of political thinking, the sight of a Christian minister in the early 19th century taking part in what was essentially a political rally created quite a stir, and Gadsby attracted some criticism for standing up for Christian compassion in this particular setting.[25] Less controversial from the standpoint of their Christian contemporaries were Barnardo, Müller and Spurgeon, who started orphanages, and Lord Shaftesbury (1801–1885), who fought in Parliament for better working conditions for children. Where the owners of a factory were Christians, the accommodation and facilities provided for workers and their families could be far superior to the norm, as can still be seen at the Cadbury factory in Bourneville, Birmingham, or in Saltaire, near Bradford, where Sir Titus Salt (1803–1876) built a new town for the workers in his spinning mill.

Another person concerned about the harsh conditions endured by the working classes was Robert Owen (1771–1858) who married into the family of a wealthy cotton manufacturer and who subsequently became the manager of the mill at New Lanark in Scotland. Owen improved the housing conditions for the workers, banned the employment of children under ten years of age and established an infants' school in the community. Unlike Salt or the Cadburys, Owen's compassion did not arise out of Evangelical conviction, for he was no friend of Christianity, publicly declaring in one meeting his "hostility to all the received forms of religion[26]" which in church-going Victorian Britain inevitably restricted his political influence. Owen was another idealist who, rather like Fourier, proposed a re-modelling of society based on communal living. His communities would have a public kitchen, but every family would have their own private apartments. Children would be brought up by the community after the age of three. He was open-minded about how these communities were to be set up. The state, parishes or individuals could set them up if they so desired, and ideally they should number 500–3000 persons[27]. All the implements and machinery needed within the community were to be held in common. Owen was confident that his communities would offer an environment whereby work would be pleasurable for all and poverty would be eliminated. Two attempts to start communities along the lines proposed by Owen were attempted in 1825, one in Scotland, the other in Indiana in the USA, which was led by Owen himself. Both failed completely within two years[28].

Undaunted by these failures, Owen started another community in Hampshire in 1839 which also failed. Indeed, his only enduring legacy is the modern co-operative movement. The first co-operative store was opened in New Lanark, and the idea was developed by the 28 pioneers who opened a store in Rochdale in 1844 with £28 of capital, very much along principles Owen and his followers had attempted some twenty years earlier. Owen continued to produce pamphlets and to hold lectures, and in spite of his atheism, retained a significant following among the working classes, to whom he sadly bequeathed his disdain for Christianity. Indeed, Owen offended Victorian England not only with his views on religion but also by denouncing marriage as a form of slavery for women. In his dream of society in the future, "Women will be no longer made the slaves of, or dependent upon men.... They will be equal in education, rights, privileges and personal liberty.[29]" It is hardly surprising that socialism would be regarded with suspicion in England when its most articulate spokesman held views that were so offensive. The bottom-up approach of the co-operative movement has much to commend it, but Owen's concept of community, like Fourier's, is far less satisfactory. While born out of an understandable concern at the disruption to family life caused by the migration to the cities, Owen's thinking undermined the role of the family through delegating the responsibility of bringing up children to the entire community, rather than to parents.

It was Owen who first popularised the word "socialism" in the discussions of the *Associations of all Classes of All Nations*, an organisation he founded in 1835[30]. Interestingly, it was also in England where the name "capitalism" was first applied to the system it sought to replace. The word was first used in a novel by W M Thackeray (1811–1863) referring merely to the idea of "having ownership of capital". It was to acquire particularly pejorative associations thanks to the writings of another man who, while not born in Britain, was to spend the latter part of his life as a British resident and who was to become the most important influence in the subsequent development of socialism.

Karl Marx and communism

Friedrich Engels (1820–1895), like Owen, had a management role in a British cotton mill, having been sent from Germany to Manchester in 1842 to work for the textile firm of Erman and Engels, in which his father was a shareholder. He was shocked at the poverty he saw, which he described graphically in 1845 in *The Condition of the Working Class in England*. That same year he met a young German writer and political activist called Karl Marx and the two men began a literary and political partnership that only ended with Marx's death 38 years later.

Marx (1818–1883) was a precocious child, born in Trier,

Germany into a Jewish family with a voracious appetite for reading. His father was very well-versed in the writings of Rousseau and Voltaire[31] and the young Marx nursed literary ambitions for himself. When he went to university in Bonn, he had wanted to study literature and philosophy, but his father insisted that he studied law instead. He still took a keen interest in philosophy and literature, and besides the writings of Voltaire and Rousseau, he became familiar with the German philosophers Immanuel Kant (1724–1804) and Friedrich Hegel (1770–1831) – two men who exercised a strong influence on the Bible-denying German theologians of the 19th century. Marx also set himself to understand economics, familiarising himself with Adam Smith along with David Ricardo (1772–1823) and James Mill (1773–1836), the founders of classic economics.

Marx's thought had moved in a radical direction during his youth. After his appointment as editor of a newspaper called *Rheinische Zeitung* while still in his early 20's, he found himself out of a job in a matter of months for having offended both the autocratic Prussian state and the Russian Czar[32]. He spent a while in Paris before another article he wrote in another newspaper criticising the Prussian state led to his expulsion from France. After a short stay in Belgium he settled in London, and England was to be his home for the rest of his life.

Marx's two most important works were the *Communist Manifesto*, co-authored with Engels in 1848, and *Das Kapital* – a lengthy and unfinished work written over a period of many years. His influence on the development of socialist thought cannot be underestimated, moving it on from idealism to a project with an action plan and a clear goal. Surprisingly, in view of the importance of the state in the thinking of most socialists, Marx believed that ultimately the state should wither away. Socialism, which increased the power of the state, was nothing more than a necessary "halfway house" between the capitalist order of his day and the utopia he desired to create. Once workers were no longer exploited, once private property had been eliminated and the middle classes, or *bourgeoisie*, the enemies of progress, had been defeated, the all-embracing socialist state would have completed its task. It is ironic, considering the subsequent history of states that have professed themselves to be Marxist, that Marx's ideal society would also be free of oppression. To this idealised stateless society he gave the name "communist." Before Marx, the words "socialism" and "communism" had been used interchangeably, the latter word first having been used in French (*communisme*), and derived from the word *commun*, meaning "common" and thus to all intents and purposes, synonymous with socialism.

In common with Rousseau, Marx believed that the earliest societies had been essentially communistic in nature, with all things in common, and although he acknowledged the tremendous technological progress and increased wealth that had occurred as a result of the industrial revolution, the inequalities in the distribution of that wealth demanded that a final change must take place – in other words, the wheel must come full circle and communism become the ultimate development in human history.

Marx believed that in countries like Britain with a stable democracy, communism could be introduced through peaceful means – in other words, by electing a socialist government. Where no stable democracy existed, violent revolution was the only way of establishing it. However, even where the means would be peaceful, there would always be an element of conflict. "The history of all existing society is the history of class struggles" he proclaimed in *The Communist Manifesto*, and the establishment of communism would likewise be a class struggle. Marx viewed the entire population of the industrialised nations as split into two categories – the *bourgeoisie* and the proletariat, or the haves and the have-nots, the owners of the means of production and the workers. The latter must take power from the former. "The Communists disdain to conceal their views and aims. They openly declare that their ends can only be achieved by the forcible overthrow of all existing social conditions. Let the ruling classes tremble at a communist revolution. The proletarians have nothing to lose but their chains. They have a world to win. Working men of all countries, unite![33]"

Marx is totally unapologetic about his opposition to the idea of private property. "You are horrified at our intending to do away with private property," he writes. "But in your existing society, private property is already done away with for nine-tenths of the population; its existence for the few is solely due to its non-existence in the hands of those nine-tenths.[34]" "Hard-won, self-acquired private property? Do you mean the property of the petty artisan and of the small peasant, a form of property that preceded the bourgeois form? There is no need to abolish that; the development of industry has to a great extent already destroyed it and is still destroying it daily.[35]"

Marx was familiar with the early socialist writers, and was scathing in his criticisms of the disciples of Owen and Fourier, who he claimed had become reactionary rather than revolutionary, especially as they sought to minimise the concept of class struggle. They dreamt of "founding isolated *phalanstères*, of establishing 'Home Colonies'...pocket editions of the New Jerusalem" but "are compelled to appeal to the feelings and purses of the bourgeois[36]" to have any hope of fulfilling their vision. Marx was also familiar with the history of the French Revolution, which he calls "the Great Revolution", which, he claimed, had taken France from being an agrarian society to a bourgeois society. He hoped to replace this bourgeois society with a communist society. He chose to emphasise this difference rather than the similarities between his thinking and that of the Jacobins, in spite of their common desire to design a new society where all men would be equal and Christianity's influence minimised. Marx was well aware of the Bible's teachings, and referred to it in several of his works, but he was no friend of the Gospel, having been an atheist since childhood. His quote about religion being the "opium of the people" is possibly the most well-known phrase in all his writings. In full, he actually wrote, "*Religious distress is at the same time the expression of real distress and the protest against real distress. Religion is the sigh of the oppressed creature, the heart of a heartless world, just as it is the spirit of a spiritless situation. It is the opium of the people. The abolition of religion as the illusory happiness of the people is required for their real happiness. The demand to give up the illusion about its condition is the demand to give up a condition which needs illusions.*[37]" However, while viewing religion as a poor substitute for true happiness, he never advocated persecution of those who professed the doctrines of Christianity.

Marx was convinced that capitalism contained within itself the seeds of its own destruction. "What the bourgeoisie therefore produces, above all, are its own grave-diggers. Its fall and the victory of the proletariat are equally inevitable.[38]" He was nonetheless enough of a realist to recognise that the communist society he dreamt of would not come into being overnight. Hence, even in the event of a revolution, the *Communist Manifesto* proposed the following socialist measures among other things as necessary:–

1. Abolition of property in land and application of all rents of land to public purposes.
2. A heavy progressive or graduated income tax.
3. Abolition of all right of inheritance.
4. Confiscation of the property of all emigrants and rebels.
5. Centralisation of credit in the hands of the state, by means of a national bank with state capital and an exclusive monopoly.
6. Centralisation of the means of communication and transport in the hands of the state[39].

But one day, "when in the course of development, class distinctions have disappeared and all production has been concentrated in the hands of a vast association of the whole nation, the public power will lose its political character. Political power, properly so called, is merely the organised power of one class for oppressing another.[40]" So when communism has been established, "in place of the old bourgeois society, with its classes and class antagonisms, we shall have an association, in which the free development of each is the condition for the free development of all.[41]" In other words, communism would achieve the equality to which the French Revolution aspired, but failed to deliver.

Marx was much more explicit in his practical strategy for neutering the power of the bourgeoisie than he was in explaining how the all-embracing socialist state would wither away to the utopian communist society which was his goal. This obvious weakness in his thinking did not bother his contemporaries, for he lived at a time when the confidence in human progress that had characterised the Enlightenment was returning, after suffering a serious blow in the bloody aftermath of the French revolution. There was, however, a pronounced difference between the optimism of the eighteenth century and that of the nineteenth, for the former was based on reason alone, whereas the latter looked very much to science and technology as the driver of progress. Marx was able to capture the mood of the age and sell it to the working classes in a form that particularly appealed to them. After all, at a time when the industrial revolution was allowing the possibility of a lifestyle undreamt of a century earlier, it was only right that they too should share in the benefits of progress and enjoy an improvement in the quality of their often harsh and humdrum lives. Marx expressed this through his theory of surplus value, which he defined as the difference between the cost of producing a product (which largely consisted of the wages paid to the workers) and cost of buying it. The final product had gained value in the making, but none of that profit went to the workers, whom he believed had every right to it.

Social Democracy, Revolution and International Solidarity

The *Communist Manifesto* had been commissioned by the Communist League, a society of socialists from several countries who had come together in Paris in 1836 initially under the name of the *League of the Just*. The Manifesto was to be published " in the English, French, German, Italian, Flemish and Danish languages.[42]" The international character of socialism was one of its features from the very beginning. The *Manifesto* concludes with a call for the working men of the world to unite, and one very practical manifestation of this international unity was the foundation of the International Working Men's Association (later known simply as the First International) in 1864 at a meeting in London. Marx was present, and rapidly emerged as the dominant personality in the new movement. However, disagreements between various groupings within socialism caused it to fold after only nine years. This period was significant for the development of socialism inasmuch as it saw the first uprising by the proletariat. In 1870, France experienced yet another revolution as Napoleon III was forced to abdicate following defeat in a war against Prussia. The siege of Paris by the Prussian army had been particularly harsh, and when, after finally capturing the city in 1871, the Prussians retreated, the citizens of Paris rose up in revolt against the new national republican government and established a self-governing *commune*. This first assumption of power by the working classes proved short-lived, for after two months, the French army gained control of the city after fierce battles in which thousands of *communards* were killed. The *commune*'s brief existence allowed it little chance to reorganise society along socialist lines. It reintroduced the Revolutionary calendar, used the red flag rather than the *tricolour* and implemented a number of social measures, including the compulsory return of all workmen's tools pawned during the siege and the separation of church and state. The plan for education in the *commune* required it to be conducted exclusively on secular lines.

In spite of the brief existence of the *commune*, Marx hailed it as the prototype of the revolution to come. In a pamphlet written shortly after its fall, he wrote, "The Paris of the workers, with its commune, will ever be celebrated as the glorious herald of a new society. Its martyrs will be enshrined in the great heart of the working class. History has already nailed its destroyers on the pillory, from which all the prayers of their priests are impotent to deliver them.[43]" Marx's eulogy cannot hide the significant questions raised by the short-lived *commune* as to whether revolution was ever going to be the best way forward to further the cause of the working class in a civilised nation,

It was in Marx's native country where the first socialist political party committed to democratic methods was founded. Prior to the 19th century, there was no German state as such, only a number of independent states. Following the Napoleonic wars, a momentum for German political unity began to build, with Prussia, the most powerful state, taking the lead. Over a hundred years earlier, the Prussian king Frederick William I (1713–1740) had created a huge bureaucratic civil service along with a professional standing army. The press was tightly controlled, and following the disturbances of 1848, which affected many other countries in Europe as well as France, a secret police network was set up. The Prussian railway network was built by the state, unlike Britain, where the railways were built by private companies. The dominance of Prussia ensured that the same large-state model was pursued in the new united Germany.

In 1818, the philosopher Hegel had become chair of philosophy in Berlin, capital city of Prussia and later of Germany. His works provided philosophical support for the idea of a big state, including its bureaucracy. Marx, as has been noted, was influenced by his writings, even though he rejected many of his ideas. For Hegel, the state was essential for the individual to achieve their fulfilment. He was a supporter of freedom of conscience and equality of opportunity, but due to the potential for conflict between different individuals, the state was essential to enable citizens "to surmount the competitive anarchy of civil society and discover a true basis of unity.[44]" Whereas the classic liberal thinking of Locke saw freedom in negative terms – i.e. in the absence of contraint, Hegel viewed it as a positive idea – participation in civil society, and that participation meant more than just voting, or taking part in the democratic process. "The state is the actuality of concrete freedom" he wrote in *The Philosophy of Right* (1821).

A big bureaucratic state may not necessarily be socialistic, but it is hardly surprising that socialism in Germany has emphasised the importance of the state rather than the decentralised communities favoured by Owen or Fourier. Ferdinand Lassalle (1825–1864) shared Marx's opposition to private property, but never sought the withering away of the state as a long-term goal. On the contrary, he magnifies its role, rejecting the classic liberal view of the state as being limited to the preservation of the individual's freedom and property, which he likens disparagingly to the role of a night watchman, whose sole function is to prevent robbery and burglary. Rather, "the state is the insitution in which the whole virtue of humanity should be realised.[45]" Unlike Marx, he did not regard class struggles in such absolute terms that he refused to liaise with any non-socialist politicans. He held several meetings with the Prussian (and later German) Chancellor Bismarck (1815–1898) in an attempt to persuade him to adopt some socialist measures, such as providing state funding for the setting up of co-operative associations. Following the beginnings of the industrialisation of Germany in the 1850s, Lassalle toured parts of the country speaking to the workers, who were in the process of organising themselves into local committees. The upshot of these meetings was the formation of the General German Working Men's Association (*Allgemeiner Deutscher Arbeiterverein*) in 1863, a year before Lassalle's untimely death in a duel. A second socialist party, the Social Democratic Worker's Party (*Sozialdemokratische Arbeiterpartei)* was formed at Eisenach six years later, which owed more to Marx's influence, and in 1875, the two groups merged to form the Social Democratic Party, or SPD (*Sozialdemokratische Partei Deutschlands)*, which by the end of the 19th century had become one of the most powerful socialist parties in Europe. Although Marx's revolutionary ideas had been dropped, socialists were still regarded with suspicion by Bismarck, especially following their growing success in the elections. They stood uncompromisingly for common ownership not just of factories, mines and land, but of machines and tools as well[46]. Schools were to be run by the state, with attendance compulsory and no religious education to be given[47].

Whether or not newly-united Germany was one day going to convert itself into a socialist state by democratic methods, it was quite clear that revolution was to be the only way forward for socialism in Russia, a country which only abolished serfdom in 1861 and which proved fertile ground for anarchism, the most extreme form of socialism. Proudhon, as noted, was the ideological mentor of anarchism, but it was the Russian Mikhail Bakunin (1814–1876) who turned it into a violent and revolutionary force. Bakunin came from an aristocratic background, and after a brief period of service in the Russian military, decided to pursue an academic career. Travelling widely in Europe, he met Proudhon and Marx, both of whom influenced him profoundly. Abandoning any thoughts of a position in a university, he spent the rest of his life attempting to spread the ideals of socialist revolution. More radical than Marx, his revolutionary socialism aimed "at the destruction of external authority by every available means.[48]" His most influential work, *God and the State*, was militantly atheistic, rejecting all restraints on individual "freedom", including marriage. Bakunin claimed that "the liberty of man consists solely of this, that he obey the laws of Nature, because he has himself recognised them as such, and not because they have been imposed upon him by any foreign will whatsoever, human or divine, collective or individual.[49]" While sharing the socialist ideal of communal ownership of resources, anarchism essentially wanted to short-cut the Marxist route to the stateless society by going straight there rather than setting up an interim socialist state. Bakunin was critical of Marx, whose ideas he regarded as authoritarian, and which he feared would lead to the setting up of a new form of government which would be no better than that which it sought to replace. He was forced to spend much of his life in exile, but a number of Russian students studying in Western Europe adopted his ideas and took his message back to Russia. In 1878, the St Petersburg police chief was assassinated – an event which marked the beginnings of a campaign of revolutionary violence by an anarchist group called *Narodnaya Volya* – the People's Will, which culminated in the assassination of Czar Alexander II in 1881. His son and successor, Alexander III (1881–1894) clamped down hard on the revolutionaries, particularly when it became apparent that they only enjoyed limited support. However, he also retreated into a reactionary autocratic rule, abandoning the liberalising policies of his father, and bequeathing to his son a lethal cocktail of unsolved problems which were eventually to re-surface with a vengeance that was to shake Russia to its very core.

Summary – Socialism in the light of the Bible

Thomas Kirkup, in his *History of Socialism* (1909), claimed that "It is a most serious mistake to suppose that there can be any real antagonism between the ethical and spiritual teaching of Christianity and the principles of socialism rightly understood.[50]" The whole argument of this book is that Kirkup and others like him are completely and utterly mistaken. While this chapter has shown that there are a number of important variations in socialist thinking just as there are variations in Christian political thought, the fundamental principles that undergird socialism are totally at odds with the Bible. The first and most fundamental point of disagreement concerns the nature of man. Thanks to the Fall, man is born affected with original sin[51] and remains a sinner all his life[52]. Nowhere among the founding fathers of socialism can one find the Biblical idea of man as a fallen creature. Instead, they display a naïve optimism about what society could be like if the ills of poverty and illiteracy could be conquered. They ignored the fact that mankind's biggest problem is not private property or competition but rather our fallen nature. The whole socialist edifice was therefore built upon a rejection of the teaching of the Bible, and of the God who is revealed in it.

173

Divergence over this fundamental point will mean that there will inevitably be a sharp divergence in thinking between Evangelical Christianity and socialism if the latter is measured against the three headings under which the Christian worldview has been analysed in the three previous chapters. This is apparent even considering the subject of compassion. Care for the less fortunate is a point of common ground between Christianity and socialism. No Christian should question the very real revulsion felt by Owen and Engels at the poverty they observed among the workers in the textile mills, or their genuine desire to improve their lot. All men are born with a sinful nature, but as Calvin rightly points out, the image of God, while deformed in fallen man, is not totally annihilated and destroyed.[53]" A capacity for genuine compassion is one manifestation of this broken image, even in atheists.

However, the common ground between Christians and socialists with regards to compassion stops at this point because of their different views of man. The Christian will seek to do good to others both out of obedience to Christ and from a compassionate spirit, but will recognise that no amount of Christian compassion can solve the problem of the heart of fallen man, which will always be "deceitful above all things and desperately wicked.[54]" This is not to view Christian compassion as a futile attempt to put a sticking plaster on a gaping wound – far from it; Christians like Wilberforce and Shaftesbury have left an enduring legacy for mankind as a whole inasmuch as no-one, Christian or non-Christian alike, would now argue in favour of slavery or child labour. Nonetheless any Christian who reads their Bible will be only too aware that sinful men are never going to organise themselves into the utopian society envisaged by Fourier or Owen, let alone Marx's stateless communism. Christians, therefore, while rightly proud of their forebears' track record in tackling injustice, oppression and poverty in a way that has made a lasting difference, are of necessity realistic about what can be achieved in a fallen world. A society totally free of injustice and oppression and poverty will only come with the return of Jesus Christ at the end of history. Christians should be caring people, but for all their efforts, the poor we will always have with us[55] until all things will be made new.[56]

A still more pronounced contrast will be found in comparing Christian and socialist ideals of liberty. Socialism quite openly opposes all the individual components comprising the Christian ideal of liberty – small government, the right to private property and the respect for the individual. Marx. as noted, was no fan of big government *per se*, viewing it only as a necessary intermediate step. He was very critical of the bureaucratic but non-socialist big government that emerged in the France of Napoleon III in the aftermath of the 1848 revolution, describing it in *The Eighteenth Brumaire of Louis Bonaparte* (1852) as "the executive power with its enormous bureaucratic and military organization, with its wide-ranging and ingenious state machinery, with a host of officials numbering half a million, besides an army of another half million – this terrifying parasitic body which enmeshes the body of French society and chokes all its pores.[57]" However, for Marx, the state was the only tool available for divesting capitalism of its capital.

This belligerent opposition to private property was inspired, as were Rousseau's writings, by the myth of an early stage in the development of mankind when there was no such thing as private property. There is no hint in the Bible that the earliest men practising communal living. The two sons of Adam, Cain and Abel, appear to have lived independently of each other[58]. "Their employments were different, that they might trade and exchange with each other.[59]" Abraham, the friend of God, had a great deal of private property,[60] even if he was never able to take possession of the land of Canaan himself. It may be granted that in the most backward cultures, the concept of private property may be unknown, but the Bible nowhere teaches that such societies represent the last remnants of a lost era of innocence, nor does it oppose the idea of private property as long as it is used to God's glory: "Honour the Lord with thy substance and with the firstfruits of all thine increase.[61]". In practical terms, this means a generous spirit, remembering the poor: "He hath dispersed, he hath given to the poor, his righteousness endureth for ever.[62]" It cannot be denied that there were many coal mines, mills and factories in Victorian England whose owners were not obeying the Bible in this area, but does this give the state the right to take their legally-held property by force? Proudhon may have declared private property to be theft, but the label better fits the appropriation by the state of a man's property on his death, as advocated by Marx. Nowhere in the Bible is there the slightest opposition to the idea of inheritance – indeed, the frequent use of it as an illustration of the Christian's hope of glory would be bizarre if God was opposed to the whole concept. While verses like Proverbs 28:8 talk of the man who increases his possessions "by usury and unjust gain" ends up gathering it "for him that will pity the poor" the writer's thinking is, as Matthew Henry puts it, that "his estate shall go to decay and another man's shall be raised out of the ruins of it.[63]" In other words, God's providence will redistribute his wealth in due course. There is no mandate here for the state to do God's job for Him.

Besides the lack of Biblical support for the abolition of private property, there is also the question of whether communal ownership of goods and capital demanded by Marx and some other socialists would ever prove to be viable. As was noted in the previous chapter, the Pilgrim Fathers attempted communal living during their first years in America, and struggled to feed themselves. The decision to allow each family of settlers the right to own their own land saw a significant improvement in their living conditions. The early socialist communities all ended in failure; indeed, the only example of a group that have successfully lived communally for any length of time are the Amish Mennonites, who seek to remain in a time-warp which eschews the conveniences of modern technology and who only marry within their communities – not the sort of model which offers any support to the socialist conviction that the abolition of private property would advance mankind to the final stage in its development.

One interesting feature about Marx, Engels, Owen, Lassalle, Saint-Simon and many later notable socialists is that they were from bourgeois intellectual backgrounds. They unquestionably felt sympathy for the poor, but to what degree were they able to step into their shoes? It was not unreasonable to assume that for a poor person, a share in communally-owned property would seem a better option than having nothing, but there is nothing intrinsic about the psyche of the poor which precludes them aspiring to private property of their own, given the right circumstances. One hundred years after Marx's death, Margaret Thatcher's government offered council house tenants the chance to buy their own homes – an offer which many gladly took up. The Labour party initially opposed these sales, but abandoned its opposition in 1983 for fear of losing votes from its erstwhile supporters. It may seem quite strange at first glance that this foundational principle of socialism was ultimately rejected by the very people it professed to be helping, but on further consideration, it is not really surprising. Socialism, as has been noted in this chapter, is very much the child of the more radical strain of Enlightenment thinking that rejected the value of traditions and aspired to re-design society according to reason. As such, socialism has an obvious attraction to intellectuals inasmuch as it appeals to their pride. Hayek makes the observation that "in general, the more intelligent an educated person is, the more likely he or she now is not only to be a rationalist, but also to hold socialist views....The higher we climb up the ladder of intelligence, the more we talk with intellectuals, the more likely we are to encounter socialist convictions.[64]" He also points out that "intelligent people tend to overvalue intelligence[65]" – in other words, they place too much confidence in their ability to solve the world's problems. This has been highlighted two centuries after the dawn of socialism by the left wing intellectuals who dominated the Blair/Brown administration of 1997–2010. They possessed little of the idealism of socialism's founding fathers, being characterised instead by a terribly know-it-all, patronising attitude towards those they professed to he helping. Such an attitude is in stark contrast to the servant leadership model of Augustine and Calvin, let alone the Bible's advice not to be wise in one's own eyes[66]. The growing disillusion among the British working classes with the Labour Party in recent years comes therefore as no surprise considering it now is led by men and women who think they know best and disdain to listen to the concerns of their supposed supporters.

Socialism, again following Rousseau, also set itself against individualism. St Augustine had argued that because individuals had different values, priorities and aspirations, government should be limited to those areas on which there was common consent, such as preserving peace and order. This individualistic view of society, which the Puritans also stressed, is very different from Marx's, which categorised everyone into one of two hostile groups, the proletariat and the bourgeoisie, with little thought of the individual. Although some later Marxists have attempted to twist the Exodus narrative with its account of the liberation of an oppressed people to justify their position, the Marxist concept of a class struggle is far removed from the Bible's teaching. Furthermore, the lumping of everyone into two categories is a gross oversimplification. Socialism has had a tendency to deny that there are both "deserving" and "undeserving" poor, ignoring the very real temptations of laziness and irresponsibility. "If any would not work, neither should he eat[67]" said St Paul, while the book of Proverbs adds that, "He that loveth pleasure shall be a poor man; He that loveth wine and oil shall not be rich.[68]" Some people, in other words, are the author of their own misfortune and do not have the same claim to sympathy as others who, for no fault of their own, have no option but to work long hours in a poorly-paid job which barely makes ends meet. Likewise, among the owners of the means of production could be found some notable individuals like the Cadburys and Titus Salt who set an example of how to care for their workers.

Should such men as these be viewed as the enemy of the working classes? Would not Marx have been better off using his pen to praise such Christian philanthropy in the hope of shaming less compassionate employers into a greater sense of compassion rather than preaching the antagonism of class conflict?

Another feature of some socialists' reaction against individualism was their reluctance to reward or even recognise outstanding ability or conscientiousness. Fourier was happy to see talent rewarded, but Proudhon wanted to see workers paid at the same rate regardless of the quality of their work, and therefore, by implication, regardless of the degree of their effort. Of these two attitudes, the latter has unsurprisingly become the more prominent among socialists, even though the Bible has no problems with the rewarding of quality. "Seest thou a man diligent in his business? He shall stand before kings" says Proverbs 22:29, a verse which Benjamin Franklin's hard-working Calvinistic father instilled into him. Different gifts carry different levels of responsibility, as Jesus taught in the parable of the talents.[69] They are God-given and therefore to be used, not despised, for the net result of paying everyone the same regardless of their individual talent is that high standards are discouraged. Socialism's dislike of competition on the grounds that it forces wages down has precisely the same effect. By contrast, a free market will usually drive standards up and rightly rewards those who deliver a quality product.

Of the violence of the Russian anarchists, little needs to be said, for it is patently obvious that the beliefs of these individuals were totally at odds with Evangelical Christianity. Bakunin ridiculed the "acceptance of the Christian absurdity, the most audacious and monstrous of all religious absurdities[70]" adding, "If God really existed, it would be necessary to abolish him.[71]" His followers were prepared to commit murder in the name of liberty, and while representing a lunatic fringe, they illustrate graphically a wider problem inherent to socialism which can be traced back to Rousseau's "general will" – the dangers of disregarding the

179

individual in the name of a collective goal. Although not a Christian, Hayek provided a penetrating analysis of this danger in *The Road to Serfdom* (1944) with which Christians would heartily concur: "Once you admit that the individual is merely a means to serve the ends of the higher entity called society or the nation, most of these features of totalitarian regimes which horrify us follow of necessity. From the collectivist standpoint intolerance and brutal suppression of dissent, the complete disregard of the life and happiness of the individual are essential and unavoidable consequences of the basic premise, and the collectivist can admit this and at the same time claim that his system is superior to the one in which the 'selfish' interests of the individual are allowed to obstruct the full realisation of the ends the community pursues.[72]"

The collective goal of anarchists and Marxist alike was to lead mankind to a final stage of development where no laws would be needed. Here socialism finds itself at odds with the third component of the Christian worldview – moral restraint – because of the conflicting views of the nature of man. It is no coincidence that a number of early socialists rejected the whole ideal of marriage and some lapsed into sexual immorality. Engels never married his long-term partner, Mary Burns, regarding marriage as unjust and unnatural. In *The Origins of the Family, Private Property and the State*, (1884) he attempted to link the rise of private property to the domination of women by men. While his opposition to marriage is unquestionable, his arguments are unclear and his sources now largely discredited.[73] Although Marx, unlike Engels, was a married man, in the *Communist Manifesto*, he was happy to join forces with him in attacking this very bedrock of society: "On what foundation is the present family, the bourgeois family, based? On capital, on private gain....The bourgeois family will vanish as a matter of course when its complement vanishes, and both will vanish with the vanishing of capital.[74]" They then go on to argue that as the bourgeois are adulterers and exploiters of working class women, they have "wives in common" and therefore should not be shocked at the communist idea of "an openly legalised community of women[75]"

Even Proudhon, whom Kirkup depicts as a man characterised by upright conduct and a fierce opponent of the immorality of the Saint-Simon and Fourier schools[76], aspired towards a day when government would become unnecessary. At best, such aspirations can be regarded as naïve idealism while, at worst, they provide a cloak behind which to hide a desire to cast off all moral restraint. The link between socialism and immorality did not die out in the 19th century. The early 20th Century group of British intellectuals known as the Bloomsbury Set were predominantly socialists, with the exception of the economist John Maynard Keynes, and even more predominantly immoral. Even in recent times, the upper echelons of socialism has produced its fair share of immoral men, such as the homosexual Peter Mandelson, Ed Miliband, who was living in sin at the time of his election to the leadership of the Labour Party, or the late French president François Miterrand, who fathered a child by his mistress, In fairness to socialism, it should be pointed out that in the early 21st Century, such immorality in high places is regrettably not just confimed to socialists. History teaches us that any society composed of sinful men and women must be restrained for its own good. God has established government for this very purpose and it will need to continue in its role until Jesus returns. This is why God's Word provides guidelines for this restraint and emphasises the importance of marital fidelity and the family. The "broken society" in early 21st Century Britain, with its vandalism, teenage pregnancies, drunkenness and drug taking is an eloquent testimony to the disastrous results of ignoring the Maker's instructions.

We have already briefly anticipated some of the themes of subsequent chapters in order to underline the tragic consequences of embracing a system of government so fundamentally opposed to the Bible's teachings. A bad tree was inevitably going to bear bad fruit[77]. Unfortunately, socialists are so confident of their ability to re-shape society that they never admit that they are wrong and never learn from the mistakes of history. They will not grasp that in attempting to solve a problem they will always end up creating a bigger one. The French Revolution, which anticipated many of socialism's ideals, and which was driven by the same hostility to God's guidelines, should have been a warning to them, ending up with the bloodbath of the Reign of Terror, Napoleon's military dictatorship and a legacy of social chaos.

However, it is all too easy to make these points with the benefit of hindsight, and before looking at socialism in power in chapter 7, we must consider those who did not have the benefit of hindsight – in other words, Christians living in the 19th Century, and especially those living in countries whose political structures had been powerfully affected by Evangelical Christianity. For several reasons, very few Christians during this period understood the depths of the antagonism between socialism and the Bible, let alone the threat it would ultimately pose to the practise of their faith.

Notes

[1] Rousseau, J J *Discourse on inequality*, 1754. On line translation http://www.constitution.org/jjr/ineq.htm Accessed 15/02/2011.
[2] *idem.*
[3] *idem*
[4] *idem.*
[5] *idem*
[6] Rousseau, J J *Social Contract*, 1762. On line translation http://www.constitution.org/jjr/socon.htm Accessed 15/02/2011.
[7] *idem.*
[8] *idem.*
[9] *idem.*
[10] *idem.*
[11] *idem*
[12] *idem.*
[13] *idem.*
[14] The 5 extra days (or 6 in a leap year) were tacked on to the end of the year.
[15] Orna-Ornstein, F, *France—Forgotten Mission Field*, p108, European Missionary Fellowship, Watford (undated).
[16] http://en.wikipedia.org/wiki/Cult_of_Reason Accessed 16/02/2011.
[17] *Gay Marriage in All but Name*, p26. The Christian Institute,

Newcastle 2004.

[18] Kirkup, T, *A History of Socialism*, p9 Elibron Classics 2006 (originally published by A&C Black, London 1909).

[19] *ibid*, p24–25.

[20] *ibid,* p26.

[21] *ibid,* p32–34.

[22] Quoted in Kirkup, T, *op cit*, p56.

[23] Kirkup, T *op cit*, p54–55.

[24] *ibid*, p53.

[25] Ramsbottom, BA, *William Gadsby* p208–209, Gospel Standard Trust Publications, Harpenden, 2003.

[26] Kirkup, T, *op cit*, p66.

[27] *ibid*, p65.

[28] *ibid*, p66.

[29] http://www.robert-owen.com/quotes.htm Accessed 23/02/2011.

[30] Kirkup, T, *op cit*, p67.

[31] Wheen, F, *Marx's Das Kapital*, p8, Atlantic Books, London, 2006.

[32] Wheen, F, *op cit*, p11–12.

[33] Marx, K and Engels, F, *The Communist Manifesto*, p30. Translated by Samuel Moore, Merlin Press, London 1998.

[34] *ibid,* p15.

[35] *ibid*, p14.

[36] *ibid*, p28.

[37] Marx, K *The critique of Hegel's philosophy of right*, Cambridge University Press, 1970.

[38] Marx, K & Engels, F, *op cit*, p13.

[39] *ibid*, p20.

[40] *idem*.

[41] *idem*.

[42] Marx, K and Engels, F, *op cit*, p3.

[43] Quoted in Kirkup, T, *op cit*, p188.

[44] Held, D, *Models of Democracy*, (3rd Edition) p104. Polity Press, Cambridge 2006.

[45] Kirkup T, *op cit,* p101.

[46] *ibid,* p224.

[47] *ibid*, p225.

[48] *ibid*, p240.

[49] *idem*.

[50] Kirkup, T, *op cit* p341.

[51] Psalm 51:5, Romans 5:12.

[52] Romans 3:10, 23, 1 John 1:8.

[53] Calvin, J, *Institutes of the Christian Religion* 1:15:4 Translated by Battles, F.L. Westminster Press, Philadelphia 1960. (Based on the 1560

French version) .

[54] Jeremiah 17:8.

[55] John 12:8.

[56] Revelation 21:5.

[57] http://www.marxists.org/archive/marx/works/1852/18th-brumaire/ch07.htm Accessed 24/02/2011.

[58] Genesis 4:2ii.

[59] Henry, M, *A commentary on the Whole Bible*, Volime 1 p36 (Genesis 4:1–2) World Bible Publishers, Iowa. Originally published 1708.

[60] Genesis 12:5, 13:2, 25:5.

[61] Proverbs 3:9.

[62] Psalm 112:9, see also Deuteronomy 15:7–8, Psalm 41:1, Proverbs 22:9, Luke 14:13, Galatians 2:10.

[63] Henry, M, *Commentary on the Whole Bible*. Volume 3, Proverbs 28:9, World Bible Publishers, Iowa Falls.Originally published in 1706.

[64] Hayek, F A, *The Fatal Conceit*, p53. The University of ChicagoPRess, Chicago 1988.

[65] *idem*.

[66] Proverbs 3:7.

[67] 2 Thessalonians 3:10.

[68] Proverbs 21:17.

[69] Matthew 25:14–30.

[70] Bakunun, M, *God and the State*, Chapter 3 On-line translation http://www.marxists.org/reference/archive/bakunin/works/godstate/ch03.htm accessed 03/03/2011.

[71] Bakunin, M *op cit*, chapter 2.

[72] Hayek, F.A. *The Road to Serfdom*, p149. University of Chicago Press, Chicago 1944.

[73] Held, D, *Models of Democracy* (4th Edition), p97–98. Polity Press, Cambridge, 2006.

[74] Marx, K and Engels, F, *op cit*, p17.

[75] *ibid*, p18.

[76] Kirkup, T, *op cit*, p53

[77] Matthew 7:18.

Chapter 6:

Socialsm and the Gospel – friends or foes?

The rich man in his castle,
The poor man at his gate,
God made them, high or lowly,
And ordered their estate.

(The now rarely sung verse 3 of "All Things Bright and
Beautiful" by Mrs C F Alexander, 1818–1895)

Philanthropy and self-help in Victorian Britain

Adam Smith had claimed that very little else but "peace, easy taxes, and a tolerable administration of justice" was needed to carry a state to "the highest degree of opulence". While it would be an exaggeration to describe 19th century Britain as "opulent", the Industrial Revolution, which greatly increased the prosperity of the country, was in many ways a vindication of Smith's teaching inasmuch as it was the product of private enterprise. The state administered justice and kept taxation low – indeed income tax was only levied intermittently during the 19th century – but otherwise played no part in the proceedings except for passing legislation which, thanks to the influence of Lord Shaftesbury and others, attempted to restrain the exploitation of workers. Finally, following the defeat of Napoleon in 1815, Britain enjoyed a century free from the threat of war, only sending its soldiers into action in distant lands like the Crimea, India and South Africa.

This new prosperity was very unevenly distributed, with little of it trickling down to the poorest in society – indeed, as was noted in the previous chapter, it was the harsh conditions endured by the workers in the factories and mills of Manchester and other industrial towns which had provided the inspiration for the work of Marx and Engels. However, although the British working classes were after all every bit as dissatisfied with their lot as their European contemporaries, it was not until the final quarter of the 19th century that socialism finally established a firm and lasting foothold in the UK. For all Robert Owen's pioneering work in the early years of industrialisation, his only surviving legacy was the co-operative movement, which in less than 20 years expanded from a single shop in Rochdale to 300 shops in Yorkshire and Lancashire alone[1]. Although the co-operative movement spawned a political party in the early 20th century, which has a permanent electoral pact with the Labour Party, its origins are connected not with mainstream socialism but rather with a lone utopian voice who had unusually emphasised the importance of communities rather than the power of the state.

The bottom-up nature of the co-operative movement was characteristic of the resourcefulness of the British working classes. This resourcefulness was encouraged by one of the most popular works of the period, *Self-Help* by Samuel Smiles (1810–1904), which was first published in 1859 and sold over 250,000 copies by the time of the author's death. In this book, Smiles encouraged individuals to look to themselves, rather than the state. He begins by quoting the well-known phrase "Heaven helps those who help themselves," and goes on to say that "Help from without is often enfeebling in its effects, but help from within invariably invigorates.[2]" He affirms the limited role of the state beloved of classic liberal democracy: "The function of Government is negative and restrictive, rather than positive and active; being resolvable principally into protection – protection of life, liberty, and property.[3]"

Smiles had been brought up in a Christian family, and his

upbringing no doubt helped to shape his views. Indeed, Christianity can claim significant credit for retarding socialism's progress in England, for it had bequeathed a legacy of bottom-up compassionate initiatives going back to the early centuries, while Nonconformity had set a precedent for peaceful campaigning in the 18th century with its patient campaigns to repeal of the Test and Corporation Acts. Consequently, most early 19th century political activism was content with Britain's limited government, and while seeking a fairer system of representation, universal suffrage and better conditions at work, did not, as a rule, look to create a large, powerful state. In the first half of the 19th Century, the UK was blessed by a number of revivals, some widespread but some more localised, which strengthened the Evangelical witness in the land. Many chapels built during this period still stand today as a testimony to the "Golden age of British nonconformity." Puritan devotional works and Calvin's commentaries were reprinted, although there was little interest in the political writings of these great men – indeed political activism by Christians was still frowned upon by some pastors, although in spite of some disapproving voices, Christians were involved in the growing trade union movement. Early trade unions were not necessarily linked with socialism in its earliest years. even if the more outspoken leaders in the movement were strong opponents of capitalism. There is, after all, nothing explicitly socialist in the concept of groups of workers acting collectively to demand better working conditions from their employers if they feel they are being treated unfairly. The Christian influence acted as a leaven, helping to temper the more extreme trades unionists, who made threatening speeches and occasionally resorted to violence. The Methodists, many of whom were from working class backgrounds, were the most politically active among the nonconformists and played a major role in the early years of trade unionism. The Methodist tradition of lay preachers, which dated back to John Wesley and the earliest years of the Methodist movement, provided valuable training in public speaking for working men. This link between Methodism and the trades unions lasted into the 20th Century. Sir Leonard Neal (1913–2008) had considered training for the Methodist ministry before embarking on a career as a full-time official in the Transport and General Workers' Union. After becoming disillusioned with the unions, he ended up as Margaret Thatcher's advisor on union reform[4].

Another bottom-up initiative from this period was the Friendly Society. Many such organisations emerged "to offer ways in which members could counter the major risks of life[5]" – in other words' a mutual insurance company. Some, like Friends Life (formerly the Friends Provident Institution) were started by Christians, but others were not. The Manchester Oddfellows Society, for instance, was apparently set up following a discussion in a public house in that city[6]. The Friendly Societies grew rapidly and without any sort of central organisation, covering all manner of mishaps, including death and sickness. By 1892, over 3 million people were members of registered friendly societies, and a further 3 million belonged to unregistered societies[7]. In the early days of the trades union movement, the boundary between a friendly society and a trades union was, from a 21st century perspective, remarkably blurred. The association formed by the Tolpuddle Martyrs – the six celebrated Dorset farm labourers who were sentenced to be transported to Australia in 1834, was actually entitled the *Friendly Society of Agricultural Labourers.*

The most vulnerable in society were not capable of bottom-up initiative. Outside help was needed to deal with the squalor of the slums, child labour or the care of orphans. The work of Shaftesbury, Barnardo and Müller was mentioned in the previous chapter. There were many other philanthropists in early 19th century Britain seeking to improve the lot of their fellow men, and Christians feature prominently in many initiatives. For example, in the field of education, Evangelical Christians, ever since the days of the Reformation, had been active in founding schools, recognising their role in lifting children out of poverty. In 19th

century Britain, both the Church of England and the Nonconformists were responsible for the construction of many new
schools. Although from 1833 government grants were available to help establish a school, the state did not interfere in
the curriculum, and acted only in a supporting role, with local
initiatives being the main driving force. In early Victorian
Britain, any interference by the government was regarded
with suspicion – indeed, even talk of compulsory education
was viewed as an attack on individual freedom[8]. Consequently, it was up to societies and individuals to establish
schools. Francis Close, Dean of Cheltenham from 1826 to
1856 and a noted Evangelical, played a role in the establishment of the celebrated public schools in that town, Cheltenham College (for boys) and Cheltenham Ladies' College.
On a more modest level, Richard Dawes, who was appointed
vicar of King's Somborne in Hampshire, during the same
period, decided to start a school in the village, as one did not
exist. He not only secured a suitable site from the lord of the
manor, but gave no less than £500 of his own money to
ensure that, in 1842, his vision finally became a reality[9].
Nonconformists, who were keen to avert the establishment
of an educational monopoly by the Church of England, were
equally resourceful. Kent College, Pembury, now a highly
regarded independent girls' school which includes Sophie,
Countess of Wessex among its former pupils, began life as a
Methodist school in Folkestone. Denominational rivalries
fortunately did not bother Lord Shaftesbury who agreed to
become president of the Ragged Schools Union in 1844,
which brought together a number of independent charity
schools founded to provide a basic education for children
from the very poorest backgrounds[10].

Philanthropy was not confined exclusively to Christians.
The writer Charles Dickens (1812–1870) had experienced the
harsh régime of factory work when his father ended up in a
debtors' prison and he had been forced to take whatever
work he could find in order to support his family. The experience left a deep mark on him, and his novels depict with
great sympathy the harsh living conditions suffered by the

urban poor. To take just one example, in *Oliver Twist*, he vividly depicted the squalor of Jacob's Island, a slum area in South London: "Crazy wooden galleries common to the backs of half a dozen houses, with holes from which to look upon the slime beneath; windows, broken and patched, with poles thrust out, on which to dry the linen that is never there; rooms so small, so filthy, so confined, that the air would seem too tainted even for the dirt and squalor which they shelter; wooden chambers thrusting themselves out above the mud, and threatening to fall into it – as some have done; dirt-besmeared walls and decaying foundations; every repulsive lineament of poverty, every loathsome indication of filth, rot, and garbage.[11]" Such graphic language – and Dickens was not exaggerating – stirred the consciences of his contemporaries, and the open sewers in the vicinity were filled in a few years after the publication of Dickens' work[12]. Another philanthropist of note, Henry Brougham (1778–1868), founded the mechanics' institutes, where small libraries of books would be collected, and working men could meet for lectures and discussions. The first such institute was opened in London in 1824, and by 1860, no fewer than 610 were in existence[13].

It would be wrong to point too rosy a picture. Philanthropy and bottom-up resourcefulness did not prevent some pretty ugly outbreaks of violence. Supporters of the Chartist movement, the most radical working class movement in the first half of the 19th Century, started riots in Birmingham, and Newport (Wales) – indeed, the latter was intended to be the beginning of a popular uprising. Chartism was a fairly diverse movement which made a powerful impact at the time, although its period of influence spanned a mere decade – between 1838 and 1848. It took its name from the *People's Charter* – a document written in 1838 calling for six reforms to the political system to make it more democratic:–

universal male suffrage;
a secret ballot;
no property qualification for members of Parliament;
payment for members of Parliament;

constituencies of equal size;
annual elections for Parliament.

There is no mention of public ownership of the means of production or compulsory wealth distribution in this document – indeed, the only point in the charter which would have expanded "the state" was the payment of MPs, as politics in mid-19th century Britain was very much a part-time business. With such small government, there was no need for full-time politicians. Unfortunately, as the Chartists rightly pointed out, this meant that only moneyed men could become MPs, as they had the necessary financial resources to support themselves. By this time, Britain's two-party system was well established. The Tories were very much the party of the landed gentry and the Anglican Church. The Whigs (or the Liberals as they became) were the party of nonconformity, and who supported free trade and the extension of the franchise. However, the Whig leaders were often aristocrats, like Lords Derby and Palmerston, and even if some Whig grandees like Brougham were sympathetic to the needs of working men, the Chartists wanted working class representation in Parliament, rather than having to rely on sympathetic noblemen to fight their cause.

Over 1,200,000 men and women signed the first Charter petition, but in 1839, only 46 out of 281 MPs in the House of Commons supported it,[14] and frustration over the rejection of the charter provoked the riots mentioned above. A second petition in 1842 attracted more than 3 million signatures. Again it was rejected. The Chartists threatened a general strike, but although strikes broke out in Lancashire, Glasgow and the Midlands[15], they soon fizzled out. Some Chartists stood for Parliament, and a few, including Feargus O'Connor, one of the Principal figures in the movement, were elected. O'Connor organised a third petition in 1848, but failed to gain as much support as the 1842 petition, in spite of addressing a vast crowd of some 50,000 people on Kennington Common, London. With several countries on the Continent engulfed in revolution at this time, its fate was sealed, as

Parliament was understandably fearful of a similar uprising in Britain. Significantly, O'Connor, although one of the wilder characters in the movement, did not support nationalisation of land, but rather sought to buy land from landowners to be leased out to smallholders. To purchase land, he started the National Land Company (originally the Chartist Co-operative Land company), but although it succeeded in buying an estate near Watford, O'Connor's lack of financial acumen meant that its failure was inevitable[16]. Chartism itself did not fold totally, and one of its leaders, G J Harney, attempted to re-orientate the movement in a more socialist direction. In 1850, he lauched a weekly newspaper, the *Red Republican*, having previously entered into correspondence with Marx and Engels[17]. However, it proved a short-lived enterprise, and Chartism was never able to command anything like the same degree of support after the failure of the 1848 petition.

The Chartist leaders had little sympathy with the Anglican church, calling for its disestablishment. Some went still further, despairing of all the Protestant denominations and setting up a number of Chartist Christian churches, which attempted to combine Christianity with radical politics[18]. Like the Chartist movement itself, these proved very short-lived. However, the sense of frustration felt by the Chartist leaders towards Evangelical Christianity can be understood inasmuch evidence suggests that, notwithstanding the work of Shaftesbury, Barnardo and others, something of an indifference to poverty had developed among some of their middle class Evangelical contemporaries. Edward Miall (1809–1882) is largely forgotten today, but was regarded as a highly controversial figure during his lifetime, challenging Christian indifference to the plight of the poor. Miall was converted in his teens, studied for the ministry and briefly considered serving abroad as a missionary before the social injustice he saw all around him made him decide to spend the rest of his life campaigning on behalf of the disadvantaged. After several unsuccessful attempts, he was elected as MP for Rochdale in 1852, being a member of the Liberal Party.

Miall did not use the scriptures, as Calvin and the Puritans had done so, to attempt to devise a comprehensive Christian worldview. Indeed, in his book *The Politics of Christianity* (1863), he argued that Christianity does not provide a blueprint for social and political action and made no attempt to develop any sort of political programme[19]. His prime contribution was critical – that English Christianity was becoming too middle-class and materialistic. His criticisms highlighted the results of the fragmentation of Christian political thinking since the end of the 17th Century. 18th Century liberal democracy exalted the right to private property and small government, but all too easily minimalised the concept of stewardship. The regression from the balanced Bible-based worldview of Calvin and the Puritans had opened the doors in some churches for a materialism which was to all intents and purposes the capitalism so vigorously denounced by Marx and other socialists.

If capitalism is defined in the narrowest terms as private ownership of capital and property, then the Bible does most certainly support capitalism with the proviso that individuals must remember that all their wealth is held on trust and to be used for God's glory. In Matthew Henry's words, "It is our duty to make our worldly estates serviceable to our religion, to use them and the interest we have by them .....to do good to the poor with what we have and abound in all works of piety and charity.[20]" However, this is not the capitalism which drew the wrath of Marx, Engels and the early trades unionists through its accumulating of wealth for itself by forcing workers to work for long hours in harsh conditions for little more than a subsistence wage. It appears from Miall's writings that sections of some nonconformist churches were at least acquiescent with this latter form of capitalism. "Man comes before property" he insisted[21].

In 1849 Miall intended to deliver a series of lectures in the Exeter Hall, London, entitled *The British Churches in relation to the British People,* but when the committee in charge of the hall saw a copy of his manuscript, they withdrew their permission for Miall to use the building[22]. He had intended to point out that while British Christians gave willingly in support of missionary work overseas, they showed less concern for the needy on their own doorstep. Indeed, he went further, claiming that for all its outward piety and regular church attendance, Victorian Christianity had become very formal, with law being substituted for love[23].

Two years later, results from the 1851 census – the only attempt ever to calculate the number of church attendees in Britain – sent shockwaves across Britain as it highlighted the growing alienation of the working classes from any form of religion. Nonconformity's golden years were clearly coming to an end, and although churches across the country were blessed by a great revival in 1859–60, once its effects had died down, the introverted piety that shut the doors to Miall withdrew still further from the last area of the Christian worldview where it had remained active – compassion. Apart from Josephine Butler (1928–1906), celebrated for her campaign against legalised prostitution, and the founder of the Salvation Army, William Booth (1829–1912), who will be considered in more detail below, Evangelical Christianity produced hardly any philanthropists of the calibre of Shaftesbury. British Christians still gave to support missionary work and Müller's orphanages, and played a prominent role in the Band of Hope, the Independent Order of Rechabites and other temperance organisations, but stepped back from their long-held position in the forefront of philanthropy.

The socialist revival in late Victorian Britain

Until the final quarter of the 19th Century, Victorian Britain was working its way slowly through the upheavals of industrialisation and urbanisation without needing socialism. In fact, in spite of the presence of Marx and Engels, indigenous socialism, while never totally extinct, commanded little popular support in the three decades following the failure of the final Chartist petition, being generally regarded as "a revolutionary curiosity peculiar to the continent with little practical interest for a free and normal country.[24]" Ironically, it was not the working classes but middle-class intellectuals who brought about its revival during the 1880s. Prominent among the new generation of socialists was William Morris (1834–1896), celebrated as a poet, painter, writer and above all for the delightful "Arts and Crafts" textiles which adorned the walls of many middle class homes in late Victorian England. Morris had originally been destined for the church, he "abandoned religion in favour of art.[25]" During the 1870s he developed an interest in politics, and after a brief flirtation with the Liberal party, he threw himself into socialism, and from then onwards until his death he toured the country lecturing on socialism.

Morris was an idealist and a romantic, and like Dickens and Brougham before him, he had a genuine concern for the poor, in spite of not being a professed Evangelical. Like his socialist counterparts on the continent, he queried whether it was right that the working classes should be adding to the prosperity of the rich by their often extremely hard labour. Should they not be entitled to a bigger slice of the cake?

Morris, together with the architect Philip Webb (1831–1915) founded the Socialist League in 1884. It manifesto demanded that, "the machinery, factories, workshops, stores...all means of production and distribution of wealth, must be declared and treated as the common property of all.[26]" Morris was not the first socialist to attempt to form a political party. Three years earlier, H M Hyndman (1842–1921), a Cambridge-educated journalist who had studied Marx's writings in a French translation, had founded the Democratic (later Social Democratic) Foundation, and Morris had originally belonged to this party before splitting off to form his own[27]. Neither party lasted very long, being beset by internal divisions, caused primarily by the adoption of anarchist opinions by some members of Morris' party, A more durable socialist institution, the Fabian Society, was also founded in 1884, and survives to this day. It was named after the Roman general Fabius Cunctator, renowned for his tactics of avoiding head-on confrontation and focusing instead on harassment and gradual attrition. Fabians likewise aimed to promote socialism step by step rather than through revolution. With the property qualification for MPs having been abolished in 1858 and the franchise being further extended in 1884 by the Representation of the People Act to include all male householders, the openings for a socialist party were far greater than they had ever been, and the failure of the early socialist parties was clearly only going to be a temporary setback.

The revival of socialism coincided with a revival of unrest among the working classes, who had been relatively quiescent since the Chartist agitations. There were dock strikes at Tilbury in 1888 and in London in 1889. Shaftesbury's campaign for labour reform had addressed the most extreme examples of exploitation, such as the use of women and young children in the coal mines, but even at his death in 1885 many men and women were still working long hours in quite appalling conditions. Socialism provided a new outlet for their discontent, particularly as its new middle-class advocates were better leaders and organisers that Chartists like O'Connor. Annie Besant (1847–1933), who joined the National Secular Society in her youth before later developing an interest in occultism, was another prominent socialist contemporary of Morris. She is remembered especially for her involvement with the "Match Girls" strike of 1888. This resulted from an article she had written in her radical newspaper, *The Link*, entitled "White Slavery" describing the unhealthy working conditions at Bryant & May's match factory at Bow in the East End of London, where the girls had to work with deadly white phosphorus that was widely used in matchstick manufacture. The management tried to force their workers to sign a statement that they were happy with their working conditions. A group refused to sign and were sacked. This in turn led to a three-week long strike which eventually resulted in the employers both improving the conditions for their workers and abolishing the punitive system of fines that had been in force. During the period of the strike, Besant petitioned Parliament on behalf of the striking girls, and organised a boycott of Bryant & May matches. In the aftermath of this strike, the Salvation Army opened up a match factory in the same neighbourhood in 1891, using the less dangerous red phosphorus and paying better wages than Bryant & May. Twenty years later, the use of white (or yellow) phosphorus in the manufacture of matches was banned by law.

Socialists and Christians between them had scored a victory for justice. Was it possible that in spite of the two very different worldviews they represented, there could be an alliance for good? The answer is an unequivocal no. By the late 1880s the Salvation Army was the only Evangelical Christian organisation still active in the field of compassionate care. William Booth's *In Darkest England and the Way Out*, published in 1890, painted a picture of urban misery every bit as shocking as Dickens' writings 50 years earlier[28]. However, outside his own denomination, he found little Evangelical support. Evangelicalism had retreated into a rather introverted pietism. The essentials of the Gospel were still preached in many churches, but salvation of individual sinners now dominated most Evangelical agendas to the exclusion of the more general care for fellow men and women.

The church's response: 1) retreat

Unlike the dramatic decline in Christian political thinking at the end of the 17th century, which is difficult to explain satisfactorily, the reasons for the Evangelical retreat from compassion in the second half of the 19th century are far more clear cut. Firstly, it could be argued that Evangelical Christianity had its hands full fighting to save the essentials of the Gospel by the time of the English socialist renaissance in the 1880s. Ten years after the Exeter Hall closed its doors to Miall Charles Darwin published his *Origins of Species*, in 1859, which was followed the next year by an equally controversial volume called *Essays and Reviews*. Darwin's work popularised the theory of evolution and attacked the book of Genesis, while *Essays and Reviews*, with contributions by seven different authors including Oxford academic Benjamin

Jowett (1817–1893) and Rugby School's headmaster Frederick Temple (1821–1902), undermined the authority of the New Testament by introducing the English-speaking world to "Higher Critical" theology which had already poisoned the church in Germany with its denials of many fundamental doctrines of the Christian faith. Thanks to this twin assault, within a single generation, Evangelical Christianity found itself fighting for its life. Bible-denying ministers in the historically Evangelical denominations were not a new phenomenon, but the sheer scale of the numbers of men training for the ministry in both the Church of England and the free churches who adopted "liberal" views – that the scriptures were not inspired, that Christ was not born of a virgin, that His miracles and His resurrection were myths and that His death was not a substitutionary atonement paying the ransom price for sinners – forced Evangelicalism onto the back foot. The "Downgrade" controversy which convulsed the Baptist Union at the end of the 1880s and which, in all probability, hastened the demise of the great C H Spurgeon, is a good example of how rapidly these views established a foothold even in hitherto solidly Evangelical denominations. Spurgeon was concerned about the growing number of men in Baptist Union chapels who were subscribing to this "new theology", and attempted to persuade the Baptist Union to adopt an unequivocally Evangelical statement of faith that would exclude liberals. Instead the Union's leadership produced a declaration deliberately loose enough for a liberal to subscribe without saying anything offensive to evangelicals. To Spurgeon's sadness, the declaration was passed overwhelmingly, although by this time he had already withdrawn his church, the Metropolitan Tabernacle, from the Baptist Union. He could see that barely a generation after the great revival of 1859, most of his colleagues had no stomach for a fight.

Evangelicalism was so easily undermined from without because it had already been undermined from within. During the 1820s and 1830s, a new understanding of the Bible had emerged which, while clinging to the essentials of the

Gospel, had conditioned the church to expect defeat and weakness. This was a profound contrast to the period from the seventeenth to the early nineteenth centuries, when Britain and later the USA had been blessed by a number of revivals, and a good few pastors on both sides of the Atlantic, while never losing sight of the great hope of Christ's second coming, believed from the Bible that the blessings they had experienced were merely the firstfruits of a greater harvest to come before history's final consummation. Iain Murray's excellent book *The Puritan Hope* traces this sense of expectation to the writings of Calvin, and charts its development through the Puritan age in the 17th century, the great 18th century preachers such as George Whitefield and Jonathan Edwards, and onto the early missionaries like William Carey (1761–1834).

It is one of the most bizarre developments in church history, especially at a time when the Kingdom of God seemed to be advancing so significantly in many parts of the world through the growth of missionary work, that so many Christians should abandon the optimism of the "Puritan hope" and embrace a far more pessimistic view of the future. It is even more extraordinary to consider that two of the most significant men responsible for this change were dead members of the Church of Rome. The first of these, a Spanish Jesuit named Francisco Ribera (d 1591), wrote a book which claimed that in a future period the temple would be rebuilt in Jerusalem with animal sacrifices re-established. His ideas were taken up by another Jesuit, the Chilean-born Manuel de Lacunza (1731–1801) whose book "The Coming of Messiah in Power and Glory" (*La venida del Mesías en gloria y majestad*) appeared posthumously in 1812 under the pseudonym of Rabbi Ben-Ezra, ostensibly a converted Jew. De Lacunza does appear to have seen through the corruption of the Roman Catholic Church, and believed that things were so bad that the return of Christ must therefore be imminent. However, his book would have disappeared into obscurity had not a copy fallen into the hands of Edward Irving (1792–1834) who translated it into

English as he found much in it that corresponded with his own views.

Irving was a strange figure – a powerful speaker but prone to doctrinal vagaries. An ordained minister of the Church of Scotland, he had accepted a call to minister to the Scottish church in London, and quickly established a reputation for his outstanding preaching. In his later years, he drifted into error over the humanity of Christ. His highly speculative mind began to question whether His humanity was sinless. However, by the time Irving was excommunicated by the Church of Scotland for these views, he had already started a new church – the Catholic Apostolic Church, which in some aspects could be viewed as a forerunner of Pentecostalism, inasmuch as it taught that the "gifts of the Spirit," such as healing and speaking in tongues, had been restored to the church as a sign that these were the last days before the return of Christ.

Irving's church has all but died out, for so convinced was he of the imminence of Christ's return that authority to ordain ministers was left in the hands of twelve "apostles" who were called supposedly by prophecy, but without any provision being made for any apostolic succession, as it was not deemed necessary. Once they died, so died with them any ordination mechanism. However, Irving's teachings did not die. A young Anglican clergyman in Ireland, J N Darby (1800–1882), who also seceded from his denomination to start a new church – the Brethren – was strongly influenced by Irving's translation of de Lacunza's work. He added in the writings of Ribera and ended up with a novel understanding of the Scriptures known as dispensationalism, which become popular not only among the Brethren in the UK, but also across parts of the USA as a result of his influence on C I Scofield (1843–1921) whose *Reference Bible* is still in use today. Thanks to the Scofield Bible, dispensational teaching has spread across a number of different sections of the Evangelical church.

Classic dispensationalism teaches that there is a different future for the Jews and the church. It studies the Old Testament with particular regard to seeking signs in the present day of the fulfilment of unfulfilled prophecies, and is convinced that the return of Christ is imminent. The return of Christ is just about the only hope it offers its followers. Church history from now on, it teaches, will be little else but apostasy and decline. The church must expect defeat, and should use what little time it has left to try and save a few more sinners before the saints are "raptured" and Christ returns to inaugurate His Millenial reign among converted Jews.

Dispensationalism's approach to the scriptures combines extreme literalism in its understanding of some passages along with the most fanciful interpretation of others[29]. For the purposes of this book, the importance of dispensationalism has been that it provided a theological basis for retreat from the world. When Sir Henry Vane wrote *A Healing Question Propounded* in 1656, the Puritan hope was shining brightly. Vane was strongly convinced that a time of great blessing was imminent, and even if not all the other Christian political writers considered in Chapters 3 and 4 were as sanguine as Vane, the link between an expectation of revival blessings and a vision to see God's word established as the basis of the nation's laws is unsurprising. So conversely, if it is all doom and gloom until the Lord comes, and the Lord is expected at any time, it is hardly surprising that Christians taking a dispensational viewpoint have shown no desire to engage in politics, even in the area of Christian compassion. Why sift political theories through the net of the scriptures to see how they weigh up? Why bother with trying to renew government according to a Christian worldview when Christians are going to be more and more marginalised? No one will listen, as these end times are going to be so dominated by evil men. Furthermore, while dispensationalism is adamant about the inspiration of the Scriptures, it regards portions of them as relevant only to a particular age (or "dispensation"). Some sections applied to the Jews in the past and others will apply to the Jews after the "rapture". The Calvinistic idea of a holistic Christian worldview based on the unity of the Scriptures was abandoned. This is hardly surprising when many of the texts used by Calvin and his successors to develop their ideas came into the "Not for this dispensation" category. Evangelicalism, at least in English-speaking countries, was to lose what was left of its balanced approach, holding in tension being "in" but not "of" the world, until the latter part of the twentieth century.

The establishment of a theology of defeat has been almost as great a tragedy for Evangelicalism as Darwinism and Higher Criticism. It left it singularly vulnerable at a time when its voice desperately needed to be heard. This is not to say that dispensationalism swept the board – the two most significant British preachers in the 19th and 20th Centuries – C. H. Spurgeon and Dr Martyn Lloyd-Jones, did not follow its teaching, nor did A A Hodge (1823–1896), R.L. Dabney (1820–1898) and B B Warfield (1851–1921) in America. However, even among those who did not accept its eccentricities, there were few Evangelical figures of note in the late 19th Century who held to the older theology of hope. The commentaries of J C Ryle (1816–1900), the Evangelical Bishop of Liverpool, offer a decidedly pessimistic outlook for the years to come:– "While the nations of Europe are absorbed in political conflicts and world business, the sands in their hour-glass are ebbing away....Yet a few years and the 'times of the Gentiles' will be fulfilled. Their day of visitation will be past and gone[30]". "Let us not be carried away by the common idea that ...the earth (will be) be filled with the knowledge of the Lord. It will not be so.[31]"

The church's response: 2) engagement

There were a few exceptions to the Evangelical retreat from the field of Christian compassion. The Salvation Army has already been mentioned in this respect. Founded in 1865, it recognised that care for the vulnerable through charitable aid created a favourable environment to preach the Gospel. Although William Booth stated that "There is nothing in my scheme that will bring it into conflict with the socialists,[32]" the Salvation Army has stayed out of party politics. Indeed, although any reader of Booth's *In Darkest Britain*, will appreciate his genuine concern for the poor, the Salvationists made no call for the building of a Godly society as the Puritans had advocated. Instead they saw the addressing of physical needs primarily as an opening for evangelism. "In providing for the relief of temporal misery I reckon that I am only making it easy where it is now difficult, and possible where it is now all but impossible, for men and women to find their way to the Cross of our Lord Jesus Christ[33]" wrote Booth.

A very different approach was taken by James Keir Hardie (1856–1915) a Scottish miner and Trade Union activist who became a Christian in 1897 and who in 1900 subsequently founded and became the first leader of a socialist political party that was to prove more enduring than the short-lived parties of the 1880s – the Labour Party. Keir Hardie, a lay preacher with the Evangelical Union Church, saw no contradiction between his Christian faith and socialism. "The impetus which drove me first into the Labour movement, and the inspiration which has carried me on in it, has been derived more from the teachings of Jesus of Nazareth than from all other sources combined," he said in 1910. Three years earlier, in his book *From Serfdom to Socialism*, he used a most extraordinary title to describe the Saviour – Jesus the Communist.

Keir Hardie was not the only Christian who believed that socialism offered the best way of addressing injustice. His Methodist colleague Philip Snowden (1864–1937), who co-authored a book called *The Christ that is to be* with Keir Hardie in 1903, held similar beliefs, as did Sir Stafford Cripps, Chancellor of the Exchequer from 1947 to 1950 in Clement Attlee's Labour government.

In the main, however, marriages between socialism and "Christianity" tended to occur among those whose beliefs cannot be called Evangelical. In the period between Owen and the British socialist renaissance in the 1880's, one of the more notable, albeit short-lived socialist movements was a group of distinctly heterodox Anglicans who described themselves as "Christian Socialists." The leaders of the movement were the writer Charles Kingsley (1819–1875), the lawyer John Ludlow (1821–1911) and the academic theologian F.D. Maurice (1805–1872), a man who denied the doctrine of the Atonement and who was sacked from his post as lecturer in English history at King's College London for his unsound views. These men expressed sympathy with the Chartist movement, and felt a special concern about the Chartist hostility to the Anglican church. Maurice had observed the large Chartist rally on Kennington Common in London in 1848, and it was this event which attracted his sympathy and those of his friends. They published two short-lived journals to expound their views, *Politics for the People* (1848–49) and the *Christian Socialist* (1850–51). Ludlow was acquainted with the teachings of Fourier[34], and Maurice was an admirer of Owen's work. These men strongly supported the co-operative movement, and Maurice in particular, who had argued in favour of socialism a decade earlier in his work *The Kingdom of Christ*, was a strong opponent of both individualism and competition. He wrote to Kingsley that "competition is put forth as the law of the universe. This is a lie.[35]"

These men did not design any economic policies nor write any political manifesto as Marx had done. By 1854, their period of influence was over. However, they left an interesting legacy inasmuch as English socialism right up to the 1960s remained largely devoid of the militant atheism that characterised its continental counterpart. Indeed, well into the 20th Century, openly atheistic British socialists had to tread carefully. One of the first British socialists openly to attack Christianity since Robert Owen was a Marxist, Robert Williams, the Labour Party candidate for Aberavon, South Wales in the 1918 General Election. He turned in a disappointing result because crowds of children turned out on polling day to boo him as "the man who doesn't love Jesus[36]". The British working classes may have been sympathetic to a party that professed to have their interests at heart, but particularly in an area touched by a revival only a few years earlier, they were not going to look too kindly on militant atheism.

When socialism revived in England in the 1880's, "Christian Socialism" also made a comeback. Some notable Evangelicals who embraced socialism have been mentioned above, but in this period, with false teaching now more widespread within the church, most of what emerged was little more than baptised socialism – in other words, socialism overlaid with a veneer of Christianity. More concerned with addressing the evils of this life than any concern for the next, the leaders of this movement were men who rejected Jesus the Saviour who died for sinners, while exalting Jesus the social reformer. They regarded Jesus' command to "love thy neighbour[37]" as far more important that Paul's statement that "Christ Jesus came into the world to save sinners.[38]" Stewart Headlam (1847–1924) was one of the most prominent among this second generation of "Christian Socialists". He had been taught by Maurice at Cambridge and came to adopt the same socialist views. Sacked by his bishop for calling Jesus a revolutionary, Headlam toured the country with his socialist message, arguing for a tax on land and the redistribution of wealth to end poverty. He denounced wealth as robbery and inconsistent with Christianity[39] and later joined the Fabian Society. Headlam combined ritualism with theological liberalism. He was a founder of a short-lived movement called the Anti-Puritan league, whose membership also included the writer G. K. Chesterton. He also stood bail for the writer Oscar Wilde when he was remanded on the charge of homosexuality, causing quite a sensation in so doing[40].

Even if this book argues strongly that Christianity and socialism are incompatible, the misguided attempts to merge the two unquestionably resulted in the British Labour Party developing in a more benign and less ideologically rigid manner than its continental counterparts. In many ways it could be described for the first half century of its existence as a hotch-potch of individuals united in their commitment to improve the lot of the British working classes, but in little else. The former deputy leader of the Labour Party Roy Hattersley writes, "From the day that the Labour Party was born – and partly as a result of its complicated parentage – powerful voices have always insisted that to define the philosophical framework within which its policies could be assembled would only lead to trouble.[41]" While unquestionably including a strong socialist element, pragmatism rather than ideology was the party's guiding principle. Indeed, it had been in existence a full 18 years without any commitment in its constitution to the foundational socialist principle of state ownership of the means of production – indeed, compulsory wealth redistribution was emphasised every bit as strongly, if not more so, than nationalisation in the British Labour Party. This lack of dogmatism regrettably allowed the Labour Party to be subtly transformed at the end of the 20th century by a more hard-line ideology that, because of its emphasis on enforced equality (and not just enforced equality of wealth) and thus its dissimilarity to classic socialism, was to creep in unnoticed – with fearful consequences.

Socialism only established a foothold in America following large-scale industrialisation in the latter half of the 19th Century, which sadly saw the development of the same type of slum dwellings as characterised many English industrial towns. Immigrants from Eastern and Southern Europe formed the bulk of America's new urban poor, and prominent among the first American socialists to reach out to them were the "social gospellers." Like their English counterparts, they were rightly concerned about the living conditions of the urban poor but had no message of salvation for them. Church historian Earle Cairns says of these men: "Basing their work on the theological dogmas of the fatherhood of God and the brotherhood of man, many turned their attention from the salvation of the individual to the application of the teaching of Christianity to the economic life of the state, in order to bring the kingdom of God to earth.[42]" The most celebrated American "Christian" defender of state intervention was Walter Rauschenbusch (1861–1918), a strong opponent of competition and the free market in general[43]. Rauschenbusch, trained as a Baptist minister, was called to a pastorate in a run-down area of New York known as Hell's Kitchen in 1885. The poverty, disease and crime that he saw all around him led to him shifting the emphasis of his pastorate from what he called saving "souls in the ordinarily accepted religious sense" to social action. A man who enthusiastically endorsed the overtly liberal theology of the German theologian Albrecht Ritschl (1821–1889), he turned to socialism, and his most celebrated book which attempted to marry socialism with the teachings of Jesus as he understood them, *Christianity and the Social Crisis* was a best-seller when it was published in 1907.

Take away the doctrines of the Fall, redemption through the death of Christ, a final judgement, Heaven and Hell and it is no surprise that "Liberal" Christianity and socialism converged so naturally. Both devoted their energies to creating Utopia on Earth with the state, not the Saviour, becoming the Messiah.

The overtly liberal theology of Rauschenbusch, Headlam and other "Christian" socialists provided a further reason for Evangelicals on both sides of the Atlantic to withdraw from the social arena. With the exception of the Salvation Army, any Christian involvement in social action would from now on engender suspicion of theological unsoundness. The final cords linking Evangelical Christianity of the late nineteenth and early twentieth centuries to the joined-up thinking of the Reformation and Puritan eras had now been cut. Although very different theologically, a significant strand of Evangelical thought and preaching was now characterised by the same other-worldliness that had characterised mediaeval piety

The Evangelical retreat from a holistic Christian worldview – at least as far as the English- speaking world was concerned – took away both the tools and the motivation for anyone still wishing to defend the idea of private property as Biblical. In this period, for a Christian to do so would have been very much swimming against the tide, for as Hayek observed, "By the Nineteenth Century, serious intellectual appreciation and

discussion of the role of property in the development of civilisation would seem to have fallen under a kind of ban in
many quarters.[44] Furthermore, to argue for the right to
private property or competition in the market from a Biblical
standpoint at the end of the 19th Century could well have
been misconstrued as support for some of the more exploitative practises of the time. Bearing in mind that British
nonconformity in particular drew much of its membership
from such of the working classes as still attended a place of
worship, the lack of a consistent Biblical challenge to
socialism in the late Victorian period is thus hardly surprising.
Sadly, with "liberal" Christianity taking over in many Free
Church pulpits, the net result has been the further alienation
of the working classes from the church, for without the hope
of the Gospel, it had nothing to say that socialism could not
say just as well. The hymn quoted at the beginning of the
chapter may have been sound biblically, but it spoke of a
divinely-ordained status quo that was now being widely
questioned.

The church's response: 3) Opposition

There were a few notable Christians swimming against the
tide. The American theologian R.L. Dabney (1820–1898)
prophesied that that the socialist ideal of communal ownership of property would fail to alleviate poverty and would
instead create misery: "It is forgotten that nature has made
the desire for the special welfare of one's self, and of one's
own family, far stronger than the desire for the general good.
Hence the only possible result of the theory is not that
private property shall be happily substituted by communism;
but that happy civilised societies may be plunged into
anarchy; and what little private property is left be held with
a far fiercer grasp, and defended by personal violence instead
of by regulated and benignant law. Natural selfishness will
never lift itself into disinterestedness, least of all by an infidel
creed which makes selfish pleasure its *summum bonum*.[45]"
He also predicated that any future welfare state would not

only cause massive rises in taxation, but would impinge on the liberty of its citizens: "All history teaches us that the more 'paternalistic' a government becomes....the more will its officials engross the power of the State, and the earnings of the citizens to themselves....either by avowed class legislation or by unavowed chicanery, they always do it. The cause of this result is plain. The more paternalistic the government, the more of the aggregate services and rights of its citizens does it handle[46]"

Similar warnings were sounded by the Dutch pastor, theologian and politician Abraham Kuyper (1838–1920), who has already been discussed in Chapter 4 and who brought back almost from nowhere the concept of a Biblical worldview which extended into all areas of life. Indeed, Kuyper can be regarded as the most able spokesmen for this position since Calvin and the Puritans. In 1880, he founded the Free University of Amsterdam, which "took the Bible as the unconditional basis on which to rear the whole structure of human knowledge in every department of life[47]." Kuyper was therefore no friend to socialism. He opposed the idea of Marxist class conflict and encouraged workers to be content with their lot, in the knowledge that for a Christian, there was a better life to come. While a strong advocate of Christian compassion, he had no sympathy with the idea of a welfare state. "The holy art of 'giving for Jesus' sake' ought to be much more strongly developed among us Christians. Never forget that all state relief for the poor is a blot on the honour of your Saviour," he said in a speech in 1891, which has subsequently been published in English under the title of The Problem of Poverty. In his lecture Calvinism and Politics, delivered in 1898, Kuyper warned of the dangers of a powerful state. He argued, as Calvin and Augustine had done that government was a necessity only because of the Fall. "Without sin, there would have been neither magistrate nor state-order.... God has instituted the magistrates by reason of sin.[48]" He points out that the division of mankind into nations after the building of the tower of Babel had its good and bad points. "This multitude of states ought not to exist; there should only be one world-empire,[49]" by which he means a sinless society under God's direct rule. However, thanks to the Fall, both this division into states and government *per se* are good things: "for a sinful humanity, without division of states, without law and government and without ruling authority, would be a veritable hell on earth.[50]" Hence his opposition to socialism, which with its "international cosmopolitan endeavours" were trying "to attain the unattainable... now and in a sinful world.[51]" Anarchism likewise was in his opinion, "nothing but a looking backwards after a lost paradise.[52]"

He goes on to tell his audience that, "We must ever watch against the danger, which lurks, for our personal liberty, in the power of the state,[53]" and with Rousseau obviously in mind adds, "Nor can a group of men, by contract, from their own right, compel you to obey a fellow-man. What binding force is there in the allegation that ages ago one of my progenitors made a '*Contrat Social*'with other men of that time?[54]" He then goes on to consider two other views of the state, which in his view were one and the same: "Directly opposed to this Calvinistic confession there are two other theories. That of popular sovereignty, as it has been antitheistically proclaimed at Paris in 1789 and that of state sovereignty as it has of late been developed by the historico-pantheistic school of Germany. Both of these theories are at heart identical.[55]" In other words, both the growth of the bureaucratic German state of the 19th Century and the French Revolution of 1789 shared a common anti-Christian ideology which viewed all power as flowing down from the state. Calvin had argued that the Scriptures state the opposite – namely that rulers are accountable to their subjects and to God. Kuyper, taking a similar line, correctly prophesied that when socialism eventually gained power, the socialist state would end up usurping God's role: "That which exists is good because it exists; and it is no longer the will of God; of Him who created us and knows us, but it becomes the will of the State, which, having no-one above itself, actually becomes God and has to decide how our life and existence shall be.[56"]

Kuyper's holistic understanding of the Scriptures also led him to distance himself from the capitalism of his day, which, as was noted earlier, was a debasement of Christian political thought inasmuch as it endorsed the Bible's support for private property and commerce but ignored the gracious mitigating influence of Christian compassion. However, one important contemporary was quite unequivocal in arguing that Evangelical Christianity and capitalism were strongly linked. The German Max Weber (1864–1920) was no theologian, but rather a sociologist, looking at Christianity not from the inside like Dabney or Kuyper, but from the outside as a detached observer. His most important work, The Protestant Ethic and the Spirit of Capitalism, (*Die protestantische Ethik und der Geist des Kapitalismus*), published in 1904–5, starts off by asking the question as to why the countries of Europe that embraced the Reformation were so much more active in the field of commerce and entrepreneurship than those that did not. He answers the question by looking at the Protestant – and particularly Calvinistic – theology of work. Acknowledging that although Evangelical Christianity is concerned first and foremost about salvation, Weber argues that by seeing every area of life under God's control, the Protestants introduced a new sacredness to a secular calling. While warnings about the danger of wealth abound in the writings of Protestant theologians, the "work ethic" characterised by frugality, restraint, honesty – in other words, a "worldly asceticism" – would inevitably cause the Christian to prosper. The Old Testament view of material prosperity as a sign of God's favour enabled the believer to feel comfortable with his wealth as it was a sign of assurance of his salvation. However, wealth was not to be used ostentatiously. Besides being saved, it should be shared. Weber quotes John Wesley's exhortation to "gain all they can so that they should also give what they can[57"].

He acknowledges that capitalism pre-dates the Reformation, but argues that the way it developed in the Protestant nations was a direct consequence of the mindset created by the Reformation. Looking at the works of Richard Baxter, he claims that "Baxter expresses himself in terms which more than once directly recall Adam Smith's well-known apotheosis of the division of labour[58]" – in other words, Baxter anticipated by over 100 years the principal theme of a book regarded as the epitome of capitalism – the *Wealth of Nations*.

Weber has had his critics, and no Christian reading his work would endorse every aspect of his argument. In his frequent use of words like "gloomy" and "harsh" when describing Calvinism and the Puritans, he is guilty of falling for the all too common caricature painted by the enemies of Reformed doctrines and the men that followed them. He also failed to discern that capitalism as popularly understood was a debasement of Christian political thinking. He makes an unjustifiable link between the Puritan tradesman and the capitalist factory owner when he claims that Puritan moral restraint in the workplace "is now bound to the technical and economic conditions of machine production which to-day determine the lives of all.[59]" On a different note, André Bieler's criticisms of Weber centre round his attempts to link some aspects of capitalism to the writings of the great reformer of Geneva, although he concedes a link with Puritanism, which he calls the "illegitimate son of Calvinism[60]" on account of its greater individualism.

For all the criticisms and reservations about Weber's work, a very searching question has to be asked: If Bible-believing God-honouring Christians have played such a major part in the development of commerce organised apart from the state, can any true believer endorse a rival system which not only exalts the state but owes its very existence and much of its development to men and women who were strongly opposed to Gospel truth? Or to put it another way, were people like Keir Hardie or Sir Stafford Cripps aberrations attempting to have one foot in each of two contradictory camps?

At the time Weber published his thesis, few other people

apart from Kuyper were considering this question. The ever-increasing support for state intervention, particularly in the area of welfare, during the late 19th and early 20th centuries, now seems quite extraordinary a century later. Even the *Girls Own* annuals, which are strongly tinged with Christian morality and hardly in the vanguard of socialist thinking, contained an article by Lily Watson which declared that, "It is through the action of the State that the task of neighbourly responsibility must be taken up....It has for some time been recognised that these matters (i.e. *health care and housing*) are the business of the State.[61]" Fifty years earlier, the philosopher John Stuart Mill (1808–1873) had warned of the danger of giving power to the State in his classic work *On Liberty*. Mill's work, which was well received at the time, was a strong affirmation of individual rights. "The worth of a State, in the long run, is the worth of the individuals composing it.[62]" Mill's bottom-up view of the state made him a strong critic of any attempt by the state to limit individual freedom, citing among his examples the Puritan restrictions on entertainment during the 17th Century, notably their opposition to the theatre. Less than fifty years after his death, his works were still being studied, but few were heeding his warnings that a big state would be restrictive.

Indeed, in spite of the growing conviction that the world would be a better and fairer place if the state was given more power, socialism before 1917 was still an unknown quantity. Its rhetoric so far consisted only of promises. What would happen if it seized power and its theories put into practise? Would it usher in a golden age or would the result instead be the tyranny envisaged by Mill, Dabney and Kuyper?

Notes
[1] http://en.wikipedia.org/wiki/History_of_the_cooperative_movement Accessed 01/03/2012.
[2] http://emotionalliteracyeducation.com/classic_books_online/selfh10.htm Accessed 01/03/2012.
[3] *idem.*
[4] Cockett, R *Thinking the Unthinkable*, p270–271. Harper Collins London 1994.

[5] Bartholomew, J. *The Welfare State We're* in, P46 Politico's publishing, London 2004.

[6] *idem.*

[7] *ibid*, p47.

[8] Woodward, Sir L. *The Age of Reform*, p477, The Oxford History of England, Volume 13. Oxford University press, Oxford, 1962.

[9] Bartholomew, J. *op cit*, p154.

[10] Whelan, R, *The Corrosion of Charity*, p24. Insititute of Economic Affairs, London 1996.

[11] http://www.literaturecollection.com/a/dickens/oliver-twist/50/ Accessed 01/03/2012

[12] http://www.hsomerville.com/meccano/Articles/JacobsIsland.htm Accessed 01/03/2012

[13] Woodward, Sir L. *op cit*, p494–495.

[14] Woodward, Sir L. *op cit*, p4128–129.

[15] *idem*, p141.

[16] *idem*, p143–5.

[17] http://www.socialistworker.co.uk/art.php?id=10272 Accessed 03/03/2012.

[18] http://en.wikipedia.org/wiki/Chartism Accessed 03/03/2012.

[19] Smith, D.W. *A Prophet without Honour: Edward Miall* in Clark S (ed) *Tales of Two Cities*, p159, IVP Leicester 2005.

[20] Henry, M, *Commentary on the Whole Bible*. Volume 3, Proverbs 3:7–12, World Bible Publishers, Iowa Falls. Originally published in 1706.

[21] Smith, D.W. *op cit*, p161.

[22] *ibid*, p166.

[23] *ibid*, p168.

[24] Kirkup, T, *A History of Socialism*, p328 Elibron Classics 2006 (originally published by A&C Black, London 1909).

[25] http://www.marxists.org/archive/morris/other/heritage.htm Accessed 03/03/2011.

[26] *idem.*

[27] Ensor, Sir R. *England 1870–1914*, p100, The Oxford History of England, Volume 14. Oxford University press, Oxford, 1962.

[28] Ensor, Sir R, *op cit*, p335.

[29] W W Fereday's *The Lord will come and the Lord will reign*, a Dispensational book published in 1898, claims that Rosh, and Meshech and Tubal mentioned in Ezekiel 38:3 refer to Russia, Moscow and – Tobolsk! Hal Lindsey's 1970 best seller *Late Great Planet Earth* makes a similar identification of Russia and Moscow.

[30] Ryle, J C, *Expository thoughts on the Gospels, Luke* Volume 2 p371. James Clarke, Cambridge Reprinted 1983.

[31] Ryle, J C, *Expository thoughts on the Gospels, Mark* p276. James

Clarke, Cambridge Reprinted 1983

[32] Smith, D W *op cit,* p176 (footnote).

[33] http://en.wikipedia.org/wiki/William_Booth Accessed 05/03/2011,

[34] Kirkup, T, *A History of Socialism,* p71 Elibron Classics 2006 (originally published by A&C Black, London 1909).

[35] Vidler, A, *The Church in the age of Revolution,* p96 Penguin Books, Harmondsworth, 1961.

[36] Murray, I, *D. Martyn Lloyd-Jones, the First Forty Years 1899–1939,* p115, the Banner of Truth Trust, Edinburgh 1982.

[37] Luke 10:27.

[38] 1 Tim 1:15.

[39] http://www.spartacus.schoolnet.co.uk/REheadlam.htm Accessed 05/03/2011.

[40] Vidler, A *op cit,* p99.

[41] Hattersley, R *Choose Freedom – the Future for Democratic Socialism,* p3, Michael Joseph Ltd London 1987.

[42] Cairns, E E *Christianity through the Centuries,* (Revised edition) p425, Zondervan, Grand Rapids 1981.

[43] *idem.*

[44] Hayek, F A, *The Fatal Conceit,* p50, University of Chicago Press, Chicago. 1988.

[45] Dabney, R L, *Discussions of Robert Lewis Dabney,* Volume 3, p323. Banner of Truth, 1982, Edinburgh and Carlisle, Pennsylvania. (originally published in 1892 and 1897)

[46] *ibid,* p310.

[47] From the biographical notes in the prelude to Kuyper A, *Lectures on Calvinism,* Eerdmans, 1931 Grand Rapids,

[48] Kuyper. A *Lectures on Calvinism,* p80/81. Eerdmans, 1931 Grand Rapids (originally delivered in 1898).

[49] *ibid,* p81.

[50] *idem.*

[51] *ibid,* p80.

[52] *idem.*

[53] *idem.*

[54] *ibid.* p82.

[55] *ibid.* p85.

[56] *ibid.* p87

[57] Weber, M *The Protestant Ethic and the Spirit of Capitalism,* Chapter 5, 1904–5 (taken from on-line English translation, http://www.archive.org/stream/protestantethics00webe/protestantethics00webe_djvu.txt) Accessed 05/03/2011.

[58] *idem.*

[59] *idem.*

[60] Bieler, A *La Penseé Economique et Sociale de Calvin*, p494–496 Librarie de l'Université Georg & Cte S.A. Geneva, 1959.

[61] Watson, L *The Citizenship of Women* in the *Girls Own Annual,* Volume XL p120–121, London 1919.

[62] Mill, J.S. *On Liberty*, on-line version http://www.bartleby.com/130/ Accessed 14/08/2012.

Chapter 7:

1917–1989: Socialism in the driving seat

Until August 1914 a sensible, law-abiding Englishman could pass through life and hardly notice the existence of the state, beyond the post office and the policeman. He could live where he liked and as he liked[1]

This quote from A J P Taylor still amazes those that read it for the first time. It sounds like a description of an idyllic, golden age. In reality Edwardian England was far from idyllic. Slums and poverty were still part of life in many cities, while nearly two thirds of the nation's capital wealth was owned by a mere 1.4% of all families[2]. Nevertheless, the degree to which Britain – and the USA for that matter – functioned successfully in this period with its small state is rarely appreciated to-day. At the start of World War I, the standard rate of income tax was only 6%[3] and the poor paid no tax at all. VAT was unknown, and healthcare was not organised by the state. The quality of life in small-government Britain was certainly not inferior to more bureaucratic top-down nations like Germany or Belgium. What is so supremely ironic is that the problems Britain and many other countries are facing one hundred years later are caused to a considerable degree by an ideology that, as was noted in the previous chapter, promised to make things better.

Taylor goes on to list some functions of the pre-1914 British state which show that Christian compassion had left its mark, thanks in no small measure to men like Lord

217

Shaftesbury. No Christian who understands the fallen nature of sinful man would deny that it was right that the state "intervened to prevent the citizen from eating adulterated food or contracting certain infectious diseases" or that "it imposed safety rules in factories, and prevented women and adult males in some industries, from working excessive hours.[4]" However, Taylor then goes on to list some areas where the state had already begun to expand in ways with which the great Christian political thinkers of the past would have been less comfortable:– "The state saw to it that children received education up to the age of 13. Since 1 January 1909, it provides a meagre pension for the needy over the age 70. Since 1912, it helped to insure certain classes of workers against sickness and unemployment". This tendency towards more state action was increasing. Before it had even seized power, socialism was already acquiring a second string to its bow. Besides wishing the state to control the means of production, socialists were now seeking for the state a mandate to redistribute wealth from rich to poor by compulsion. Expenditure on social services had roughly doubled since the Liberals took office in 1905.[5] Taylor's list is not exhaustive. He does not mention, for instance, the Finance Act of 1894 had imposed estate duties "on the full capital value of land and applied to all property, real or personal, settled or free, which passed or was deemed to pass on the death of the deceased.[6]" However, increased meddling by the state had boosted public spending in the UK between 1870 and 1913 from 9.4% to 12.7% of GDP[7] (Gross Domestic Product – which may be defined as "the total market value of all final goods and services produced in a country in a given year, equal to total consumer investment and government expenditure plus the value of exports minus the value of imports.[8]")

The expansion of the state had been given a considerable impetus by the formation of the "Labour Representation Committee" whose origins were considered in the previous chapter and which won two seats in the 1900 general election only a few months after coming into existence. In the

1906 election, the Labour Party, as it had by then become, won no less than 26 seats. This newcomer had not taken long to upset the two-party system which had dominated British politics since the 18th Century, and it was the Liberals who felt the pressure most acutely, as they had historically enjoyed more support from the working classes than the Conservatives. The Liberals had actually won a huge majority in 1906, but when Herbert Asquith (1852–1928) took over as Prime Minister in 1908, some Liberal policies started to smell strongly of socialism, such as the introduction of a state pension. Was such a move necessary? In 1895, a royal commission had looked at the subject, and had not recommended the introduction of a state pension. After all, the thrifty and generous Victorians had survived pretty well without the help of the state. Many of them were members of one or more friendly societies, some of which already provided a pension. And as for compassion, the average middle class household in late Victorian Britain gave 10% of its income on charitable giving – more than it spent on clothing or housing[9]. Voluntary wealth redistribution was working pretty well, so why replace it by state-enforced compulsory wealth redistribution?

Things came to a head when Asquith's chancellor David Lloyd George introduced the so-called "people's budget" in 1909, which was decidedly socialist in style, proposing a land tax, a "super tax" and an increase in estate duties to pay for an ambitious welfare programme, including the controversial state pension. The Conservative majority in the House of Lords threw out this budget, although it is debatable how much opposition to compulsory wealth redistribution was based on ideological principles as opposed to a simple but understandable reluctance to pay more tax. The response of Asquith and Lloyd George was to seek a reduction in the power of the House of Lords, but King Edward VII was reluctant to create a large number of Liberal peers merely to vote away the veto of the Upper House. On Edward's death in 1910, his successor George V was pressured into signing the Parliament Act, which, by curtailing the veto of the House of

Lords, removed the last remaining obstacle in the way of state-enforced wealth redistribution. It is remarkable that during the battle over the budget in 1909, Lloyd George had declared in one speech, "Who made ten thousand men the owners of the soil and the rest of us trespassers in the land of our birth?[10]" Such an attack on private property sounds more like Marx or Rousseau than a minister of the British Liberal Party. The death knell was sounding for lightly-governed Britain, once a source of wonder and admiration to other countries.

Although it was another decade before the British Labour Party was to enjoy its first taste of power, by then socialism had firmly established itself in another country – and in a far more ruthless way than Asquith or Lloyd George would ever have had envisaged.

The Russian Revolution and its aftermath

Anarchism and revolutionary ideals in Russia had not been suppressed by the reactionary Czar Alexander III. During the reign of his son Nicholas II, industries were developed, but no civil rights were granted to the workers. This unhappy situation led to an attempted revolution in the aftermath of Russia's defeat in a war against Japan in 1904–5. Sailors mutinied at Odessa on the battleship *Potemkin* and 200,000 disaffected workers marched on the Winter Palace in St. Petersburg. They were attacked by mounted Cossacks and many were killed. It was only a lack of leadership and the disunity among the different revolutionary groups which enabled the authorities to crush the uprising. The Czar made concessions, granting freedom of conscience, speech, meeting and association, and authorised elections for a legislative assembly, or *Duma*, which met for the first time in 1906. However, Nicholas was unable to come to any workable power-sharing agreement, even with the more moderate element in the *Duma*, so the unsatisfactory stalemate continued. After a further decade, the chaos and inefficiency of the Russian military machine following Russia's entry into the First World War brought the country close to collapse and provided the Marxist revolutionaries with a further opportunity to seize power. This time, they were successful.

Russia actually experienced two revolutions in 1917. The first of these, the February Revolution, resulted in the abdication of the Czar and the formation of the so-called Provisional Government, which consisted of a rather uneasy alliance between assorted socialists and a more liberal element. The leader of this assembly was an aristocratic prince, Gyorgy Lvov. Only a few weeks after this first revolution, Vladimir Ilyich Lenin (1870–1924) returned from exile in Switzerland. A convinced Marxist since 1887, he had been imprisoned and later exiled for plotting against the Czar. When the Russian Social Democratic Labour Party split into two in 1903, Lenin became leader of the majority (Bolshevik) faction, and took an active role in events in 1904–5. In the aftermath of the failure of the revolution, he fled to Western Europe, where he remained until 1917. From the moment of his return, he worked to undermine the Provisional Government. His first speech on returning to Petrograd (now St Petersburg) left his hearers in no doubt about his vision for the future: "Sailors, comrades, we have to fight for a socialist revolution, to fight until the proletariat wins full victory! Long live the worldwide socialist revolution!" However, he had many enemies, not only among his political opponents but among some of his fellow Marxists. The Provisional Government still had sufficient power to outlaw his Bolshevik party and once again, he was forced to flee the country – this time to Finland. However, in his absence, the Provisional Government was unable to maintain any real stability, and Lenin soon returned to play a prominent role in the second revolution, the October Revolution, which finally ushered in a socialist government, of which he became the leader.

In theory, Russia should have been a more open country as a result of these dramatic changes. The *Soviets* – workers' local councils – had begun their life in the early years of the 20th Century as a grassroots movement operating under a type of direct democracy. However, Lenin's Bolshevik regime, while retaining the term and making frequent use of the phrase "all power to the Soviets!" rapidly developed a top-down structure which reduced the democratic element to a mere formality. In 1918, industry, banking, agriculture and much of the retail sector were placed under the power of the state and centrally controlled, even if in theory they now belonged to "the people."

Liberals and less radical socialists, who had supported the first revolution, found themselves completely sidelined by the Bolsheviks following the October revolution and rose up in rebellion. The civil war between the Bolsheviks' Red Army and their opponents (the "Whites") was a bloody affair, with atrocities on both sides. In spite of support from Britain, France and America for the opponents of the October revolution, the Bolsheviks eventually emerged triumphant and their enemies were eliminated, imprisoned or exiled. The Czar and his family were all executed, as were a number of leading figures from pre-revolutionary days. Other political opponents were sent to labour camps. In 1922, all other political parties except the Communist party, as the Bolsheviks had now been renamed, were banned. Even the anarchists fell under this ban. One of their most influential leaders, Pyotr Kropotkin (1842–1921), had been offered, but declined a post in the Provisional Government. He was most uncomfortable with events following the October revolution. "This buries the revolution", he remarked, as his hatred of government in any shape or form naturally included the authoritarian regime of Lenin. Lenin permitted anarchists to march in procession at Kropotkin's funeral, but after that, anarchist leaders were forced to flee the country to escape assassination squads.

For the Evangelical churches in Russia, the first years following the revolution appeared to offer an improvement in their circumstances. The Russian Orthodox Church, which was the nation's established church until 1917, had shown very little tolerance of "sects" as it termed them. One of the first acts of the Lenin's government after the October Revolution was to separate church and state. In January 1918 a decree was passed allowing freedom of religion, which further weakened the overbearing influence of the Orthodox Church. However, a hard-line Marxist regime was never likely to show any great enthusiasm for religion in any shape or form, and a programme of atheistic indoctrination in schools was inaugurated before Lenin's death, accompanied by harassment of anyone professing to believe in God. The Russian Orthodox Church was the main loser, being a particular object of hatred due to having been hand-in-glove with the hated Czarist administration, but Evangelicals soon found themselves suffering restrictions too, in some cases, joining Russian Orthodox priests in the labour camps,

Lenin was convinced that he had a blueprint that would completely transform this previously backward country, by now known as the Union of Soviet Socialist Republics. The name is significant, for although the only political party permitted under the new order was now called the Communist Party, true to Marxist principles, Lenin and his successors recognised that they had not yet arrived in the promised land of communism, where government would wither away. They had managed to establish the intermediate state of socialism, but the final leap was to remain elusive. When Josef Stalin took over as leader following Lenin's death in 1924, rather than trying to abolish the state, he brought in the first of his "five year plans" for industry and agriculture, designed to bring the Soviet Union up to date and able to compete with the West. Lenin's *New Economic Policy* of 1921 had allowed for a very limited role for the private sector, particularly in agriculture, but these concessions were ended as Stalin sought to eradicate the last traces of capitalism by bringing everything, even agriculture, under collective control. The targets he set were very ambitious. The factory workers were poorly paid and had to endure long hours and often dangerous conditions, and even though some of the industrial targets were met, his agricultural policies resulted in a disastrous famine in 1932–3, far more devastating than the rise in food prices caused by Lenin's policies a decade earlier. Meanwhile, the purge on dissidents, including Christians, continued unabated.

As if this was not enough, just like the Jacobins in the French revolution, the original leaders of the Bolshevik revolution started to fall out with one another. The first of the leaders of the 1917 revolution to fall from grace was Leon Trotsky (1879–1940), who believed that a socialist society could not survive without worldwide permanent revolution. Stalin, who was more committed to "socialism in one country" – in other words, focussing his attention on the Soviet Union – managed to marginalize Trotsky and force him into exile. He was eventually assassinated in Mexico by an agent acting under orders from the Soviet leadership. Two of the men who had allied themselves with Stalin in 1924 to outmanoeuvre Trotsky, Grigory Zinoviev and Lev Kaminev, likewise found themselves at loggerheads with Stalin the following year. Although they submitted to Stalin and acknowledged their "mistakes," several years later Stalin put both men on trial on trumped-up charges, and in 1936, they were shot – two of the more prominent of an estimated 5,000,000 men and women that died in Stalin's "great purge".

Marx's *Communist Manifesto* had offered hope to the "proletarians" that a revolution would cause them to "lose...their chains." The first revolution led by men professing to be his disciples ended up chaining them more tightly than ever.

A brief look at socialism between the wars

Marxist sympathisers across Europe were optimistic that the October Revolution in Russia would precipitate similar uprisings elsewhere. They were to be disappointed. Marxist régimes in Hungary and Bavaria were briefly established in 1919, but lasted only a matter of months. The only other country successfully to embrace Marxism in the inter-war period was Mongolia, where, with Soviet support, a "People's Republic" was proclaimed in 1924 which lasted until the 1990s. It is hardly surprising that such optimism was misplaced. The execution of the Russian Royal family was hardly going to commend revolutionary Marxism, sending shockwaves of horror around Europe. Their deaths have been cited by authors such as the American Robert Massie as one reason why Germany swung to the opposite extreme and embraced the ugly, but strongly anti-Marxist ideology of Adolf Hitler[11].

By the end of the 19th century, socialism had fragmented into three fiercely antagonistic variants – anarchism, revolutionary Marxism and social democracy. In Britain, the influence of Evangelical Christianity, weak though it now was in comparison with the 18th and 19th centuries, acted as a restraint on the more extreme forms of socialism. Apart from an incident when a few armed émigré Russian anarchists fought a gun battle with the police in Tottenham in 1909[12], anarchism was never a serious force in Britain. A few Marxist groups were established, most of which merged to form the Communist Party of Great Britain in 1920. The Labour Party refused to grant it affiliation status, although some Communist Party members joined the Labour Party at a later date, and two such men were elected to parliament in 1922. Among the party's early supporters was Sylvia Pankhurst, daughter of the suffragette Emmeline Pankhurst. It never gained any widespread electoral support in its own right, unlike similar parties in Southern Europe, although two Communist Party candidates were elected to parliament in 1945, beating the Labour Party candidates. They were to be the party's last MPs.

The reluctance of the Labour Party to take the Communist Party under its wing is hardly surprising. While the party reflected the widely-held view that the state should take the lead in the provision of social care, as was noted in the previous chapter, it was hesitant to commit itself to any single prevailing ideology. Unlike the German SPD, which was heavily influenced by Marx and Lassalle, many Labour Party supporters would have disdained the name "socialist" and even fewer would have shared the Marxist goal of a society without government. Even when Labour briefly enjoyed its first taste of power under Ramsay MacDonald in the 1924 General Election, it remained a pretty broad church ranging from a tiny core of hard-line Marxists to a significant number of people opposed to widespread nationalisation and committed to state-provided welfare for pragmatic rather than ideological reasons. Labour's breakthrough – admittedly as a minority administration with Liberal support – lasted less than a year. Fear of Marxism was widespread in Britain at the time, so anything smelling even remotely of socialism was naturally going to be regarded with suspicion. The administration's only significant achievement was to authorise a large-scale council house building programme. Significantly, the 1928 Representation of the People Act, which marked the achievement of the Suffragettes' goal of equal voting rights for men and women, was passed by a Conservative administration. Earlier extensions to the franchise in 1832, 1867 and 1884 had all been the initiatives of the Liberal party, who believed that they would benefit from the removal of various property qualifications as a requirement to vote. It proved a miscalculation on the part of the Conservatives that on this occasion they would benefit from extending the female franchise to include 21–29 year olds and abolishing the property qualification for women voters[13], as Labour was returned to power again in the 1929 General election, again led by MacDonald. He had only been in office for a few months when the Great Depression began, triggered by the Wall Street Crash. Share prices on the American stock market plunged as a result of a dramatic contraction in the American money supply aided by the passing of protectionist import tariffs. MacDonald's decision two years later to head up a government of national unity in order to address the Depression led to accusations that he had betrayed the socialist cause. Both he and his chancellor Philip Snowden were expelled from the party. Snowden's principal crime in the eyes of his Labour colleagues was his desire to balance the budget, even if it meant cutting unemployment pay. The resulting in-fighting meant that the nationalisation programme longed for by hard-core British socialists had to wait for a further decade.

Since 1854, American politics have been a battleground between the Democrat and Republican parties. The ideologies of these two parties have fluctuated over the years, but between them, they have successfully maintained a stranglehold on both the Presidency and Congress. This did not prevent socialist parties attempting to break into the American political system. A Communist Party was established in 1919, and managed to recruit no less than 60,000 members in its first year, outstripping the more moderate Socialist Party of America which could only boast 40,000 members in spite of having been founded 18 years earlier[14]. Despite its lack of electoral success, the Communist Party managed to gain a great deal of influence within American trade unionism. It received financial aid from the Soviet Union for some years. Both the Communist Party and anarchism derived most of their initial strength from recently-arrived immigrants from Eastern Europe, many of whom were of Jewish origin. The most notorious anarchist incident in America was the assassination of President William McKinley in 1901. His murderer, Leon Czolgosz, was an anarchist of Polish origin who claimed to have been influenced in his actions by a speech from another immigrant anarchist, the Lithuanian born Emma Goldman (1869–1940). Although immigration continued to import further supporters of the more extreme variants of socialism to the USA, suspicion of all variants of socialism was, if anything, greater than in the UK, not only because of a rather irrational but widespread fear in the early 1920s that America was about to suffer a Bolshevik revolution, but also due to the threat it posed to the small government enshrined in the American constitution. When five Socialist party members were elected to the New York State Assembly in 1920, the rest of the assembly voted to expel them on the grounds that they had been "elected on a platform that is absolutely inimical to the best interests of the state of New York and the United States.[15]" Sadly, in spite of this recognition of the incompatibility between socialism and America's foundational principles, even the safeguards built into the constitution ultimately proved insufficient to prevent the Federal government from growing significantly in size, as will be considered shortly. The more extreme forms of socialism gained a far greater foothold in Southern Europe without ever succeeding in taking overall power. Many émigré Russian anarchists settled in Paris, and consequently for a while France became a stronghold of anarchism, along with Italy and Spain, although the movement was ultimately suppressed in all three countries. Italy suffered particularly from anarchist atrocities. There were a number of unsuccessful anarchist insurrections in the late 19th century, and King Umberto I was killed by anarchists in 1900. In these lands, Marxist Communist parties also enjoyed widespread support. Soviet financial aid was conditional on the parties refusing to take part in *bourgeois*–led coalitions. The French Communist party refused even to join a broad socialist coalition government that came to power in 1936, although they gave it their support.

In Italy, Germany and Spain, socialism in all its variant forms found itself gradually marginalized by fascism and Nazism. The term "fascism" was derived from the Latin *fasces*, a bundle of rods tied round an axe, a symbol associated with the ancient Roman magistrates, and which emphasised the idea of greater strength through unity – one rod could be easily broken, but not a bundle. Like socialism, fascism did not support small government or individualism, but unlike socialism, it was strongly nationalistic and did not emphasise the class struggle. Benito Mussolini (1883–1945), who became prime minister of Italy in 1922, had started his political career as a socialist, but changed his thinking to fascism. Once established in power, he gradually replaced constitutional government with a dictatorship. He outlawed anarchism, stifled press freedom and dealt firmly with any dissenters, particularly socialists. Hitler likewise cracked down on all variants of socialism following his seizure of power in 1933. The full title of his "Nazi" ideology was, of course, National Socialism (*Nationalsozialismus*) but it was the "national" that was always paramount. This emphasis on national identity, with its insistence on the alleged superiority of some races over others, was in fact a sharp contrast to socialism, which had always had a pronouncedly transnational flavour from the days of the First International onwards. The nationalism of Nazi ideology is remembered above all for its outworking at Auschwitz and other concentration camps, where at least 6 million Jews were put to death, along with other racial "undesirables" such as gypsies.

Hitler's rise to power was aided by a reaction against socialism in the years following the end of World War I, when Germany had suffered from a number of short-lived Marxist uprisings. The German SPD (Social Democratic Party) by now enjoyed sufficient support to find itself a partner in three of the short-lived coalition governments during the period from 1919 to 1930, but gradually lost its influence among the working class to the newly-formed German Workers Party (*Deutsche Arbeiterparti*) whose fierce nationalism touched a chord in a nation that felt itself to have been given a harsh deal from the Treaty of Versailles that ended the First World War. It was this party which Hitler was later to lead and which, after 1933, under its new name, became the only permitted political party in Germany. Hitler did not embark on widespread nationalisation, but taxation and regulation gave the state considerable power over private industry. Although socialism was suppressed, the style of government in Germany – or indeed Italy – during this period cannot remotely be compared with the small non-intrusive state found in pre–1914 Britain and depicted so eloquently by A J P Taylor.

Spain, which had become a republic in 1931, held an election in 1936 which resulted in the formation of a coalition government including both communists and democratic socialists. A rebellion by a number of military leaders opposed to socialism saw the country plunged into a civil war that ended with the triumph of the generals and the military dictatorship of Francisco Franco (1892–1975). Italy and Germany provided military support to Franco's forces while the Soviet Union gave support to the opposing republicans, along with volunteers drawn from every part of the socialist spectrum from other parts of Europe and beyond. The governments of Britain and America stood aloof, and Britain in particular strongly discouraged its citizens from becoming involved, although some chose to ignore this advice. The most celebrated such men were George Orwell, (1903–1950), the author of *Animal Farm* and *Nineteen Eighty-Four*, and Laurie Lee (1914–1997), author of *Cider with Rosie*.

It is no coincidence that the influence of theological liberalism in Germany and rejection of the Reformation by Spain and Italy resulted in these nations finding themselves caught between two conflicting forms of tyranny. Denied the influence of Evangelical political thought, genuine freedom and the concept of limited government for which the Puritans had struggled and which had inspired America's founding fathers had found few echoes in these lands. As will now be obvious to the reader, although the term "right wing" is now widely used as a blanket term for anyone rejecting socialism, the small-state ideology of both Christian political thought and classic liberals like John Locke and John Stuart Mill has no more in common with the tyrannical regimes of Hitler, Mussolini or Franco than it has with socialism. F A Hayek's *Constitution of Liberty* offers a more accurate picture than the misleading left/right division. He presents socialism, fascism and what David Smith calls "Gladstonian Liberalism[16]" as three points of a triangle, with the latter on the bottom, making the point that as one moves downwards, the greater the degree of personal liberty.

Sweden voted in a socialist government during the interwar period. It is often cited as the one country where socialism has "worked." Certainly, socialism seemed to enjoy widespread support among the Swedish electorate during much of the 20th Century, for once the Swedish Social Democratic Workers' Party (*Sveriges socialdemokratiska arbetareparti*) came to power in Sweden in 1932, it saw few interruptions to its rule for some 70 years. However, Swedish socialism was hardly typical. While it created Europe's most comprehensive welfare state – at the cost of very high levels of taxation – 90% of industry remained in private hands, albeit under strict government control[17]. Sweden's increasing prosperity during this period was not thanks to socialism but primarily due to a being a country with a small population, large mineral deposits, a long tradition of free trade and an even longer history of neutrality, which allowed it in particular to emerge unscathed from World War II, having done very well in supplying weapons to both sides in the conflict.

A well-sourced article suggests that there were darker sides to Swedish socialism, with no less than 60,000 Swedes suffering compulsory sterilisation between 1934 and 1974. The Social Democrats, it seems, were prepared to resort to eugenics in their attempt to create the ideal society[18]. The generous benefits offered to all and sundry, including to unmarried mothers, led to a decline in the institution of marriage to the point where, by the year 2000, less than half of all Swedish babies were born to married parents. Even the most "successful" socialist state has therefore proved that socialism in practise ends up destroying Christian values. Indeed, socialism also ends up destroying society. The Swedish researcher Jonas Himmelstrand claims that Sweden to-day "is riddled with stress-related health problems in adults, declining psychological health and school results in youth, a high number of people on sick leave, and an inability for parents to connect with their children.[19]" Reality slowly seems to be dawning in Sweden that socialism has not proved good value for money, which for many years saw public expenditure rise to a staggering 60% of GDP. The huge cost of the Swedish welfare state, which rose dramatically in the first decade of the 21st century in the wake of large-scale immigration, has caused the country to slip down the table of the world's most prosperous nations, and consequently in 2010, for the first time since before World War II, a non-socialist Prime Minister, Frederik Reinfeldt, won a second consecutive term of office. Sweden's change of heart is more than a question of economics. Younger people in particular are starting to reject the dependency culture and disincentives to enterprise produced by the mollycoddling of Sweden's welfare state. Interestingly, such disillusion was predicted as long ago as 1946 by the post-war socialist prime minister Per Albin Hansson, who said "We have had so many victories that we are in a difficult position. A people with political liberty, full employment and social security has lost its dreams.[20]"

If it walks like a duck and quacks like a duck…..

With the political legacy of Calvin and the Puritans having ebbed away, even favoured countries such as Switzerland, Holland, Britain and the USA saw significant increases in the size and scope of government during the first half of the 20th century. State-enforced compulsory wealth redistribution and increased government spending became the norm, naturally accompanied by higher taxation. Gone, even in the USA, were the days when income tax was a short-term expedient to finance occasional wars. Higher taxes and redistributive welfare schemes became part of life in the developed world, often accompanied by the transfer of all or part of the means of production from private enterprise to state control. Not all these changes were undertaken in the name of socialism – indeed some advocates of state-controlled wealth redistribution repudiated any suggestion that they were socialists, even if the end product of their labours often bore a close resemblance to the ideology they disowned.

One organisation to come under this heading was the Roman Catholic Church. Twenty seven years after his predecessor Pius IX condemned communism and socialism in the *Syllabus Errorum* (syllabus of Errors) calling them a "most fatal error", Pope Leo XIII went still further in his encyclical *Rerum Novarum* in 1891. Paragraph 16 states specifically, "It is clear that the main tenet of socialism, community of goods, must be utterly rejected, since it only injures those whom it would seem meant to benefit.[21]" He then went on to mount a spirited defence of private property: "The first and most fundamental principle, therefore, if one would undertake to

alleviate the condition of the masses, must be the inviola-
bility of private property.[22]" The encyclical goes on to insist
that the state has no right to intrude into the family, and talks
about care for the poor without mentioning compulsion.
Calls for compulsory wealth redistribution are few indeed
and considerably more muted than those from socialists:
"The right to possess private property is derived from nature,
not from man; and the State has the right to control its use
in the interests of the public good alone, but by no means to
absorb it altogether.[23]" A generation later Pius XI (1922–
1938) went further, saying, "no one can be at the same time
a good Catholic and a true socialist". However, in his 1931
encyclical *Quadragesimo Anno*, Pius took a much more negative line on the rights to private property. "Provided that the
natural and divine law be observed, the public authority, in
view of the common good, may specify more accurately what
is illicit for property owners in the use of their possessions...History proves that the right of ownership, like other
elements of social life, is not absolutely rigid.[24]" He rather
surprisingly claimed that *Rerum Novarum* "completely over-
threw those tottering tenets of Liberalism which had long
hampered effective interference by the government.[25]" This
is not how most open-minded readers would understand the
earlier encyclical. With Pius XI, a distinct change of tone can
be detected, with pronouncements on the subject of private
property and the free market becoming definitely more
hostile in tone, For example, he insisted that "the right
ordering of economic life cannot be left to a free competition of forces...It is most necessary that the economic life be
again subjected to and be governed by a true and effective
directing principle, [26]" and by this "directing principle" he
clearly meant state intervention, for he elsewhere spoke of
the state as the bulwark against the individualism he so vehe-
mently opposed:– "When we speak of reform of institutions,
the State chiefly comes to mind, not as if universal well-being
were to be expected from is activity, but because things have
come to such a pass through the evil of what we have termed
'individualism'.[27]" "For it is rightly contended that certain

forms of property must be reserved for the state.[28]" Recognising the problem of reversing Pius IX's condemnation of socialism in the *Syllabus Errorum*, he circumvents the issue with some very accommodating language: "It can even come to the point that imperceptibly these ideas of more moderate socialism will no longer differ from the desires and demand of those who are striving to remold society on the basis of Christian principles.[29]" The pope chose totally to ignore those Evangelicals considered in chapters 3 and 4 of this book who had been striving precisely to build society on Christian principles, and who drew from the Bible a model for the organisation and government of a nation which was corresponded precisely to that which he was attacking so vigorously.

His successors have been even more accommodating to socialism and strident in their attacks on private property. Paul VI spoke strongly against capitalism in his 1967 encyclical *Populorum Progressio*. He insisted that "certain landed states" may be expropriated (presumably by the state) not only if they "bring hardship to peoples", but also simply because they are "extensive.[30]" The encyclical then implicitly calls for a planned economy:– "Individual initiative alone and the interplay of competition will not ensure satisfactory development...It is for the public authorities to establish and lay down the desired goals, the plans to be followed, and the methods to be used in fulfilling them; and it is also their task to stimulate the efforts of those involved in this common activity.[31]" An attack on free trade completes this barrage of assaults on individual liberty: "It is evident that the principle of free trade, by itself, is no longer adequate for regulating international agreements.[32]" while the closing sections of the encyclical include an appeal to rulers to support state-enforced compulsory international wealth redistribution:– "Government leaders, your task is to draw your communities into closer ties of solidarity with all men, and to convince them that they must accept the necessary taxes on their luxuries and their wasteful expenditures in order to promote the development of nations and the preservation of peace.[33]" It is hard to imagine that the pope was really so naïve as to be unaware that only a small percentage of state-to-state international aid actually ends up in the hands of those most in need of help. John Paul II's *Sollicitudo Rei Socialis* (1987) reaffirmed the teaching of his predecessor, saying that, "even though many situations have changed in the world, (it) has the same force and validity today as when it was written.[34]" Looking a lot further back, this encyclical also reaffirmed Aquinas' lukewarmness to private property, stating that, "It is necessary to state once more the characteristic principle of Christian social doctrine: the goods of this world are originally meant for all.[35]" He then goes on to express some sympathy for armed revolution: "Peoples excluded from the fair distribution of goods originally intended for all could ask themselves: why not respond with violence to those who first treat us with violence?[36]" The *Catechism of the Catholic Church*, which came out during his pontificate, did not go this far, but took the same line regarding private property. While condemning "totalitarian and atheistic ideologies associated in modern times with 'communism' or 'socialism'", the "universal destination of goods" is reaffirmed, and "the right to private property...does not do away with the original gift of the earth to all mankind[37]" – in other words. only allowed as a grudging concession. In language almost reminiscent of Rousseau, the Catechism affirms that "It is the role of the state to defend and promote the common good of civil society[38]" which it defines in much broader terms that Locke's "Life, liberty and estate" or the definition of this book – moral restraint and the prevention of unjust exploitation of the poor.

In those European countries where Roman Catholicism prevailed, socialist parties were characterised by a strong anti-clerical tendency, which meant that most Roman Catholic politicians would be found in the opposing "Christian Democratic" parties. These days, such parties are often labelled "right of centre" by the media, but while being socially conservative in areas such as abortion and the family, the rest of their ideology rarely shares much common ground with the Christian political thought outlined in chapters 3 and 4, which, in view of 20th century Roman Catholic social teaching, is quite understandable. However, Papal encyclicals do not speak for every Roman Catholic. The American Roman Catholic scholar Michael Novak (b. 1933) took a different line in his 1993 paper entitled "The Catholic Ethic and the Spirit of Capitalism[39]" which drew strongly on *Rerum Novarum* and pointed out how as recently as 1991 John Paul II not only condemned socialism but even the "social assistance state." Nevertheless, notwithstanding the emergence in recent times of Roman Catholic centre right politicians such as Rick Santorum and Paul Ryan in the USA and Tony Abbott in Australia, the track record of Roman Catholicism in power has not been a happy one as far as its support for liberty and limited government is concerned. Admittedly, Rome's fiercest critics have focussed most of their attention on the collaboration of the Vatican with Mussolini and Hitler in the 1930's, but John Robbins' stark words are pretty close to the mark:– "If there be any Roman Catholic readers who are inclined to favour freedom and free enterprise, may they understand that their church does not, and they must choose to be either good Catholics or good Christians.[40]"

It was the measures taken to combat the Great Depression by the Democrat Franklin D Roosevelt, American president from 1933 to 1945, known as the New Deal, which saw the American state take on a number of features associated with socialism. The New Deal marked a watershed in American politics, in so much as from 1933 onwards, thanks to Roosevelt, the predominant ideology of the Democratic Party has always been to the left of the Republicans. Indeed, following Roosevelt's election, the Democrats were to hold power for all but eight of the next 36 years, an indication of how far America had fallen from the decentralised small-government ideals of its founding fathers and the Christian influence which inspired them.

The New Deal was Roosevelt's response to the Great Depression. President Herbert Hoover had initially responded to the 1929 Wall Street Crash by raising income tax dramatically and spending the extra revenue in an attempt to stimulate the economy. Roosevelt ran against Hoover in 1932 on a platform of "cutting taxes, cutting subsidies, cutting government and balancing the budget.[41]" On winning the election, Roosevelt promptly broke his pre-election promises and continued Hoover's policies, albeit repackaged under the name by which they will be remembered. The top rate of income tax was raised to no less than 90%, and the National Industrial Recovery Act of June 1933, "forced manufacturing industries into government-mandated cartels and empowered a massive federal bureaucracy to dictate production and pricing standards covering two million employers and 22 million workers.[42]" The New Deal may have been sold as an attempt to help the poor and needy through job creation, but it turned into a power grab by the Federal government. One of Roosevelt's right hand men was Father John A. Ryan (1869–1945), in many ways a Roman Catholic Rauschenbusch. By the time of his appointment, he had already written in support of a "legally mandated eight-hour workday...the legalisation of picketing during strikes....public housing programs, government ownership of natural monopolies, graduated income taxes, graduated inheritance taxes[43]" to name but a few. If most Roman Catholic politicians in mainland Europe have been associated with parties opposed to socialism, in America, the most influential Roman Catholic political advisers and politicians – including the first Roman Catholic president John F. Kennedy (1917–1963) – have until recently been very much to the left of the American political spectrum.

Roosevelt's New Deal met with stiff opposition from Congressmen, some of whom accused him of being a "communist." The American Supreme Court went as far as nullifying some legislation, but these were only temporary setbacks. The Great Depression had undermined belief in *laissez-faire* economics and allowed America to end up with a far bigger federal government than the writers of its constitution ever imagined. Soviet propaganda played a role in this process. Many Western intellectuals at this time were deceived by false claims that Stalin's five year plans had been successful in boosting prosperity, and became convinced that a planned economy (which inevitably requires a large bureaucratic state) was not merely the only answer to the immediate crisis, but also the way forward.

In reality, like all attempts to solve a financial crisis through a fiscal stimulus, the New Deal totally failed in its objective of alleviating America's unemployment problems or its poor economic performance. Britain, whose government did not embark on a spending binge, emerged far more quickly from the Great Depression. Roosevelt's treasury secretary Henry Morgenthau Jr was to write in his private diary in 1941, "We have tried spending money. We are spending more than we have ever spent before and it does not work...I say after eight years of this administration we have just as much unemployment as when we started... and an enormous debt to boot.⁴⁴" However, the obvious failure of the New Deal did not lead to an immediate reversal of high taxes and large-scale state spending. Enthusiasts for the big state, whether or not they go under the name of socialist, never seem to learn from history. For some 30 years after the war, even during the Republican Eisenhower administration (1953–1961) the top rate of taxation in traditionally small government America never fell below 70% and for a while peaked at over 90%. Such high rates of taxation are a strong disincentive for businessmen and entrepreneurs to work. Who would want to go to the effort of earning extra money when 9/10 of it would be taken away from you by the state? One popular movie actor decided that it wasn't worth his while to star in more than two films a year for this very reason. His name was Ronald Reagan.

Another major figure who disavowed the name "socialist" but whose ideas contributed to the growth in the size of the state was John Maynard Keynes (1883–1946) – the most significant economist of the first half of the twentieth century. Keynes was part of the "Bloomsbury Set", a group of predominantly left-wing British intellectuals notorious for their immorality. Keynes' dissent from the prevailing socialism of his friends was reflected in his vigorous criticism of Marx's writings and revolutionary ideals. He described *Das Kapital* as "an obsolete textbook which I know not only to be scientifically erroneous but without interest or application to the modern world[45]" and elsewhere he added "The class war will find me on the side of the educated bourgeoisie.[46]" He visited the Soviet Union during the 1920s, and came back distinctly unimpressed: "For me....Red Russia holds too much that is detestable...Comforts and habits let us be ready to forgo, but I am not ready for a creed which does not care how much it destroys the liberty and security of daily life ...It is hard for an educated, decent intelligent son of western Europe to find his ideals here, unless he has first suffered some strange and horrid process of conversion which has changed all his values.[47]" A further visit in 1928 only confirmed him in his opinions.

Considering his refusal to embrace his friends' socialism and his forthright condemnation of the Soviet Union, it is perhaps surprising at first glance that Keynes should end up aiding and abetting the growth of the state. However, he had argued for a "somewhat comprehensive socialisation of expenditure" well before this phrase appeared in his most well-known work *The General Theory of Employment, Interest and Money* (1936). He had worked with the Liberal Party to help them produce their 1929 election campaign document *We Can Conquer Unemployment*, which included a commitment to significant public spending on road building, house building and the development Britain's telephone network in the hope of reducing unemployment as well as stimulating the economy. Unlike most Victorian economists, he did not believe that, left to itself, the economy would inevitably regain its equilibrium following a severe recession. In the aftermath of the Wall Street Crash, with the private sector reluctant to invest, Keynes therefore maintained that the state should spend money in order to maintain economic stability. His arguments were very different from that of classic socialism. To put it simply, Keynes proposed a larger role for the state because he believed state spending would promote economic growth – generating an output considerably in excess of the amount spent. He did not subscribe to classic socialism's ideological commitment to the means of production being under common ownership. When road haulage was nationalised in 1945, Keynes was furious, regarding it as one step too far and totally unnecessary[48].

Keynes also challenged earlier economic thinking in another area – the need to balance the national budget. Exceptional circumstances, such as wars, required extra borrowing, but as a rule, deficits in public finances had previously been regarded as a bad thing – quite correctly from a Biblical point of view. This reluctance to incur debt had been the cause of Philip Snowden's expulsion from the Labour Party in 1931. Keynes' ideas met with some scepticism from the Treasury – after all, what happens if a state borrows money to stimulate growth and the growth fails to materialise? – or the extra growth in state-financed public works is offset by a decline in the private sector? As has been noted, Roosevelt found himself facing similar problems in America in the 1930s. Keynes had written an "open letter" to Roosevelt advocating an "accelerated programme of loan-financed public expenditure[49]" and had broadly supported the New Deal when it was first launched. In his own country, opposition to the principle of increased public spending, with its larger and more frequent government deficits, was largely overcome by the time of his death.

Keynes left a complex and somewhat ambiguous legacy. The "managed capitalism" he proposed was borne out of his desire to save, rather than destroy capitalism. On the other hand, those aspects of his thinking most in accord with socialism were the most influential on the generation of economists and politicians that followed him. While a book like this cannot attempt either a detailed analysis of the complexities of Keynes' economic thought or the differences between Keynes and those who subsequently professed to be his disciples, the word "Keynesian" has become synonymous with, among other things, a far greater role for the state in managing a nation's economy than the Bible condones. Wherever a social democratic government has taken power since Keynes' death, its economic advisers, if they wish to be labelled anything at all, will usually profess to be "Keynesians."

The Red Revolution rolls on – a litany of suffering

Socialists of all persuasion had played an honourable part in the fight against Nazi and Fascist aggression during the Second World War. However, no sooner had Hitler been defeated than it became apparent that militant Marxism posed an equally serious threat. The so-called Cold War was beginning. Marxist parties enjoyed widespread electoral support in several Western European nations, regularly gaining 25% of the votes cast in post-war France for example. Marxism was ultimately defeated at the end of a 5-year civil war in Greece, but Poland, Czechoslovakia, Hungary, Bulgaria, Romania, Yugoslavia, Albania and East Germany soon found themselves under the control of Marxist régimes, although the fate of the three Baltic states of Estonia, Latvia and Lithuania was even worse – they were forcibly incorporated into the Soviet Union.

In every country where Marx's followers came to power, Christians were persecuted, although the degree of suffering varied from country to country. At one end of the spectrum, Poland remained stubbornly Roman Catholic and church members, while excluded from positions of authority and generally being frowned upon, were allowed to meet without any serious restrictions. At the other end of the scale, Albania under Enver Hoxha proclaimed itself the world's first atheist state in 1967, and ordered the transfer of all churches, monasteries and mosques to the government. A particularly grisly martyrdom was suffered by some who refused to abandon their Christian faith. They were imprisoned in weighted wooden barrels that were then thrown into the sea.

Romania did not go quite this far, but clamped down brutally on Christians as soon as it had established itself as a "popular republic." Pastor Richard Wurmbrand suffered no less than 14 years in prison, and in his autobiography *In God's Underground*, gives a chilling first-hand account of the torment he and many other Christians went through in the countries behind the Iron Curtain. "We're not murderers like the Nazis," a colonel in the secret police informed him. "We want you to live – and suffer.[50]" He did live, and certainly suffered. "I stood for hours, long after my arms had lost all feeling, and my legs began to tremble and then to swell. When I collapsed on the floor, I was given a crust and a sip of water and made to stand again.[51]" "I was ordered to squat and place my arms around my knees. A metal bar was thrust between elbows and knees and then lifted on to trestles, so that I swung head down, trussed, with my feet in the air. They held my head while someone flogged the soles of my feet. The blows were like explosions. Some fell on my thighs and the base of my spine. I fainted and was revived by drenchings in cold water.[52]"

Meanwhile, further afield, Marxism scored another victory when the People's Democratic Republic of China was proclaimed in 1949. Its leader Mao Zedong (formerly known as Mao Tse Tung) proved himself every bit as ruthless a tyrant as Stalin. Between 1951 and 1958, all the 4,000 or so Protestant missionaries were expelled from the country[53]. Mercifully, few of them suffered physical violence. Chinese Christians did not have the chance to leave the country. A puppet church, known a the Three Self Patriotic Movement[54], was set up by the government, and pastors who would not affiliate their churches to it were persecuted severely. Pastor Wang Ming Dao (1900–1991), one of China's most eminent Evangelical leaders, spent no less than 22 years in prison for his faith. Following the failure of the "Great Leap Forward" of 1957–1961, which closely resembled Stalin's Five Year Plans with their nationalisation (or collectivisation) of agriculture, Mao decided that something more radical was needed to purge out any subversive capitalist elements in Chinese society. His "Cultural Revolution" of 1966–1976 turned up the heat on the church, and even the Three Self Patriotic Movement was closed down for a while. The number of Chinese who were killed during this period will never be precisely known, but estimates range from 750,000 to 3,000,000.

From China, revolutionary socialism spread out across South East Asia. When the Korean Peninsula was partitioned at the end of World War II, North Korea was placed under Soviet control. It launched an attack on its southern neighbour in 1950, with China also providing support after 1951. American military might saved South Korea, but it proved less successful in saving South Vietnam, which was lost to the free world in 1975, after a 16-year war. The same year, Cambodia also fell, and a particularly brutal regime took power led by Pol Pot's Khmer Rouge, whose purge of "reactionary elements" included not only anyone associated with the former government but anyone with a university education or wealth. The church in the country was quite small, but had experienced some growth in the final years before the Khmer Rouge takeover. Only 2,000 of the estimated 9–12,000 believers survived the slaughter[55].

In Latin America, a civil war in Cuba saw self-confessed Marxist-Leninist Fidel Castro seize power in 1959. Cuba provided a bridgehead for the export of revolutionary Marxism to other neighbouring countries. Guerilla wars were waged in Peru by the Maoist Shining Path (*Sendero Luminoso*) movement, and in Colombia by the Revolutionary Armed Forces or FARC. Where these groups gained control of a town or region, anyone refusing to join their army could face execution, and the Colombian guerrillas in particular have helped to swell the ranks of the noble army of Christian martyrs by targeting pastors.

Latin America is also home to Liberation Theology, which at its most extreme can best be described as an attempt to marry Roman Catholicism with revolutionary Marxism. There can be no doubt that the military dictatorships in the region could be every bit as oppressive as Marxist regimes, and poverty abounds to this day in many parts of the continent. But should priests be taking up arms and joining the insurgents in order to help the poor and marginalised? The Brazilian Archbishop Dom Helder Camara (1909–1999) chose a more peaceful path in his desire to build a better society, founding a philanthropic organisation committed to the physical needs of the urban poor. "When I feed the poor, they call me a saint. When I ask why they are poor, they call me a communist," he famously stated. Another outspoken defender of the rights of the poor, Archbishop Oscar Romero of El Salvador, was shot dead in 1980 while saying mass. While Evangelicals regard Roman Catholicism as doctrinally erroneous, the fearless commitment of these men to the values of Christian compassion has to be admired. However, it is a different issue with men like the priest, Camilo Torres, who was killed in a battle with the Colombian army in 1966, fighting alongside Marxist guerrillas. "Revolution is not only permitted for Christians, but obligatory[56]" he said. In the 17th Century, Samuel Rutherford had defended the Scottish rebellion in *Lex, Rex*, arguing from a Christian perspective that Charles I had failed to fulfil his God-given obligation as a ruler to defend "true religion." His thinking is a world apart from that of Torres, who while professing the name Christian, took up arms alongside violent men whose objective was to replace a particularly ugly dictatorship not with the godly society the Puritans longed for, but with an equally unpleasant and godless régime.

Africa too suffered from Marxism, particularly in the former Portuguese colonies of Angola and Mozambique. Agostinho Neto, the Marxist dictator who ruled Angola from its independence in 1975 to his death in 1979, once declared that: "Within 20 years there will not be a Christian or a Bible left in Angola! I have destroyed the Bible![57]" Mercifully, his claim proved false, and the church is growing in both these countries, although Marxism has left a legacy of appalling poverty, particularly in Mozambique. In Zimbabwe, Christians are still suffering under the rule of Marxist Robert Mugabe, although their problems have been rather overlooked amidst the widespread violence and economic breakdown which has afflicted this once relatively prosperous country.

In country after country, Marxism in all its different variants has ended up persecuting Christians. Its ideological singlemindedness leaves no room for a minority that believe in a higher authority than Marx (or the Marxist state.) Marxism's conflict, however, is not just with Christians, but with God Himself. This is particularly well illustrated by Brother Andrew, the founder of *Open Doors*, a Christian organisation which ministers to the persecuted church. Visiting East Germany in one wet early Autumn during the 1950s, he encountered posters everywhere proclaiming

Ohne Gott und Sonnen Schein
Holen Wir Die Ernte ein
(Without God and without sun
We will get the harvest done)

He comments, "This slogan had really shaken the people. It was a brazen duel between the new régime and God Himself. The rains continued and the harvest did not get in. Overnight, as suddenly as they had appeared, the posters vanished – all except for the sodden few that you could still see clinging to lamp posts.[58]" The Marxist conflict with God explains why Christians have been so frequently singled out by Marxist states. The socialist state tried to replaced the Saviour as the Messiah, and even if it failed abysmally to lead its citizens into the promised land of a government-less society, it still demanded the exclusive worship of every one of those citizens – which for a Christian meant a violation of the First Commandment. In North Korea, this state-worship is still expressed in a particularly idolatrous form – the massive statues of Kim Il-Sung, whose dynasty has ruled that tragic land since partition in 1948, and which are found across the country. The mausoleums of Lenin and Chairman Mao still survive as temples of state-worship in the former Soviet Union and China respectively, and even where state-worship never acquired a human symbol, it found other modes of expression, such as the East German *Jugend Weihe* (Youth Consecration), a deliberately godless imitation of the Lutheran confirmation service where young people pledged themselves to "the great and noble cause of socialism" and "the revolutionary heritage of the people." For Christians, worship is reserved for God alone, and just as their predecessors paid a heavy penalty for refusing to bow down to Caesar, the noble army of martyrs and confessors has been strengthened in recent years in lands where Marxism has held sway by believers who have conscientiously refused to worship the state.

Marx's communist dream was to build a free and fair society without government and without God. This vision has not come to pass in any country and never will. Intead, it has left a legacy of poverty and repression. The seemingly mindless brutality of Pol Pot in Cambodia from 1975 to 1979 was actually driven by a determination to achieve Marx's ideals in record time. The Khmer Rouge would be the best communists of all, and by eliminating the professional classes at one stroke, the interim process of socialism could be quickly bypassed and Utopia brought in. Some estimates put the number of deaths under his four-year reign of terror as high as 2 million (over 20% of the population), and all tragic victims of a vision that in country after country has failed utterly and completely to reach fulfilment.

Attlee's Socialist Utopia and its aftermath

The 1945 British General Election took place in the final year of Keynes' life, in the immediate aftermath of the end of war in Europe. In spite of widespread appreciation of Winston Churchill's leadership during the war, his Conservative Party was trounced by Clement Attlee's Labour Party, whose promises of social reform, full employment and the creation of a comprehensive welfare state appeared to the electorate to be the best way of rebuilding Britain following the end of the conflict. Of all the Labour governments ever to rule Britain, Attlee's must be regarded as the most effective and the most sincere, albeit misguided. Attlee himself was a quiet unassuming man who had served as mayor of Stepney in London's East End, where he had been appalled by the poverty he encountered. He genuinely viewed the creation of a welfare state as the building of a New Jerusalem – indeed one speech he made to a Labour Party conference was brought to a climax by reading out the final lines from William Blake's poem *Jerusalem*[59]. Such was the scale of change wrought in Britain during Attlee's six years in power that in Britain today, many people are unaware how different life was before 1945.

Nationalisation of major industries had been promised in Labour's manifesto, and the coal mines, the railways, road haulage, the canal network, steelmaking and public utilities including gas and electricity were taken into public ownership[60], along with the Bank of England, which had been a private institution since its foundation in 1694. Apart from steelmaking, nationalised in 1951, all the other industries were taken into public ownership before 1948. The pace slowed after this date due to the economic difficulties faced by the Attlee government after 1947. One of Keynes' last achievements had been to negotiate a loan from America to help rebuild Britain and avert what was widely called at the time a "financial Dunkirk." However, when it became known that there were strings attached, which hampered Britain's trade with the USA, the pound found itself under pressure. Hugh Dalton, Attlee's chancellor, was forced to rein in public spending and then resigned. From 1948 to 1951, financial austerity was the watchword of the day, and such grandiose plans that had not already been accomplished were put onto the back burner.

Much had nonetheless been achieved. Besides the widespread programme of nationalisation, which brought 20% of the economy into public ownership, a comprehensive welfare state had been created. A report on welfare had been produced during the war by William Beveridge (1879–1963), a leading economist and civil servant. Its main proposals, such as universal flat rate National Insurance to pay for unemployment benefit, were implemented by the

Attlee government. Alongside National Insurance came the National Health Service, the brainchild of the Welsh socialist Aneurin Bevan. Although there were times when hospitals had struggled for funds, healthcare in Britain during the years prior to 1948 contained many good features which were fully acknowledged by Bevan and other advocates of nationalisation. "Hospitals and beds were plentiful. Britain was a leader in a wide variety of specialities. A great richness of hospitals existed in 1948. They were world leaders and world teachers.[61]" The problem as far as a socialist like Bevan was concerned was that healthcare was "unplanned" and "a medley of public and voluntary institutions.[62]" The medical profession was strongly opposed to the transfer of hospitals to state control. One meeting of a thousand doctors in Wimbledon in 1946 called Bevan's plans "The biggest expropriation of property since the dissolution of the monasteries.[63]" Their opposition was to no avail, and Bevan pushed through "the most radical state take-over of healthcare outside an avowedly communist country.[64]" Such opposition from the medical profession presents a striking contrast to the furore over proposed NHS reforms following the 2010 General Election. Talk of returning healthcare back to the private sector is now greeted with horror. When the Tory MEP Dan Hannan called the NHS "a sixty year mistake" during a 2009 speech in America to opponents of Barack Obama's plans to adopt a similar healthcare policy in the USA, British politicians from all ends of the political spectrum, including his party leader David Cameron, queued up to distance themselves from his remarks. Thanks to Attlee and Bevan, it is no easy task to argue in early 21st century Britain that you are compassionate if you do not support state-funded healthcare. Nonetheless, in recent years, critics of the NHS have been growing in number, and with good reason, as will be considered in more detail in a second volume of this book.

The Labour Party had supported the 1944 Education Act, (commonly known as the Butler Act after the Conservative chancellor "Rab" Butler, whose report on education earlier that year had provided the basis for it) and implemented many of its proposals on coming to power, thus increasing the role of the state in education. The first state schools had been built in the late 19th century in places where neither church nor private philanthropy had established one – in other words, to fill the gaps. However, as so often is the case, once the state begins to interfere, it cannot stop. Secondary school education was now to be provided free of charge (or rather, paid for by the taxpayer), and pupils were required by law to remain at school until the age of 15[65]. Free school milk was introduced (again, in reality, paid for by the taxpayer – nothing really comes free with socialism), and daily prayers were made mandatory. The Act did not introduce a national curriculum, and compulsory sex education would never have crossed the minds of British politicians in 1944. However, it marked an unnecessary increase in state interference in an education system which, like healthcare, could have managed well enough on its own. The 1944 Act brought in the 11 plus exam, and proposed three types of secondary school – grammar schools for the more academic, secondary technical schools for the more practical and "secondary modern" schools for other pupils. A school building programme was begun, but few technical schools were ever built. The Act also introduced the Direct Grant system, whereby certain independent grammar schools were offered state funding in return for taking in a percentage of pupils free of charge. It is significant to note the Attlee government's support for selective education – in sharp contrast with attitudes in today's Labour Party. It is far from the only contrast. Following the suspension of the death penalty in 1948, Attlee and the foreign secretary Ernest Bevin were among those who voted for its restoration[66].

Another important task facing the new government was the need for more houses to be built – following the damage caused by the Luftwaffe during World War 2. No less than 80% of the houses built in the late 1940's were council houses. Some were well built[67], but by no means all, and the plan to use social housing as a visual statement of how the state had liberated the poor from their slums was to result in disaster. The high-rise blocks of flats, which first appeared in Britain's cities in the 1950s, not only broke up families and communities but rapidly gained such bad reputations for crime and filth that most have now been demolished. Such was one unintended consequence of giving the state a greater control of town planning through the Town and Country Planning act of 1947.

It was the issue of free healthcare that finally brought Attlee's premiership to an end in 1951. With military spending increased as a result of Britain's involvement in the Korean War, prescription charges were introduced for false teeth and spectacles. A number of Labour ministers, including Bevan, resigned in protest. The government collapsed and the Conservatives were returned to power under Winston Churchill. However, although the steel industry and road haulage were de-nationalised, and identity cards and rationing scrapped, no attempt was made to dismantle the welfare state. Successive Conservative leaders up to the 1970s took a similar line – trying to manage the welfare state and other socialist creations better than Labour. So slight were the perceived differences between the two big parties in the UK that during the 1950s the term "Butskellism" was coined – an amalgam of the names of Hugh Gaitskell, Labour leader from 1955 until his death in 1963, and the Tory chancellor "Rab" Butler. This widely-held perception of the post-war consensus does not entirely do justice to Butler, who succeeded in cutting government spending from 41.1% of GDP in 1951 to 36.4% in 1955. Indeed, in his memoirs, Butler makes clear his belief in the value of low taxes and deregulation if an economy was to prosper and grow[68].

Even in defeat, however, Labour in the 1950s could nevertheless look back with satisfaction on having brought about a seismic shift in public attitudes. Writing in 1956, the Labour MP (and subsequent cabinet minister) Tony Crosland (1918–1977) said that in his opinion, "capitalist features and attitudes no longer predominate[69]" in Britain. He went on to single out competition – one of the "evils" denounced by socialists in the Victorian era in particular, and observed, "There is probably now no country in the world where competition is less aggressive or individual exertion more suspect...To a large extent, security has replaced competition as the guiding rule of economic conduct.[70]" Furthermore, Crosland believed that, "the national shift to the Left, with all the implications for the balance of power, may be accepted as permanent.[71]" Peter Hitchens offers one reason why there was so little ideological opposition to state intervention:– "In the post–1957 years... the governing class had lost their nerve and will. They doubted their religion and their right to rule.[72]" The Conservative Party still contained a number of men who were singularly uncomfortable with the growth of the state from its pre–1914 level, but alongside them were many supporters of a "mixed economy" – where part of the economy remained in private hands while the rest was controlled by the state. Harold MacMillan (1894–1986) was one of the more prominent spokesmen for this new outlook. He had been educated at Eton and then married a daughter of the Duke of Devonshire. Like most politicians with such a background, MacMillan ended up in the Conservative Party, but he was a pragmatist, a supporter of Keynesian intervention and the author of a book *The Middle Way* which was one of the earliest Conservative *apologiae* for the mixed economy, appearing in 1938. Soviet propaganda also played a role in building support for government intervention in the post-war years. The supposed success of Stalin's Five Year Plans were trumpeted abroad, and the relatively few westerners to visit the Soviet Union, such as diplomatic staff, were only allowed to see examples of apparent successes. This was sufficient to hoodwink them, and to encourage the governments they represented to believe that a planned economy was the way forward. Augustine had taught that governments should only be involved in a very limited number of areas where there was consensus, such as the preservation of peace, but from 1945 onwards, there appeared to be a consensus right across the west for the state to be involved in far more areas of life than Augustine would ever have dreamed. David Held comments that, "nearly all the political parties throughout the 1950s and 1960's believed that in office they should intervene to reform the position of the unjustly privileged and aid the position of the underprivileged. Only the politics of a 'caring state' embodying concern and fair-mindedness, specialisation and expertise, could create the conditions whereby the welfare and good of each citizen were compatible with the welfare and good of all.[73]" The "mixed economy" appeared to be working well and enjoyed widespread support among the electorate. In Western Europe and the USA, standards of living improved dramatically in the first 20 years following the end of World War II. In 1957, MacMillan, now Prime Minister, famously commented, "You've never had it so good!" Perhaps he was right – or perhaps not.

The ambivalence of Post-War America

The United States of America was forced into the Second World War when the Japanese bombed its naval base at Pearl Harbor in 1941. From that point onwards, American military might played a major role in the defeat of the Axis powers, and after 1945, American political and financial might played an equally important part in shaping the peace. Under the European Recover Plan, better known as the Marshall Plan after American Secretary of State George Marshall, from 1948 to 1952 America provided financial aid to help rebuild the shattered economies of Western Europe, including Germany – or at least the areas of Germany not under Soviet control. Alongside economic reconstruction, America also lent its support to political developments, ensuring that Western Europe would be sufficiently strong to resist the threat of Soviet invasion.

There was a strange ambivalence about post-war America. American hostility to the Soviet Union and Marxism in general was even stronger than in Britain, and was reflected not only in its foreign policy but also in its domestic politics.

"Better dead than Red" was a popular slogan in the immediate post-war years. Fears of a "communist" takeover, already stoked by popular literature, were heightened in 1949, when the Soviet Union announced that it had successfully tested its first nuclear bomb. The following year, two American citizens, Julius and Ethel Rosenberg, were convicted of passing atomic secrets to the Soviet Union during the World War 2. They were executed three years later. The stage was set for Republican Senator Joe McCarthy (1908–1957) of Wisconsin, who personified the anti-Marxist hysteria that swept the country in the early 1950s. He began to produce lists of various individuals who he claimed were spying for the Soviet Union or else Marxist sympathisers. His first list included over 200 such individual in the State Department, and subsequent blacklists were produced of Hollywood actors, members of the American Communist Party and even serving soldiers in the American armed forces. He had a willing accomplice in the then director of the FBI, J. Edgar Hoover (1895–1972), who put together a "loyalty-security" programme to root out any employees of the Federal government who may have held subversive views.

There were unquestionably Soviet spies operating in the USA, but McCarthy's blacklisting did not always target the right people. Over 10,000 people lost their jobs as a result of his witch hunts, and hundreds were imprisoned, sometimes on the flimsiest of evidence. McCarthy's accusations of alleged Soviet supporters in the American military, along with his ever more aggressive questioning techniques saw public opinion turn against him by the middle of the decade, especially after incurring a formal censure by the Senate in 1954. He died less than three years later, probably as a consequence of alcoholism. He was vindicated posthumously in 1993 when former KGB officer Alexander Vassilev was permitted to access the records of Soviet intelligence operations during the Stalin era. His book *Spies, the rise and fall of the KGB in America*[74], is a shocking account of how widespread and successful Soviet infiltration of the American government had been.

Bearing in mind the strength of anti-Soviet sentiment in post-war America, it seems surprising that there was no real attempt to reverse the New Deal policies brought in by Roosevelt, in spite of their being identified as socialist or "communist". While America never went as far down the socialist road as Britain – creating no NHS and not bringing its railroad system under state control until 1971, by which time there was very little of it left – there was a remarkable absence of clamour for small government or a reduction in the size of the state during the 1950s. To counter the threat of a Soviet-style takeover, it would have seemed logical to revert to the founding principles of the USA, with its small federal government and emphasis on democratic accountability. In 1953 the Republican Dwight D Eisenhower was elected president because Harry S. Truman, Roosevelt's successor, was perceived as being too soft towards Marxism. However, Eisenhower, the only Republican president between 1933 and 1969, not only retained the 91% income tax bracket for top earners, but made no attempt even to raise the threshold.

American ambivalence was also reflected in its foreign policy. In its concern to contain the Soviet threat, it gave active support to the creation of several supra-national structures whose structures are completely foreign to the country's historic small-government tradition – the European Union and the United Nations. The idea of creating some sort of European federation was not particularly novel, but the horrors of World War 2 provided a new impetus for the project, as it was widely believed that such a project would prevent such a conflict occurring again. In once sense, these sentiments were mistaken inasmuch as the North Atlantic Treaty Organisation (NATO), established in 1949, and whose original members included the USA, Canada, the UK and several Western European nations, has proved an effective guarantor of peace between the nations of Europe for over 60 years. However, the USA was happy to support the project for European integration which is now known as the European Union in spite of being aware that principal driving force, the Frenchman Jean Monnet (1888–1979), while not a card-carrying socialist, had implemented a programme of state planning and nationalisation in post-war France very similar to that pursued by Attlee in Britain[75]. Monnet's blueprint for a federal Europe, with its bureaucratic structures and inbuilt democratic deficit, could not have been further removed from the American Constitution. An unelected "High Authority" which was eventually subsumed into the unelected European Commission, was set up in 1951, with Monnet as president, without any hint of concern from the USA. The Americans were also aware that because of likely opposition from the electorate, the federation was to be brought about by deceit, "Nobody after the first two years of Monnet's presidency at the High Authority would again talk of it or its equivalent as a 'European Government'....the idea of a Europe in some sense above the nations was no longer stated in the open.[76]" Indeed, in 1953, when the French government started to get cold feet over the Monnet project, the response of John Foster Dulles (1888–1959), Eisenhower's secretary of State, was a threat to withdraw US aid[77]. Dulles had known Monnet for many years[78], and offered his support for the "Common Market" project throughout his tenure of office. Sixty years later, in the contest for the 2012 Republican presidential nomination, the term "European" was bandied about by some candidates in a pejorative sense to emphasise traits in big government that they did not wish to see in America. However, their forebears must take some of the blame for the creation of the institution they rightly despise.

The United Nations was another American initiative which came into being in the immediate post-ware period, but whose founding principles are also at odds with those of the USA. It came into being in 1945, to replace the League of Nations, an initiative of American President Woodrow Wilson in 1919, which hoped, by creating an international body to deal with disputes between nations and maintain world peace, to prevent a repetition of World War 1. It singularly failed in its mission. The American public voted not to join the organisation, feeling that it was best to keep out of European affairs, and it was generally regarded throughout its life as rather a toothless organisation. Jean Monnet was appointed its deputy secretary general, and it was his frustration with the wielding of national vetoes[79] that made him determined to reduce the power of individual states in his design for a united Europe.

Following World War 2, the mood in the USA was more supportive of the creation of international and inter-governmental organisations, and consequently, the UN was able to be a far more ambitious project, aiming not only to keep the peace but to enshrine certain fundamental human rights across the planet. Like the EU it is a very bureaucratic organisation, and its objectives smell strongly of socialism and Keynesian economics. For example, Article 55 of the UN charter commits the UN to promoting full employment[80]. The existence of UN agencies such as UNICEF, the UN children's fund and the World Food Programme also point to a belief in the power of governments (or bureaucrats) rather than bottom-up initiatives to solve the world's problems. Article 24 of its charter also requires members to, "confer on the Security Council primary responsibility for the maintenance of international peace and security, and agree that in carrying out its duties under this responsibility the Security Council acts on their behalf[81]" – a rather worrying surrender of national sovereignty. Fortunately, the UN has proved as equally ineffective as its predecessor, beset by the same problems of establishing an international consensus – especially among the Security Council, which includes the USA, the UK, Russia and China among its permanent members. As noted above, NATO has preserved the peace most effectively in Europe, but the UN has not prevented the many wars which have broken out elsewhere; it has also failed to prevent famines while its support for human rights has been ignored by many nations who joined it. In recent years, its prestige has been seriously dented by the oil-for-food scandal, whereby the son of the then UN Secretary-General, Kofi Annan, was implicated with profiteering from the UN initiative to allow the Iraqis to sell oil in exchange for food and medicines, but not military equipment. However, for all its lack of credibility, there have been no major calls to disband it. The John Birch Society, a pressure group named after an American military intelligence officer killed in 1945 by Chinese Maoists, has campaigned since 1959 for American withdrawal from the UN, and John Bolton, nominated by President George W. Bush as US ambassador to the UN, strongly criticised the organisation, saying that if the top 10 stories of the 38-story UN building in New York were to be lost, it would not make any difference. For such remarks, the US Senate blocked his appointment. The UN, which gets 22% of its funding from American taxpayers, which in 2010–11 amounted to $5.4 billion merely for the "regular" UN budget (excluding peacekeeping activities)[82], is here to stay – at least for the time being, even if it appears to offer the world few, if any, tangible benefits.

Both the World Bank and the International Monetary Fund were the brainchild of Harry Dexter White (1894–1948), a senior official in the US Treasury. These organisations, like the UN, are funded by the various member nations – or more exactly, by their taxpayers. From a Christian perspective, it is hard to justify this international redistribution of public funds by organisations who are not accountable to the electorates of the donor nations. Furthermore, like so many large international organisations, they suffer from an inability to take a truly impartial stance on certain issues. This has been particularly true of the IMF since the Frenchwoman Christine Lagarde was appointed Managing Director. As a citizen of a country using the Euro, she has used her influence to ensure that non-eurozone taxpayers' money has been used willy-nilly to shore up the single currency by contributing to the bailout funds for struggling Greece, without conducting an impartial cost/benefit exercise as to whether any of this money is ever likely to be paid back, or considering whether Greece would instead be better off leaving the Eurozone.

Besides these concerns about the organisations he founded, there are also concerns about White himself. He died of a heart attack shortly after being summoned before the House Un-American Activities Committee, set up by the American Congress to root out possible Marxist sympathisers. There are strong indications that he did indeed pass classified information to the Soviet Union during the Second World War[83], and that he was fully aware of left-wing sympathies among several other Treasury staff.

For all the hostility to socialism in any shape or form among ordinary American people, the huge expansion of the state under Roosevelt and his successors had opened the doors of power in the US Federal government to individuals whose ideology was vastly removed from the principles of the Founding Fathers. How much better it would have been for the country and for the world at large if the world's leading superpower after 1945 had stayed true to these principles.

The verdict: Marxism didn't work...

For all the revulsion any Christian must surely feel about the violence and godlessness of anarchism, the history of the 20th century is a comprehensive vindication of the followers of Bakunin against those of Marx. Anarchists and Marxists originally shared a common goal of creating a society without government. They differed on whether a socialist state was needed as a necessary intermediate phase before this goal could be reached, and the anarchist scepticism has proved more than justified. Not only did the state refuse to wither away wherever Marxism seized power, but in country after country it grew into a tyrannical monster.

It is depressing to record so much suffering caused by an unbiblical view of human nature, but failure to recognise the sinfulness of the human heart is truly the root cause of Marxism's failure. On coming to power, even those men initially drawn to socialism with a genuine desire to improve the lot of their fellow men have found themselves intoxicated by the power it gave them. This is not to suggest that Marxists like Stalin or Mao were unique in the harshness of their despotic rule. History was already littered with all too many infamous tyrants well before the appearance of socialism. Indeed, it is precisely in order to counteract this lust for power in fallen human nature that God has put so many guidelines in the Bible that limit the scope of government and encourage servant leadership. George Washington may not have been an Evangelical Christian, but he had been brought up in an atmosphere permeated with Christianity, and this was reflected in his actions following America's victory in the War of Independence. He "amazed and awed the courts of Europe, which expected him to seize power. Instead, he resigned his army commission, and on Christmas Eve 1783, rode home to Mount Vernon.[84]" Oliver Cromwell likewise only reluctantly took the reins of power as Lord Protector in 1653 following the failure of the Barebones Parliament. He felt that his position as head of state demanded an appropriate lifestyle, but "he had no particular appetite for the enjoyment of the luxurious trivialities which have often innocently pleased men who have acquired rather than inherited the supreme power.[85]"

While acknowledging that such men are exceptional, and that a tendency to tyranny is far more prevalent among men in positions of great power, there is one particular aspect of Marxist dictators that sets them apart from other autocrats – they rose to power in the name of the proletariat, or more precisely, in the name of an ideology that sought to build a free society where men would be equal. They ended up doing the opposite. The palace constructed by the Romanian dictator Nicolae Ceaucescu in Bucharest survives to this day as a monument to socialism's lust for power. Cited as the world's second largest building, it is decorated with gold leaf marble and contains 4,500 chandeliers. Its construction required 26 churches and 7,000 homes to be bulldozed[86], while the costs forced the country into debt. In the early 19th Century, Owen and Fourier envisaged their utopian communities living in spacious beautiful buildings. They would never have dreamt that such a grandiose folly would have been constructed as a symbol of power by a man professing to be

PROVIDENCE, PIETY AND POWER

their ideological descendent, especially bearing in mind that at the same time only a few miles away, orphans were being housed in sub-human conditions – as the world discovered to its horror after 1989.

Even now, when the main area of concern for Christian organisations seeking to help the persecuted church is now the Middle East and other Islamic countries, North Korea, ruled by a hard-line Stalinist regime with a fearsome lust for power, has maintained its position for several years as the world's most difficult country in which to be a Christian in *Open Doors'* annual survey – ahead of Saudi Arabia, Iran and Afghanistan. North Korea is currently the only surviving 100% state-owned centrally planned economy in the world, and the degree of control exercised by the regime over its citizens goes as far as to deny them any choice over their occupation, while forcing them to participate in the ritual worship of the Kim dynasty, The April 2011 *Open Doors* magazine contained a feature on North Korea, including a couple of quotes from anonymous Christians. One pastor said, "The people don't believe the leaders any more. The entire society is destroyed by the government and transformed into a living hell.[87]"

Besides the political tyranny it created, Marxism also failed abysmally in its attempts to create prosperity through the replacement of the free market with planned economies. For all the socialist-inspired welfare reforms and nationalisation programmes undertaken by Western democracies, the retention of a competitive private sector ensured their technical superiority. The Soviet Union attempted to build a supersonic airliner to rival Concorde, the Tupolev Tu–144. A prototype crashed at the 1973 Paris Air Show, and when production examples finally entered service, all were withdrawn after only 55 flights due to serious safety issues. By contrast its Anglo-French rival remained in regular commercial service until after 2000. The failure of the planned economy was equally apparent when its standards of living were compared with those of the Western nations. One recurring story from the latter years of the Soviet era is the bewilderment felt by religious (and other) dissidents allowed to emigrate to the West when confronted by the sheer variety of produce on offer when they entered a supermarket for the first time. In the Soviet bloc, queues were part of life. If you saw a queue, you joined it because it usually meant that it was your only chance to buy some essential household commodity, assuming the stocks did not run out before you reached the head of that queue. Still, even the Soviet Union never quite sank to the level of North Korea. *Open Doors'* April 2011 magazine also featured the words of another anonymous Christian describing the country's desperate plight: "The food ration has stopped completely due to the great drop in rice production. We are in the worst situation ever. The people have totally given up their expectations towards the government and are struggling to find ways to survive.[88]"

As far as sexual issues are concerned, the early years of the Soviet Union were characterised by the same anti-Christian disdain for marriage as in the most extreme phase of the French revolution – and with similar unhappy results. Sexual liberalism has been a consistently recurring theme in both the writings and lifestyles of many of the socialists studied thus far, with a sexual free-for-all featuring strongly in their aspirations for their future socialist/communist utopia. In the real world, things worked out very differently. Barely a decade after Lenin and the Bolsheviks first introduced legislation to make divorce easier and allowed couples to live together without any formal registration, Russian society began to break down. "Immense problems were posed by divorce, alimony, family instability and homeless waifs wandering the streets.[89]" Even as hard-line an atheist as Stalin was forced to recognise that this deliberate rejection of one of the most important components of Christian moral restraint had proved disastrous. In 1936, the deputy chairman on the Soviet supreme court said, "It is necessary to put an end to the anarchist view of marriage and childbirth as an exclusively private affair." Marriage and the family had to be strengthened to prevent total chaos. In 1944, Stalin published his Family Edict to strengthen marriage and the family, making divorce a less straightforward procedure. He also cracked down on homosexuality, which he regarded as *bourgeois*. In 1959, the Soviet Union finally ended its opposition to marriage – creating a secular form of marriage service[90].

In summary, an ideology which had promised so much in terms of freedom and progress created the complete opposite in practise. The history of Marxism in power is a powerful but tragic proof that any country run along principles which so deliberately disregard God's Word is going to suffer.

....and the British Labour Party ended up in a cul-de-sac

If Marxism has proved a tragic failure, what of the other end of the socialist spectrum? What had become of Attlee's New Jerusalem? The answer is that it too left a legacy of failure on several fronts. The socialist dream of a bold re-shaping of Britain was faltering badly even before Attlee left office in 1951, even if the scale of that failure was not apparent at the time. Indeed, by 1956, for all the confident statements in Anthony Crosland's *The Future of Socialism* mentioned above, there is much soul-searching in the book, including a number of statements that would have been unthinkable a decade earlier. "For the first time for a century there is equivocation on the left about the future of nationalisation,[91]" he wrote. Barely a decade after the Attlee government launched its programme of nationalisation, here was an admission that it had not been an unqualified success. "Some of the anticipated advantages did not materialise, while certain unexpected disadvantages emerged.[92]"

British Rail offers a good example of the failure of nationalisation. While the railways were in a very run-down state at the end of World War 2, a short-term emergency government loan would have enabled them to continue under private ownership where they would have unquestionably been better managed than British Rail ever was. Thanks to government interference, managers of the nationalised industries were never allowed a free rein, and the net result was confusion. On the one hand, steam locomotive construction continued until 1960, while on the other, the *Modernisation Plan*, published in 1955, proposed the rapid withdrawal of steam traction in order to save costs and to create a showpiece modern railway. Consequently, as the rush to modernise the railways gathered pace, many newly-built steam locomotives in good mechanical order were sent to the scrapyard years before their planned withdrawal date. The last steam locomotive built by British Rail, No. 92220 *Evening Star*, was withdrawn in 1965 after a mere five years' service, while No. 34096 *Trevone*, a locomotive used for much of its life on express trains between London Waterloo and the West of England, was subject to a costly rebuild as late as 1961, only to be withdrawn 3½ years later. As if this was not wasteful enough, some of the early diesel locomotive types purchased to replace steam were rushed into service before it became apparent how unreliable they were. The worst examples, the Metropolitan Vickers class 28's, were withdrawn in 1969, only a year after the end of steam, having enjoyed a working life of only 10 years. Although there were some disastrously bad locomotives built before 1948 by the private companies, they did not have to suffer either ideology-driven interference or the appalling profligacy resulting from it – indeed, such waste would have been unthinkable in a public company that had to render an account to its shareholders.

Another problem with the nationalised industries, particularly the coal mines, was their unhappy history of industrial relations, which unquestionably hastened the decline of Britain as a manufacturing nation. The emergence of hardline Marxists in senior positions in British trade unions only exacerbated the situation. In 1973, Arthur Scargill became president of the Yorkshire branch of the National Union of Mineworkers in 1973, later becoming national president in 1981. The NUM had been involved in two national miners' strikes in 1972 and 1974, but neither were as protracted or as damaging as the 1984–5 strike, from which the industry never recovered. While a downsizing of the coal industry had to take place due to the increasing costs of extracting coal from many of the pits, which made them unprofitable, this downsizing could have been far less painful had Scargill not tried to turn the dispute into an ideological confrontation, which ended with a resounding defeat for socialism. One of the few post-Attlee nationalisations, the motor manufacturer British Leyland, was equally notorious for its strikes during its relatively short lifetime. Once again, the spokesman for the trade unions, Derek Robinson, better known as "Red Robbo", was a Marxist. He was eventually sacked in 1979, and a vote for a sympathy strike among the workers was resoundingly defeated.

Scargill and "Red Robbo" illustrate the problems faced by the British Labour Party from the 1960s onwards. Labour's Harold Wilson, Prime Minister from 1964–70 and 1974–6, was positively proud of the fact that he had never read further than page 2 of *Das Kapital*[93]. When he first became Prime Minister, Marx had seemed irrelevant. His belief in the imminent collapse of capitalism had proved very wide of the mark. True. As Crosland pointed out, "Keynes-plus-modified-capitalism-plus welfare state" was not capitalism, but neither was it socialism[94]. Furthermore, Marx's comments in the *Communist Manifesto* that private property was an irrelevancy for the working classes because they did not own anything seemed very dated by 1964. The resurgence of hard-line Marxism was ultimately to put Labour into opposition for 18 years. The British socialists Sidney and Beatrice Webb had visited Stalin in 1932 and, although concerned about the lack of freedom in the Soviet Union, they had otherwise been impressed and unlike Keynes, had come back convinced that a Soviet-style planned economy was the way forward. The world was a different place by 1979, with too much known about the repression in Marxist countries for all but a small minority to aspire to introduce such a system in Britain. However, that small minority included not only powerful union leaders like Scargill, but also the *Militant Tendency* movement within the Labour

Party, who repeatedly urged the reluctant party leadership throughout the 1970s to undertake further nationalisation and who attacked any Labour party members opposed to their Marxist ideology.

It would be wrong to credit the defeat of Labour in 1979 solely to the ongoing fear among the British public of Marxism or a Soviet invasion. While organisations such as the recently-established National Association For Freedom (now The Freedom Association) regularly highlighted the Marxist sympathies of British trade unionists and their links with the Soviet Union in their fortnightly paper *The Free Nation*, the disillusion with socialism among the electorate went far deeper. There was a growing recognition that Attlee's New Jerusalem was proving to be an illusion. It was not only high-rise housing and British Rail that had failed. Even the welfare state, viewed by the post-Attlee generation as the greatest achievement of the 1945–51 government, was not held in such universally high regard. The reason is that state-run welfare, just like state-run education, is never entirely altruistic and never exists in isolation. It always comes as part of package that wants to control more and more areas of public and private life. The Labour governments of 1945–1979 may not have created power-hungry dictators, but they created a large, powerful state. Evan Luard, writing at the end of this period, observed that, "The state has become in modern times the all-powerful, all-purpose omni-competent organisation which totally rules men's lives. And yet it is, in the eyes of most men, a vast, impersonal, inhuman and almost abstract machine that is not only – except in the most theoretical sense – beyond their control, but corresponds in no way to what they feel to be their own, immediate, living community.[95]" British socialism may have been the most benign in the western world and, at least up to 1951, dominated by men of unquestionable sincerity, but it still ended up creating a monster. In 1987, Roy Hattersley was to write of the Victorians that "Their ideas on society and human progress, individual liberty and economic efficiency were all of a piece, mutually dependent, and wrong,[96"] but the opposite is true. Even if few notable Victorian politicians were Evangelical believers, they were sufficiently influenced by Christian political thought to have followed many ideas in accord with the Bible's teaching. It is Hattersley's party, and the ideology to which he subscribed, even in a relatively mild form, which is in the wrong, and which has left a damaging legacy which destroyed the residual positive influence of Christian political thinking in Britain, even if it did not attack Christianity *per se*.

So the verdict of history on socialism's big state – be it the Marxist variation, the Swedish Social Democratic version or the British Labour Party's version – is one of consistent failure. Although standards of living improved dramatically across the western world during the 20th century regardless of the ideology of the government in power, it begs the question as to how much wealthier, freer and more godly Britain or America could have been if the state had remained at the size it was prior to World War I.

Once again however, we are asking questions with the benefit of hindsight. Was there anyone asking this question in the 1970's? Was there was an alternative to the big state in a complex modern industrial society? Furthermore, was an effective Christian voice ever to be heard in politics again? To these subjects we shall now turn.

Notes

[1] Taylor, *AJP English History 1914–1945*,(Oxford History of England) p1 Pelican, Oxford 1965.

[2] http://www.shepheard-walwyn.co.uk/images/inside_image/The_ People_Budget.pdf Accessed 11/03/2011.

[3] http://www.hmrc.gov.uk/history/taxhis4.htm Accessed 11/03/2011.

[4] Taylor, AJP *op cit*, p1.

[5] *idem.*

[6] http://www.voa.gov.uk/instructions/chapters/inheritance_tax_ch _1b/sections/section_2/frame.htm. Accessed 11/03/2011.

[7] Smith, DB *Living with Leviathan*, p26, The Institute of Economic Affairs, London 2006.

[8] http://www.investorwords.com/2240/Gross_Domestic_Product. html Accessed 01/03/2011.

[9] Bartholomew, J, *The Welfare State we're in*, P40, Politico's London 2004.
[10] http://www.users.globalnet.co.uk/~semp/budget.htm Accessed 11/03/2011.
[11] http://news.bbc.co.uk/1/hi/special_report/1998/romanov/132464.stm Accessed 25/04/2011.
[12] Hitchens, P, *A Brief History of Crime*, p148 Atlantic Books, London 2003.
[13] Women aged 30 and above had been granted the vote in 1918, but they had to be either a householder or married to a member of the Local Government Register.
[14] http://en.wikipedia.org/wiki/Communist_Party_USA Accessed 30/04/2011
[15] http://en.wikipedia.org/wiki/First_Red_Scare Accessed 01/03/2012.
[16] Smith, D *Living with Leviathan*, p20, Institute of Economic Affairs, London 2006.
[17] http://www.applet-magic.com/sweden.htm Accessed 03/05/2011.
[18] http://www.lewrockwell.com/dieteman/dieteman33.html Accessed 03/05/2011.
[19] http://www.lifesitenews.com/news/sweden-a-warning-against-overzealous-state-family-policies Accessed 23/05/2011.
[20] Quoted in Crosland, CAR, *The Future of Socialism*, p64 (footnote) Schocken Books, New York 1957.
[21] http://www.vatican.va/holy_father/leo_xiii/encyclicals/documents/hf_l-xiii_enc_15051891_rerum-novarum_en.html Accessed 11/04/2011.
[22] *idem.*
[23] *idem.*
[24] Pius XI, *Quadragesimo Anno, On Social reconstruction*, 25 (1931) as quoted in Robbins, J *Ecclesiastical Megalomania*, p41. The Trinity Foundation, 1999.
[25] Quoted in Robbins, J, *op cit*, p46.
[26] Quoted in Robbins, J *op cit*, p66.
[27] *ibid*, p65.
[28] *ibid*, p68.
[29] *idem.*
[30] *Populorum Progressio*, English on-line text http://www.vatican.va/holy_father/paul_vi/encyclicals/documents/hf_p-vi_enc_26031967_populorum_en.html accessed 23/04/2011.
[31] *idem.*
[32] *idem.*
[33] *idem.*
[34] *Sollicitudo Rei Socialis* English on-line text http://www.catholic-pages.com/documents/sollicitudo_rei_socialis.pdf Accessed 23/04/2011.

[35] *idem.*

[36] *idem.*

[37] *Catechism of the Catholic Church*, (English edition) pp 514, 515, Geoffrey Chapman, London 1999.

[38] *ibid*, pp419, 421.

[39] Available on-line at http://www.acton.org/pub/religion-liberty/volume-4-number-1/catholic-ethic-and-spirit-capitalism

[40] Robbins, *op cit*, p25.

[41] Levin, Mark R, *Liberty and Tyranny*, p86,Threshold Editions, New York, 2009.

[42] *ibid*, p87.

[43] Robbins, J *op cit*, p84, The Trinity Foundarion, USA, 1999.

[44] Levin, *op cit*, p88.

[45] http://socyberty.com/economics/was-john-maynard-keynes-a-socialist/ Accessed 03/05/2011.

[46] Skidelsky R *John Maynard Keynes*, p371.Pan Macmillan, London 2003.

[47] *ibid.* P372.

[48] Skidelsky, R *John Maynard Keynes Fighting for Britain 1937–1946*, p471 Macmillan London, 2000.

[49] Skidelsky, R *John Maynard Keynes*, p507.Pan Macmillan, London 2003.

[50] Wurmbrand, R. *In God's Underground*, p69.W.H. Allen/Hodder & Stoughton, London 1969.

[51] *ibid*, p43.

[52] *ibid*, p46.

[53] Neill, Bishop S, *A History of Christian Missions*, p429. Penguin Books, London 1986 (second Edition).

[54] So called because it was allegedly self-governing, self-supporting (free from foreign interference) and self-propagating. TSPF churches were not allowed to preach from the Book of Revelation, nor teach anything subversive.

[55] Johnstone, P *Operation World*, p146 OM Publishing, Carlisle, 1993 (5th edition) .

[56] http://www.greenleft.org.au/node/12518 Accessed 08/04/2011.

[57] http://www.frontline.org.za/articles/prayforthepersecuted.htm Accessed 16/05/2011.

[58] Brother Andrew, *God's Smuggler*, p146–7, Hodder & Stoughton, London 1968.

[59] Bartholomew, J, *The Welfare State we're in*, P327, Politico's London 2004.

[60] Britain's airlines had already been nationalised in 1939.

[61] Bartholomew J, *op cit*, p102.

[62] *ibid*, p104.

[63] *ibid*, p105.

[64] *ibid*, p90.

[65] One proposal from 1944 which was not implemented at the time was that all young people who left school at 15 should continue in compulsory part-time education until the age of 18.

[66] Hitchens, P, *A Brief History of Crime*, p191. Atlantic Books, London 2003.

[67] The first home purchased by your author was an ex-council house built in Eastbourne, Sussex in 1949, which was extremely well built and gave no problems.

[68] Booth, P. (ed) *Sharper Axes, Lower Taxes*, p68. Institute of Economic Affairs, Lnndon, 2011.

[69] Crosland, C A R, *The Future of Socialism*, p35 Schocken Books, New York 1957

[70] *ibid.*, p70

[71] *ibid.*, p9

[72] Hitchens, P, *A Brief History of Crime*, p196, Atllantic Books, London 2003.

[73] Held, D *Models of Democracy* (Third edition), p186. Polity Press Cambridge 2006.

[74] Published by Yale University Press, New Haven, 2009.

[75] North, R and Booker, C *The Great Deception*, p35 Continuum Books, London 2003.

[76] Duchene, F, *Memoirs*, as quoted in North, R and Booker, C *The Great Deception*, p58. Continuum Books, London 2003.

[77] North, R and Booker, C, *op cit*, p64.

[78] *idem*, p15.

[79] *idem*, p14.

[80] http://www.un.org/en/documents/charter/chapter9.shtml Accessed 02/03/12

[81] http://www.un.org/en/documents/charter/chapter5.shtml Accessed 02/03/12.

[82] http://www.foxnews.com/world/2011/10/07/us-diplomats-blow-whistle-on-united-nations-budget-games/ Accessed 02/03/12.

[83] https://www.cia.gov/library/center-for-the-study-of-intelligence/csi-publications/csi-studies/studies/vol49no1/html_files/harry_dexter_8.html Accessed 02/03/12.

[84] Abbott, D and Glass, C *Share The Inheritance,* p88, The Inheritance Press, Lake Oswego Oregon/Shawford 2010.

[85] Fraser, Lady A, *Cromwell, our Chief of Men*, p463 Mandarin Paperbacks, London 1993.

[86] http://www.pilotguides.com/destination_guide/europe/hungary-

romania/ceaucescu_bucharest.php Accessed 11/04/2011.
[87] Source: *Open Doors Magazine*, April 2011.
[88] *idem.*
[89] *Gay Marriage in All but Name*, p25. The Christian Institute, Newcastle 2004.
[90] *idem.*
[91] Crosland, CAR, *The Future of Socialism*, p310 Schocken Books, New York 1957.
[92] *idem.*
[93] Wheen, F *Marx's Das Kapital*, p82 Atlantic Books, London 2006.
[94] Crosland, *op cit*, p79.
[95] Luard, E, *Socialism without the State*, p29 Macmillan, London, 1979.
[96] Hattersley, R, *Choose Freedom, the Future for democratic socialism*, p33. Michael Joseph Ltd, London, 1987.

Chapter 8:

Thatcherism, Reaganomics and the metamorphosis of socialism

If this is socialism, who needs socialism?
(graffiti written on the Berlin Wall)

The assault on socialism: Thatcher and Reagan

The British 1979 General Election saw the Conservatives returned to power with a substantial majority, an unsurprising result given the high inflation and poor economic performance that dogged the 1974–79 Labour administrations of Harold Wilson and James Callaghan. Margaret Thatcher made history by becoming Britain's first female Prime Minister, but her ideology was more significant than her gender. Gone was the "Butskellite" agenda of trying to manage socialism better than Labour. Mrs Thatcher was determined to reduce the size and intrusiveness of the state, and move the economy more toward a free market model – in other words, an economy driven by supply and demand where individuals and companies were not constrained by government interference[1]. She found a kindred spirit two years later when, Ronald Reagan became the 40th President of the United States and took his country down a similar path. Taxes were cut, nationalised utilities privatised and red tape was reduced.

These policies, were a marked change from the "mixed economy" favoured by MacMillan and his protégé Edward

Heath, and showed how the tide had turned in the Conservative Party. Twenty years earlier, even those who were uncomfortable with the big state created by the Attlee government felt themselves to be swimming against the tide. At that time a planned economy à la Stalin was considered to be the inevitable destiny of the western nations. However, by the time of Mrs Thatcher's victory, the centrally-planned economy of the Soviet Union was no longer seen in the same light. Far from outstripping the West, it was now apparent that it had condemned its citizens to a far lower standard of living.

Those Conservatives who had always believed in limited government had also benefitted from a renewed interest in the writings of a number of individuals who had been critical of socialism from its earliest days in power. These men, a group of Austrian economists, are known by posterity simply as the "Austrian School". The mentor of the group, Carl Menger (1840–1921), is largely forgotten. He rediscovered the late mediaeval Salamanca school[2], and adopted the same emphasis on the subjective element of determining values and prices.[3] Menger's pupil, Ludwig von Mises (1881–1973) built on these foundations, developing and defending a position which was distinctly unfashionable in the early 20th century – that only a free market and private ownership of land would produce prosperity. He was convinced that any government intervention in the economy would inevitably lead to socialism. Mises was also a strong believer in asset-backed currencies, unlike Keynes who, in his 1923 booklet *A Tract on Monetary Reform*, had called gold a "barbarous relic.[4]" His support for asset-backed currencies was in many ways an extension of the Salamanca/Menger concept of subjective value. He felt uncomfortable with the alternative – a "fiat" currency (i.e., a currency which cannot be redeemed for any commodity, but is issued at the decree of a government or central bank), feeling that such currencies could suffer from widespread inflation, which would therefore distort any subjective value placed on an object by any individual.

Mises' pupil F A Hayek, who has already been mentioned several times in this book, lived to see the Reagan/Thatcher years. Indeed, it was Hayek's *The Constitution of Liberty* that Margaret Thatcher famously slammed down on the table at a Conservative Party meeting, saying "<u>THIS</u> is what we believe!" Hayek did not mince his words when it came to socialism:– "The dispute between the market order and socialism is no less than a matter of survival. To follow socialist morality would destroy much of present humankind and impoverish much of the rest.[5]" Hayek's writings were known in Britain well before 1979. The Institute of Economic Affairs, a think tank founded in 1955 by Antony Fisher (1915–1988), had been set up to support free markets and small government and to oppose socialism and protectionism. During the Attlee years, Fisher had read Hayek's most influential work *The Road to Serfdom*, which argued that any system of central government planning inevitably leads to totalitarianism. He had initially planned to go into politics, but Hayek himself persuaded him to start a think tank instead. In retrospect, it proved the right course of action, as the IEA has played a substantial role in combatting socialism not only in Britain but in other lands too. Margaret Thatcher probably also became acquainted with Hayek in the 1940s. Churchill is also known to have read the book[6], and to have enthused about it.

However, for all Hayek's importance as a political philosopher, Austrian economic theory had been discredited for many years by the time Mrs Thatcher and Ronald Reagan took office. In 1931 a debate was held in Cambridge between Keynes and Hayek, and Keynes' arguments in favour of government intervention in the economy during a deep recession demolished Hayek's defence of the opposing point of view. This debate essentially completed the eclipse of Austrian economic thought for some 50 years. The economists who emerged to challenge Keynesian interventionism, including Ronald Reagan's economic advisor Milton Friedman (1912–2006), and Sir Alan Walters (1926–2009), who was appointed as personal economic advisor to Mrs Thatcher in

1981, were monetarists. Monetarism, in summary, believes that the best route to prosperity for a nation is a steady but gradual increase in the money supply. Unlike the Austrians, monetarists therefore oppose the inflexibility of asset-backed currencies, including any sort of gold standard, preferring to allow a government (or central bank) to control the amount of money (which in most measurements includes various types of bank deposit) by the use of variable interest rates. Although monetarists and Keynesians therefore both oppose asset-backed currencies, it is their differences which are more pronounced, particularly on the role of the state, with monetarists being generally opposed to Keynesian state spending to boost employment. To put it simply, private enterprise should drive the economy on the back of a stable money supply managed by a central bank. Monetarists are therefore no friends of socialism or state intervention in the market.

Outside the world of economics, it did not take long for other opponents of socialism to take the route that Hayek advised Fisher not to take, and they soon began to make their mark in the British political scene. In 1963, an audience in Castle Douglas, Scotland was told that, "In a free economy...the decisions of individuals in all parts of the country add up to the decision of the nation itself on how best to direct its efforts and use its resources. Experience teaches us that the decision so taken is often wiser and truer than the cleverest collection of planners would have arrived at."[7] The speaker was addressing not a group of academics but the ordinary British electorate – and addressing them with great effect. However, this most able and consistent opponent of socialism in pre-Thatcher Britain was already in a political wilderness by the time she came to power thanks to one particular speech on one particular subject. Enoch Powell (1912–1998) will always be associated with the so-called "Rivers of Blood" speech[8], which he made in Birmingham in 1968 on the subject of immigration, and which caused a tremendous furore at the time. The fact that Powell has subsequently been airbrushed from history as a result of this speech has meant that his significant contribution to many other subjects of political debate during the 1960s has largely been forgotten. After 1968 he was too hot for the Conservative Party to handle. Disagreement with their policy on taking Britain into the European Economic Community (the precursor to the European Union) led to his resignation from the party, and he ended his political career as the Ulster Unionist MP for South Down.

He did not long remain a voice crying in the wilderness. Sir Keith Joseph (1918–1994) started to take an interest in Milton Friedman's writings in 1974, and it was through him that Margaret Thatcher came to adopt the views for which she will always be remembered. Regarded as the ideological mentor of Thatcherism, Joseph famously said the following year, "It was only in April 1974 that I was converted to Conservatism. (I had thought I was a Conservative but I now see that I was not really one at all.)" That same year, together with Margaret Thatcher, Joseph founded the Centre for Policy Studies, another think tank that sought to challenge socialist policy and reduce the size of the state. Its brief was to "think the unthinkable.[9]"

In some ways, Thatcherism really only marked the beginning of the assault on socialism. While state-owned utilities such as water and gas were privatised and council houses sold off, no attempt was made to privatise either the NHS or the state pension scheme. Neither was any attempt made to put an axe through the burgeoning bureaucracy of local government. Ironically, the poll tax, often cited as the worst failure of all the Thatcher policies, could have been a success had it been accompanied by a drastic reduction in the size of town and county halls. Furthermore her scope for change was limited in the early years of her premiership by the presence of Conservative ministers in the Cabinet who did not share her ideals – the so-called "wets" such as James Prior. Ultimately, her growing antipathy to the European Union resulted in her being forced from office by a group of Europhile Tories headed by Michael Heseltine and Sir Geoffrey Howe. In spite of this rather unceremonious end of her premiership, her eleven years in Downing Street had changed Britain for the better after years of stagnation.

The end of the Cold War and its aftermath

For all the criticisms that have been levelled against Thatcher and Reagan, the assault on socialism during the 1980's provided the catalyst for the end of the Cold War by high-lighting the failure of the Soviet Union's centrally planned economy to deliver prosperity. The election in 1985 of Mikhail Gorbachev as head of state heralded a period of remarkable change. Gorbachev found himself in charge of a country whose economy had stagnated, and unlike his pred-ecessors, he was open-minded enough to realise that its revival was impossible within the existing political structure. His solution was a relaxation of tight press censorship and the ban on privately run businesses that had been a feature of life in the Soviet Union since the days of Lenin. He also made it clear that the Soviet Union would not interfere in the domestic affairs of the Warsaw Pact nations – in other words, no repeat of the events in 1956 when Soviet tanks suppressed the popular uprising in Hungary, or the equally brutal response in 1968 to Alexander Dubček's attempts at liberalisation in Czechoslovakia – the so-called "Prague Spring."

The result of this change of policy in the Kremlin was the collapse of the totalitarian Marxist regimes in Eastern Europe during 1989, followed by the collapse of the Soviet Union itself two years later. Gorbachev's abandonment of repres-sive hard-line Marxism/Leninism unleashed strong nation-alist feelings across the different republics. Meanwhile, his economic liberalisations were blamed for widespread food shortages in the country at the time. The election of Boris Yeltsin as president of the Russian Federation, the largest Soviet republic, in 1991 precipitated a major crisis. Yeltsin's desire to increase the speed of economic liberalisation coupled with ever-growing numbers of Soviet republics wanting to secede completely from the Union proved too much for a group of hard-liners within the Soviet Communist Party and their allies in the military. They attempted a coup in August 1991, which saw Gorbachev briefly placed under house arrest. It was Yeltsin's leadership that saw off the coup, and although Gorbachev was released after only three days, his power had been weakened, and the entire structure of the Soviet Union itself started to disintegrate as one republic after another declared independence.

The Cold War was finally over, leaving behind it a strong anti-Russian and anti-socialist legacy in many Eastern European countries, notably Poland, the Czech Republic and the Baltic States of Estonia, Latvia and Lithuania, which had been involuntarily annexed by the Soviet Union in 1940. Not surprisingly, the emerging leadership in these countries turned to the writings of Hayek and the monetarists as they sought to rebuild their shattered economies. In newly-independent Estonia, a 32-year old Christian, Mart Laar, became president in 1992. Previously an historian, Laar had only read one book on economics before taking office. The book in question was written by Milton Friedman, and on the strength of this, he introduced a large-scale privatisation program and a flat tax. This laid the foundation for Estonia becoming one of the so-called "Baltic Tigers" whose economies grew rapidly from 2000 until the recent recession. Although one of the most radical, Laar was by no means atypical of the new generation of leaders in Central and Eastern Europe in the 1990's. The other Baltic states, along with Poland, the Czech Republic and Slovakia in particular embraced the free market and began a rapid privatisation of their infrastructure.

No observer in the West could deny that these changes were dramatic and immensely significant, but what exactly was happening? Was this to be the beginning of a new era of freedom and small government? The optimism of those heady years is encapsulated in the writings of the American Francis Fukuyama, notably in his book *The End of History and the Last Man* written in 1992. The free market and democracy had triumphed over totalitarianism, and political ideology had reached its fulfilment. "What we may be witnessing is not just the end of the Cold War, or the passing of a particular period of post-war history, but the end of history as such: that is, the end point of mankind's ideological evolution and the universalization of Western liberal democracy as the final form of human government[10]" he wrote. Another American conservative, Midge Decter, didn't mince her words: "It's time to say: we've won, goodbye."

Over twenty years later, it is hard to feel the same optimism. Indeed, looking back on the events of 1989–91, it is remarkable that the dismantling of the Berlin Wall was regarded at the time as far more significant than the crushing of the pro-democracy demonstrations at Tienanmen Square in Beijing by the Chinese army a few months earlier. That the countries of Central and Eastern Europe now enjoy religious freedom, the freedom to travel and a much higher standard of living is unquestionably a real step forward, but neither democracy nor the concepts of small government, low taxes and a free market have proved the all-conquering forces that Fukuyama had so confidently anticipated. Socialism was not going to roll over and die – not by any stretch of the imagination.

The Frankfurt School and their heirs – cultural Marxism and Postmodernism

At the beginning of the 20th Century, Thomas Kirkup had described socialism as "one of the most elastic and protean phenomena of history, varying according to the time and circumstances in which it appears,[11]" Even before socialism came to power, its focus had broadened to include compulsory wealth redistribution as well as state ownership of utilities. Indeed, well before the end of the Cold War, the former had supplanted the latter. By 1989, socialism in Western Europe and much of the Anglophone world was undergoing a further major transformation that more or less ditched state ownership and replaced compulsory wealth redistribution's emphasis on financial equality with a wider "equality" agenda. Such has been the scale of the change that the end product appears on the surface to have very little in common with either Soviet-style Marxism-Leninism or the classic democratic socialism exemplified by Clement Attlee in Britain. The creators of this new-look socialism have nonetheless been either avowed socialists or Marxists.

The first of these influences to be considered is the work of the Frankfurt School and its ideological successors who, for the purposes of this book, will be referred to as post-modernists, although some are more accurately described as deconstructionists, post-structuralists and various other rather bewildering titles. None of the key figures associated with this variant of socialism are anything like as well-known as Marx, Lenin or even Aneurin Bevan. Indeed, with the exception of the Hungarian György Lukács (1895–1971) none of them ever held political office. Nor were they misguided genial men seeking to appeal to the rank and file, like William Morris. Their writings are not easy to read, for they were philosophers speaking to the academic world, viewing the world as detached observers. However, as is so often the case, when politicians have attempted to put philosophy into practise, some unintended consequences have resulted.

Lukács, described as "the most brilliant Marxist theorist since Marx himself[12]" held office in the short-lived 1919 Marxist government in Hungary as People's Commissar for Education and Culture. During his brief period of office, he attempted to introduce sex education into Hungarian schools, but was met with widespread resistance. "Who will save us from Western civilisation?" he asked[13]. His comment sums up this radical new Marxism. Lukács recognised that transformation of society needed to go deeper than a change of ownership of the means of production − it required a transformation of culture too, which he regarded as every bit under *bourgeois* control as industry and political power. Fleeing to Vienna after the fall of the Hungarian Marxist régime, Lukács was among those invited by a wealthy young German Marxist called Felix Weil to attend the First Marxist Work Week in the German town of Ilmenau in 1923. From the deliberations of this gathering emerged the idea of a think tank , or "institute", which, thanks to Weil's sponsorship, was established the following year in the University of Frankfurt, the Institute for Social Research (*Institut für Sozialforschung*), better known nowadays as the Frankfurt School. The Institute was in existence for only 10 years before being forced to close down in 1933 following Hitler's seizure of power. Besides being Marxists, most of the staff were also Jewish, so they fled from Germany for their own safety, relocating in America, where they found academic employment, particularly in Columbia University, New York. This enforced exile provided new opportunities to introduce this new Marxism to American students.

Although most of the Frankfurt exiles returned to Germany following Hitler's defeat, Herbert Marcuse (1898–1979) the "Father of the New Left", stayed on in America, and during the 1960s acquired a widespread following among the student protesters opposed to the Vietnam War. "Marx, Mao, Marcuse" read their placards[14]. Marcuse, along with Max Horkheimer (1895–1973) and Theodor Adorno (1903–1969), is also revered as the ideological mentor of the German Green party[15].

The thinking of the Frankfurt School differed from classic Marxism in a number of ways. Firstly, these men rejected the idea of there being any absolute truth, or "closed philosophical systems.[16]" This not only meant a rejection of Evangelical Christianity's belief in the Bible as God's infallible Word, but also the classic Marxist belief that socialist governments would wither away to usher in a utopian society. Martin Jay, an American academic who knew several leading members of the Frankfurt School personally, states that they reluctantly jettisoned "a triumphalist notion of impending human emancipation, based on a single story of species-wide progress produced by class struggle.[17]" The Frankfurt School developed so-called "critical theory", which is precisely what its name implies – criticism of earlier writers, but without necessarily offering any sort of alternative blueprint. Their writings have an "essentially open-ended probing, unfinished

quality[18]" – in other words, destructive rather than construc-
tive. Horkheimer, who became director of the Frankfurt
School in 1930, took his opposition to absolutes to the point
where he even questioned the possibility of complete justice
in society[19]. This new variant of Marxism was distinctly
pessimistic, although not without its agenda for improving
the world.

Another important difference between classic Marxism
and the Frankfurt School has already been alluded to – the
reinterpretation of the concept of class struggle in terms of
culture rather than economics and redistribution of wealth.
Classic Marxists would never have written a paper entitled
"The Culture Industry as Mass Deception," but Horkheimer
and Adorno produced a study under this title in 1944, which
was one of a series of similar publications claiming culture
was linked to the reinforcement of existing social hierarchies
– in other words, popular music and art helped preserve the
power of the *bourgeoisie*.

Thirdly, whereas classic Marxism, like all early variants of
socialism, emphasised the "common good" and denigrated
individualism, the writers of the Frankfurt School emphasised
the individual and questioned the generalisations that would
lump large numbers of people under a common heading,
such as "proletariat" in the assumption that their desires
were identical. "The new radicals critiqued the politics of
representation, the idea that anyone, any party can speak for
and represent or stand in for the mass of people and the
multiplicity of their desires, needs and aspirations.[20]" While
Augustine had argued for limited government on the grounds
that the state should only confine itself to addressing issues
where there was a consensus that it should do so, the individualism of Marcuse, built on a denial of absolutes, was very
different from Augustine's. Marcuse, along with Erich Fromm
(1900–1980), had sought to integrate the work of the
psychologist Sigmund Freud (1856–1939) into a Marxist
framework. Of particular significance was Freud's concept of
the *libido* – the sexual drive. He believed that the conven-
tional moral boundaries which aimed to confine sex to the

marriage relationship were nothing less than repression. Why should something as enjoyable and natural as sex be subject to guilt-induced restrictions? In 1955, Marcuse published *Eros and Civilisation*, which relied heavily on Freud in its vision of a non-repressive society. Individual freedom and happiness meant free and open sexuality. The immorality that characterised many 19th and early 20th century socialists was now firmly incorporated into a Marxist philosophical framework.

Such writings – indeed, much of the work of the Frankfurt School – was regarded as distinctly suspect, or "revisionist" in the Soviet Union. However, Marcuse and his ideological heirs had come to regard the Leninist (and even more so the Stalinist) interpretation of Marxism as a blind alley and a betrayal of Marx well before the Soviet Union collapsed. Another Marcuse work, *One-Dimensional Man*, attacked not only the totalitarianism he perceived to be present in the West, but also the real totalitarianism of the Soviet Union. Workers living in advanced industrial societies may enjoy a higher standard of living than the workers of Marx's era, but their individualism has been destroyed by an impersonal bureaucracy and a government over whose decisions they have no control. "The slaves of developed industrial civilization are sublimated slaves, but they are slaves, for slavery is determined.[21]"

The pessimism of this quotation needs to be balanced with Marcuse's hopes for the eventual emergence of a free society. Nine years after *Eros and Civilisation*, he wrote a paper entitled *Repressive Tolerance* which, in the name of "freedom" redefined the very concept of tolerance in a very selective way: "Intolerance against movements from the Right, and toleration of movements from the Left.[22]". He argued that restrictions on tolerance during the 1930s would have prevented the Nazi holocaust and thus preserved greater freedom, and that even in the 1960s, withdrawal of tolerance in the traditional sense of the term was required to achieve "true pacification." "Such extreme suspension of the right of free speech and free assembly is indeed justified only if the whole of society is in extreme danger. I maintain that our society is in such an emergency situation, and that it has become the normal state of affairs.[23]" Although still blighted by racial segregation in the south, it was absurd to think that America in the 1960s was in as great a danger of totalitarianism as Germany in the 1930s. Marcuse nonetheless insisted that a new version of tolerance was needed to ensure that the voice of "small and powerless minorities" could be heard. In summary, he redefined the Marxist class war so that the struggle was not so much between capitalist factory owners and the working classes but rather, between adherents to bourgeois cultural values, (including any belief-system built on absolutes), and those who were allegedly repressed by them – for example, women, homosexuals and various other "victims".

Although the Frankfurt School commenced its work in the 1920s, the reason why Marcuse did not enjoy much influence until after 1945 is that their thinking was running ahead of the prevailing mood of their contemporaries in the Western world. Whereas classic socialism, born out of the 18th Century Enlightenment, took an optimistic view of the future, the shock of two world wars shattered this idea of the inevitability of progress. Following the defeat of Hitler, questions were asked regarding how a supposedly civilised and advanced nation could have presided over the horrors of Auschwitz. From a Christian point of view such heart-searching should have come as no surprise, for the optimism that sprang from the Enlightenment (and which undergirded the thinking of 19th century socialists) was based from the start on a faulty view of man that disregarded his sinful nature. However, the Evangelical church of the 1940s and 1950's was too weak and withdrawn from society to fill the ideological vacuum created by the two World Wars and Marcuse and others filled the gap instead.

The ruthless questioning of society's long-held assumptions was taken still further by a generation of predominantly French Marxist philosophers who had been strongly influenced by the Frankfurt School. Jacques Derrida (1930–2004) in an extremely complex essay called *Différance*, questioned whether it was possible even for words to have any objective meaning. The so-called "Deconstructionists" applied the concept of criticism to literary works, challenging every historical interpretation of the author's intentions. Truth at all levels was individualised, resulting in an individualism far removed from Christian understanding, for it was disconnected from any objective values and any higher authority. According to Derrida, what an individual believes to be the truth really is the truth for them. This applied not just in a literary context – i.e. how someone understands an author's intentions – but in terms of religious belief, sexual preferences and other areas of knowledge.

This relativisation of truth nowadays usually goes under the name of postmodernism. Away from the world of philosophy, one of the best depictions at a more popular level of the mindset of the "postmodern" generation who have grown up without any ideological anchor is Douglas Coupland's novel *Generation X: Tales for an accelerated culture*[24], published in 1991. The book's three characters Andrew, Dag and Claire, share a house together. They are young and articulate, but are stuck in dead-end jobs and devote much of their time to telling stories. They have neither vision nor passion and the book itself has no real sequential storyline. It ends abruptly without ever having taken the reader anywhere.

For all the pointlessness and pessimism of postmodernism, which *Generation X* so graphically depicts, it nonetheless contains a hankering after total freedom for the individual. Marcuse and others had been able to redefine freedom in a much more individualistic, selfish and unrestricted manner than the Bible, and their teachings were eagerly taken up on university campuses from the 1960s onwards. However, like any movement seeking a freedom in opposition to God's Word, the net result is always the opposite – tyranny. As the students that grew up in the 1960s under the influence of these teachings have risen up the political ladder, so have long-held freedoms found themselves challenged on an unprecedented scale, even in countries like Britain and the USA.

The Labour Party's triple divorce

Another strand of contemporary Western socialism can be traced back to a change of thinking among British socialists in the 1950s, which was first expressed in Anthony Crosland's 1956 book *The Future of Socialism*. This book, as was noted in the previous chapter, trumpeted the successes of the Attlee government while questioning whether further nationalisation was the best way forward. It also sought to move British socialism's agenda beyond state ownership of the means of production and the Welfare State towards a broader equality agenda than merely wealth redistribution. Indeed, Crosland's re-definition of socialism said nothing about wealth redisribution or control of the means of production. Rather, in his words, socialism was "about the pursuit of equality and the protection of freedom – in the knowledge that until we are truly equal we will not be truly free.[25]" Although Crosland's ideas developed separately from the Frankfurt School and in a very different environment, there are some interesting parallels, as will be shown.

Crosland is particularly remembered for his attacks on grammar schools. While there is some question over whether he actually said, "If it's the last thing I do, I'm going to destroy every f******* Grammar School in England and Wales and Northern Ireland," this was unquestionably his objective. He regarded selective education as one factor in the preservation of the class system which was still such a feature of British society even in the 1950s. Equality of opportunity was therefore not sufficient. "Equal opportunities for self-advancement, superimposed on a segregated educational system, would still leave too wide a gap between the new élite and the average citizen.[26]" Such language was very different from that of Attlee's minister of education, Ellen Wilkinson, who had argued a decade earlier in favour of selective education saying, "There are differences in intelligence among children as well as among adults. There are distinctions of mind and these are imposed by nature. I am afraid that this is a fact which we cannot get over. Children will be different in bent, and in intellectual capacity. There is a purpose in education and that is to draw out and develop the best in every child. Because children differ in their intellectual makeup, it seems to me that different provisions must be made by the Ministry of Education.[27]" The Butler report of 1944 had allowed for the creation of comprehensive schools, but unsurprisingly, very few had been built before Crosland's book appeared, but they later became a weapon in Labour's crusade against privilege. Crosland's variation of socialism, in other words, was prepared to use state power to rearrange the very order of society and thus promote "freedom." Significantly, he did not go as far as Roy Hattersley 30 years later, who proposed the abolition of private education with the same objective in mind. However, when Crosland's proposals were implemented from the 1960s onwards, the social mobility provided by the Grammar Schools which had given children from poor backgrounds the opportunity to go to university, began to decline. There is a particular irony in this. Crosland had attacked selective education saying it deprived the working classes of their natural leaders, and that if unchallenged, it would result in the Labour Party being led "entirely by Old Etonians.[28]" While no Labour Party leader has so far come from Eton, Tony Blair, Britain's longest serving Labour Prime Minister, went to a private school, as did Alastair Darling, Harriet Harman and Ed Balls among others. Crosland's attack on Grammar Schools ultimately ended up creating an élitism in the Labour Party that was anything but egalitarian. As will be considered below, this has resulted in a wedge being driven between the party and its traditional supporters and has led to a government which far from creating freedom, has intruded into personal freedom in an unprecedented way. Once again, socialism, in trying to solve one problem has ended up creating a bigger one.

Crosland also believed that changes were necessary to the "restrictions on the individual's private life and liberty" if a freer and more equal society was to be created. The examples he cited included, "the divorce laws, licensing laws, prehistoric (and fragrantly unfair) abortion laws, obsolete penalties for sexual immorality.[29]" In 1956, such suggestions would still have seemed shocking, even to some within his own party, but barely a decade later, Britain was ripe for change. Attitudes to moral restraint in British society up to 1960, even among socialists, were still strongly influenced by Christianity even though a century had passed since Darwin and higher criticism had inflicted such damage on the church and dispensationalism had hastened Evangelicalism's withdrawal from the political arena. The "swinging sixties" saw the rise of a new generation who questioned the morality of their parents. After all, few of these parents would have been Evangelical believers, even if some 40% may have attended a Sunday School in their youth. Surely such attitudes smelt of hypocrisy? Inspired by the music of the Beatles and the Rolling Stones, the youth of the 1960s rebelled against Biblical morality, and in so doing, paved the way for like-minded politicians who had arrived at the same conclusions years earlier to come out of their closets. Immorality had been an element in British socialism since the days of the Bloomsbury Set, but only now in the "swinging sixties" was there finally an opening for it to become mainstream.

Although Crosland was the intellectual architect of Labour's revolt against Biblical morality and restraint, it was Roy Jenkins (1920–2003), Home Secretary from 1965 to 1967, who, more than anyone else can take the credit for putting these "new look" Labour policies into practise. Labour's return to power in the 1964 UK General Election, just as in 1997, owed a great deal to Conservative failure rather than any renewed enthusiasm for socialism, and ironically, the Conservatives' failure in this instance involved sexual immorality. The Conservative Secretary of State for War, John Profumo, had an affair with a prostitute called Christine Keeler, the alleged mistress of a Russian spy. When it became public in 1963, it fatally weakened the Conservative government, and the following year, Britain found itself again under Labour rule, led this time by Harold Wilson. The election result had been a close call, and for the next two years, Wilson's room for manoevre was limited, but a further general election in 1966 saw an increased Labour majority and the openings for Jenkins. Abortion, previously only permitted if the mother's life was in danger (and only under-taken with the intention to save the both lives if possible) was legalised, homosexuality de-criminalised and the death penalty abolished. The grassroots revolt against Christain morality which in the 1960s was epitomised by rock music, hippies and drug taking, played into the hands of Jenkins in the UK and Marcuse in America. This new-look socialism could inflitrate the thinking of a new generation by ideinti-fying itself with their rebellion. Jenkins even anticipated the concept of multi-culturalism more associated with the Blair years, talking of "equal opportunities accompanied by cultural diversity in an atmosphere of mutual tolerance[30]" in a speech in 1966, where he specifically rejected the concept of cultural assimilation.

The relative weakness of parliamentary oppostion to these changes is an indication of how much Britain had altered during the 1960s. Even some Conservatives were cautiously supportive. When Sir Cyril Black expressed his opposition to "the state withdrawing its existing disapprobation from acts which most people regard as loathesome and debasing[31]" during the debate on de-criminalising homosexuality, he sadly found himself with little support.

Crosland's lukewarmness towards further nationalisation also gradually gained support within sections of the Labour Party, much to the disapproval of the party's left wing. Conse-quently, just as the Frankfurt School was attacked as "revi-sionist" by Stalin, so the Labour Party "modernisers" found themselves under attack from traditional Marxists such as the members of *Militant Tendency*. Indeed, such was the discord within the Labour Party following its 1979 defeat that four leading modernisers, including Roy Jenkins, left the Labour Party in 1981 to form the Social Democratic Party, which subsequently merged with the Liberal Party to form the Liberal Democrats. This party rejected the classic Marxist/socialist emphasis on nationalisation, choosing rather to leave the private sector alone and to develop the "freedom and equality" agenda of Crosland. In due course the Labour Party they walked away from was to adopt this agenda too.

The catalyst for these changes was the success of Margaret Thatcher. Roy Hattersley, writing in 1987, noted how thirty years earlier, Crosland had felt able to dismiss Hayek as an irrelevancy but now, "many of the irreversible changes which Crosland observed have been reversed by Margaret Thatcher's government.[32]" There can be no doubt that socialism did take a big hit in the UK during the Thatcher years, and as in the 1950's, Labour went through a period of soul-searching. Had the modernisers been right after all? Was this the only way back to power? It was apparent that something drastic would have to be done after the Conservatives, somewhat against the odds, won a fourth term in office in 1992 under the distinctly uncharismatic John Major. Neil Kinnock, the party leader, had no choice but to resign, especially after prematurely suggesting during a rally in Sheffield held shortly before the result was announced that Labour was going to win. His place was taken by the Scot John Smith, who died after less than two years in office. Smith was enough of a traditional socialist to attack the Tories for cutting the basic rate of income tax to 20%, but it was he who pushed through one significant reform that heralded a further re-shaping of the party – the abolition of the Trade Union block vote at Labour Party conferences. His successor Tony Blair took the even more momentous step of revising Clause IV of its constitution. Clause IV only dated from 1918, nearly two decades after the Labour Party's formation, but its addition showed that Labour, in spite of not being a solidly socialist party, was committed to the classic socialist principle of public ownership of resources. In full, it stated that one of the party's objectives was:–

To secure for the workers by hand or by brain the full fruits of their industry and the most equitable distribution thereof that may be possible upon the basis of the common ownership of the means of production, distribution and exchange, and the best obtainable system of popular administration and control of each industry or service.

On the face of it, the abandonment of a central tenet of historic socialism looked like an admission of defeat. Well before Blair, it had become obvious that the Marxist ideal of the end of private property was always going to struggle to gain acceptance in post-war Britain, and especially post-Thatcher Britain with its enthusiasm for house ownership. However, Blair's support for the private sector disguised the amount of control which the state retained over it through tax and regulation. His economic model had close parallels not only with Swedish socialism but also with Hermann Göring's *gelenkte Wirtenschaft* (joined-up economy), introduced in Nazi Germany in 1936[33]. Furthermore, a closer look at Blair's revised Clause IV shows that, like Crosland and Hattersley, he was reluctant to jettison the socialist label, even if socialism now meant something quite different from what it had meant when the original Clause IV was drawn up. The new clause states that:–

The Labour Party is a democratic socialist party. It believes that by the strength of our common endeavour we achieve more than we achieve alone, so as to create for each of us the means to realise our true potential and for all of us a community in which power, wealth and opportunity are in the hands of the many, not the few, where the rights we enjoy reflect the duties we owe, and where we live together, freely, in a spirit of solidarity, tolerance and respect.

The discerning observer will observe that elements of classic socialism are still present – the emphasis on collectivity (as opposed to individualism), along with hints of Rousseau's "general will" and even echoes of the Communist Manifesto which stated that "the free development of each is the condition for the free development of all." Compulsory wealth redistribution is still affirmed, but the modernising agenda is also plainly set forth, particularly in the use of the word "tolerance" Here is the first hint that the drip-down influence of the Frankfurt School and their successors in the academic world was beginning to emerge into the British political mainstream. It is not just a case of great minds thinking alike, or more appropriately, of fools seldom differing. New Labour's approach to tolerance is too close to that propounded by Marcuse in his 1965 paper "Repressive Tolerance" to be mere coincidence. Martin Jay, a man sympathetic to the Frankfurt School, is dismissive about the fear of "political correctness" by the "alarmist right,[34]" but postmodernism and the agenda of the Labour modernisers have unquestionably been blended with elements of Frankfurt School teaching. The end result has been a very ugly and sterile state-enforced orthodoxy of thought which requires all opinions to be given equal weight, while viewing intolerance as unacceptable. This synthesis had been completed by the early 1980s, but widely ridiculed when first put into practise by "loony left" councils such as Margaret Hodge's Islington. However, when New Labour came to power in 1997, this pseudo-toleration moved into the mainstream. "Equality and Diversity" training became big business and Christians started to find themselves under greater pressure in Britain that they have known for over a century, particularly in relation to their opposition to homosexuality.

This metamorphosis of Labour Party ideology has resulted in a triple divorce. Firstly, Labour has now totally divorced itself from any pretence of common ground with Christianity. There can be no place for a Keir Hardie, a Snowden or a Stafford Cripps in the upper echelons of to-day's Labour Party. Classic socialism may have shared with Christianity a compassion for the poor, but the pseudo-toleration and denial of absolutes at the heart of the party today are in total conflict to the Bible in every way. Christians such as those mentioned above had previously acted as a leaven which retarded outright opposition to Christianity in British socialism, but now even in Britain the fundamentally anti-Christian nature of socialism has emerged dominant, as it always does.

Secondly, the Labour Party has divorced itself from freedom. In 1956, Crosland had ridiculed Hayek's concerns that socialism would lead to a curtailment of freedom. "We have experienced a decade of varying degrees of government control, with no sign of a weakening of our democratic fibre[35]" he wrote. Even as late as 1987, Hattersley's book on socialism was entitled "Choose freedom". A generation later, it is now impossible to equate the party of which he was once deputy leader with freedom. Power has gone to the heads of the new generation of Labour party politicians. They may not believe that the state should own all the means of production, or all the bricks and mortar in the land, but even the precise height that light switches and wall sockets must be above the ground in new houses have now been decreed by the state. A stream of legislation, culminating in the 2010 Equality Act, which forces public bodies like schools and the police to promote homosexual and transsexual issues, have reinforced a determination to force pseudo-tolerance down the British people's throats. With pseudo-tolerance everyone has their "rights," even prisoners, and the state is determined that these must be respected. This top-down approach is essential inasmuch as it is the only way of defending the biggest weakness not only of pseudo-toleration but post-modernism as a whole. Without the support of protective legislation this whole ideology is vulnerable to the emer-gence of a stronger, more positive worldview that could sweep away all competitors, restore order to society and bring in a far more genuine freedom. So, in Don Carson's words, "Instead of a rich diversity of claims arguing it out in the workplace... and instead of this diversity being cherished as the best way to ensure freedom and to pursue truth, the pressures from philosophical pluralism (*i.e. postmodern denial of absolutes*) tends to squash any strong opinion that makes exclusive truth claims.[36'] Christianity, which fits the bill precisely, must be therefore marginalised at all costs, and its influence on society reduced.

Any opponents of New Labour, whether Christian or not, have been attacked. Indeed, the tactics of the Labour Party in recent years towards any serious opposition have been reminiscent of the response of the Roman Catholic Church to the Reformation in the 16th Century. When a paper entitled *Women in Power – Milestones* was published by Harriet Harman's department in 2009, some 28 women were mentioned by name, but Margaret Thatcher was not one of them. The paper merely mentioned that Britain's first woman prime minister was elected in 1979, instead going into far more detail about Britain's first female councillor, Britain's first female MP and Britain's first female black and Asian MPs. There is no mention either that Mrs Thatcher was the first female leader of a British political party when she replaced Edward Heath in 1975, or the fact that she was the longest serving prime minister in the 20th century, and won three general election victories.[37] It is impossible to believe that this was merely an oversight. Socialists may not be burning their opponents at the stake, but this airbrushing from history of a notable leader whose ideology was not to their liking suggests that like the Roman Catholic Church at the time of the Reformation, postmodern socialists just cannot admit that they might be wrong and are determined not to allow their opponents the freedom to say so. Furthermore, postmodern socialism in the west, while not enforcing state-worship in the manner of the former Soviet bloc or North Korea, views anyone committed to shrinking its size and influence as an unwelcome dissenter.

Support for postmodern pseudo-tolerance is not confined to the Labour Party. The Liberal Democrats, who owe their very existence to the Labour modernising agenda, have replaced the tradition of freedom which characterised the old Liberal Party by this same postmodern pseudo-tolerance. Because its manifestations appear outwardly to have so little in common with classic socialism or the Marxism-Leninism of the former Soviet Union, the Marxist and socialist sympathies of the originators of pseudo-tolerance are suspected by few, and certainly not broadcast by its supporters. Perhaps the biggest tragedy is the support for these same views among the current leadership of the Conservative Party. David Cameron, instead of exposing pseudo-tolerance for the destructive and tyrannical force that it is, has chosen to embrace it, shocking his audience at the 2006 Conservative party conference in Bournemouth with his support for homosexuality, and taking a similar line five years later, stating he supported the marriage of homosexuals "because he was a Conservative." What has emerged is a new "Social Butskellism" where the leaders of all the three largest UK political parties are keen to display their support for homosexual relationships, even at the cost of marginalising Christians. Dr Martin Parsons, in a blog posted on the *Conservative Home* Website[38], suggested that the lack of support from senior figures in the Conservative party for Christians who spoke out against homosexuality may have cost the party votes in the 2010 general election, therefore denying Cameron an absolute majority.

Returning to the Labour Party, it cannot now pretend to be the party of freedom. Indeed, it is hard to say who it really represents now, for there has been a third divorce – from its traditional supporters. The metamorphosis of the Labour Party which was finally completed by Tony Blair may have succeeded in making it acceptable to middle class intellectuals, but in conceding some ground to private enterprise and refusing to re-nationalise the industries privatised by the Conservatives, he alienated the trade unions. At the same time, pseudo-tolerance and multiculturalism have alienated many working class voters, who are far more conservative in their social attitudes. There can be few better illustrations of the dilemma the party faces than Gordon Brown's widely-reported gaffe in the 2010 election campaign. After being confronted by lifelong Labour voter Gillian Duffy in Rochdale on the subject of immigration from

Eastern Europe, Brown failed to turn off the radio microphone he had been using, and the press picked up his comments as his car drove away where he called Mrs Duffy a "bigoted woman". Victorian middle class socialist intellectuals like Annie Besant and William Morris were able to convey the image of being true friends to the working classes. Their modern counterparts have not been so successful. Terry Eagleton, a Marxist who came from a working class background, is rightly scathing in his criticism of the type of men and women who came to dominate the Labour Party in the Blair era: "The history of the Labour Party in Britain is littered with smooth-talking ambitious men who climb to power on the backs of working men and women, took over their language, claimed empathy with their sufferings and then proceeded to sell them out.[39]"

It is one of the strange ironies of the metamorphosis in the British Labour Party that those formerly regarded as the furthest to the left, because of their adherence to the traditional socialist agenda of nationalisation and compulsory wealth redistribution, are now more highly regarded even by their opponents than the modernisers. Michael Foot, the last classic socialist to lead the Labour Party, died during the early stages of the writing of this book, and tributes were paid to him from across the political spectrum. "Michael Foot's legacy is of a politician unafraid to declare his conviction in beliefs that, right or wrong, were deep-rooted and proudly worn[40]" wrote one commentator. Margaret Thatcher called him "a great parliamentarian and a man of his principles" and even the Tory Eurosceptic MEP Dan Hannan talked respectfully of Foot in his blog, calling him "God's Englishman[41]". To believe in an erroneous ideology but to be open and sincere about it while looking for its triumph through democratic means is surely better than the deviousness that characterises the leadership of to-day's Labour Party, who under Gordon Brown's chancellorship and premiership, raised taxes and increased public spending dramatically, not so much out of a Keynesian desire to boost the economy but rather in the hope that a bloated public sector would never bite the hand that fed them and therefore continue to vote them back into office.

New look socialism elsewhere

The shift in thinking within the Labour Party is not without its parallels elsewhere. The German SPD, always a far more ideological party than its British counterpart, took the momentous decision with its 1959 Bad Godesberg Program to abandon all Marxist ideology and to drop its long-standing hostility to private ownership of utilities. Such a change was quite remarkable at the time, but less so than more recent changes in China. While the pro-democracy demonstrators in Tienanmen Sequare failed to understand that the shift in thinking that had taken place in the leadership of the Chinese Communist Party following Mao's death was very different from the changes in the Soviet Union, the changes have still been quite profound. Mao's successor, Deng Xiaoping (1904–1997) was a pragmatist who wanted to see economic growth at all costs. His ideas for developing a prosperous China were at odds with Mao's rigid hard-line Marxism/Leninism, and led to his marginalisation during the Cultural Revolution years of the 1960s. However, on Mao's death, it was Deng who emerged out of the ensuing power struggle as the new leader and began to open the door to private business and the development of trade with the West.

Economic liberalisation did not mean any opening up of Chinese society. Whereas the persecution of Christians had eased somewhat, although not completely, in Gorbachev's Soviet Union, the hardships of the Chinese church have continued under Deng and his successors. The Chinese Communist Party has no intention either of relinquishing power or introducing democracy, as the Tienanmen Square demonstrators found out to their cost. Whether competition and private enterprise, coupled with the growing number of Christians at all levels of Chinese society, will eventually bring socialism to an end in China only time will tell.

The new postmodern "pseudo-tolerance" has been taken

on board by socialists in other countries too. In Sweden, a Pentecostal pastor, Åke Green, was prosecuted in 2002 under "hate crime" legislation due to a sermon he preached in which he attacked homsexuality, saying it was incompatible with Christianity. The sentence was overturned on appeal, but the very fact that a man could be taken to court for stating a fundamental Biblical truth underscores yet again that wherever socialism gains power, sooner or later, Christians will find themselves under pressure.

The return of a Christian voice in politics

The course of events depicted in this chapter has shown how urgent is the need for the Christian voice to be heard again in the political arena. Throughout the first half of the twentieth century, the influence of dispensational theology with its insistence on the imminence of Christ's return and defeat for the church precluded any serious Evangelical Christian political thinking, but from the 1950's onwards, dispensationalism began to face challenges on two fronts. The first was the revival of interest in the works of the Puritans that grew out of the ministry of Dr D. Martyn Lloyd-Jones (1899– 1981) at Westminster Chapel in London. The establishment of the Banner of Truth Trust in 1957 by Lloyd-Jones' assistant Iain Murray led to the publication of many long-neglected works by these great 17th Century Christians, which in turn resulted in many, including Murray himself, realising that Christians in that period had largely held a more positive view of the end times than that which dispensationalism was teaching[42]. However, just like the early 19th century, another period when there was widespread demand for reprints of the works of Calvin and the Puritans, their political writings once again have attracted little attention.

The second challenge to dispensationalism came from the Charismatic movement, which also began in the 1950s. Members of the new churches that sprang up in the following two decades found it hard to reconcile the "new thing" they believed God to be doing with the doom and gloom of dispensationalism. The large congregation at the 1988 Downs Bible Week singing, *"World changers, we're gonna be world changers"* clearly had much higher expectations of what God could yet do in history than the Brethren assemblies in which so many leaders of these new churches had grown up.

The rise of distinctively Christian political pressure groups in the USA is a complex subject that requires a whole book to itself. American Evangelicals, already in retreat from politics since the late 19th century thanks to the influence of dispensationalism, had suffered a blow to their credibility in 1925 when the state of Tennessee banned the teaching of evolution in schools and the American Civil Liberties Union (ACLU) launched a test case to challenge this ban. The offending teacher who defied the ban, John Scopes, was found guilty, but of greater significance, the counsel for the prosecution, William Jennings Bryan, stumbled over the issue of the identity of Cain's wife (Genesis 4:17) when challenged by ACLU's lawyer Clarence Darrow. His apparent inability to defend the Biblical record was widely viewed as a humiliation for Evangelical Christianity for many years afterwards[43]. However, such was the challenge to Biblical morality posed by the legalisation of abortion and homosexuality from the late 1960s onwards that Christians on both sides of the Atlantic felt compelled to put this humiliation to one side and speak out.

The return of American Evangelicalism to the political arena was unquestionably one of the factors that propelled Ronald Reagan to the White House in 1980. Sixteen years earlier, the Republican Senator Barry Goldwater (1909–1998) had stood on a similar platform of reduced powers for the federal government and opposition to the welfare state, but had no organised support from American Evangelicals[44]. There is a strange irony in that Reagan's defeated opponent, the Democrat incumbent Jimmy Carter, had emphasised his Evangelical credentials four years earlier, and his victory owed much to Evangelical pressure groups coalescing in support of his presidency. His four years in office proved a profound disappointment for his Evangelical supporters, particularly as he made no attempt to reverse the legalisation of abortion, and thus the now well-organised Evangelical campaign groups transferred their allegiance, almost *en bloc*, to Reagan.

The American theologian and apologist Francis Schaeffer (1912–1984) was one of the first significant Evangelicals to overcome his reluctance to engage in politics. Schaeffer, a man strongly influenced by the Dutch Calvinist tradition of Kuyper, saw modern Western society as a battleground with two worldviews locked in conflict – secular humanism and Christianity. The very idea of there being such a thing as a Christian worldview, or the belief that Christians had something to say to society as a whole, were concepts that would have been completely new to many American Evangelicals at this time. Although more widely known for developing this worldview in the field of art, Schaeffer felt compelled to move into politics following the legalisation of abortion in America in 1973. His *Christian Manifesto* of 1981 was given its title deliberately as an attempt to answer Marx's *Communist Manifesto* or the *Humanist Manifesto*, the second version of which had been published eight years before Schaeffer's work.

The rise of Christian television stations in the 1970s also contributed to the development of Christian political activism in the USA. Although criticised by more astute observers like Neil Postman for presenting religion "quite simply and without apology as an entertainment[45]" televangelists like Jerry Falwell and Pat Robertson were able powerfully to rally Christian opinion in the political realm, even if at no point did they ever remotely approach the depth of Schaeffer's thought. Falwell had found himself drawn into the political arena in 1976, when he embarked on a series of rallies entitled *I love America*, where he highlighted the moral decline in the nation. Abortion, as with Schaeffer, was a particular concern of Falwell's, although he was equally vocal in his condemnation of homosexuality. In 1979 he founded the campaigning organisation *Moral Majority*, which threw its weight behind the Reagan campaign, although its influence in bringing about Reagan's victory may not have been quite as great as Falwell claimed at the time. Behind Falwell's organisation stood Paul Weyrich (1942–2008), a man who shared his concern about America's departure from its Judaeo-Christian roots, but not his Evangelicalism. Weyrich was born a Roman Catholic, but moved over to the Melkite Greek Catholic Church in protest against what he saw as Rome's "liberal" shift following the Second Vatican Council in the 1960s[46]. Weyrich also founded the Heritage Foundation, now one of the most influential American conservative think tanks. Furthermore, it was actually he, not Falwell, who actually coined the term *Moral Majority*.

The erosion of moral standards which galvanised Schaeffer, Falwell, Weyrich and Robertson was also a major factor in politicising the author and pastor Tim LaHaye, best known for the best selling "Left behind" novels and a man who openly acknowledges his debt to Schaeffer. LaHaye is a dispensationalist and somewhat prone to conspiracy theories, but he has been another hugely influential figure in American Christian political circles in recent years. For all the theological reasons that a dispensationalist may have had for opting out of politics, by the late 1970's, any Evangelical Christian would have heard the alarm bells ringing as far as the secularisation of society was concerned. Even without a full-orbed Biblical worldview such as that of Calvin or the Puritans, one leading Evanglical after another knew they had to make a stand. It is significant that both LaHaye and Falwell supported Reagan's economic policies, although it would have been interesting to see them try to defend these policies from the Bible. By contrast, the economist Gary North, a staunch Calvinist and trenchant critic of dispensationalism, has produced a whole series of economic commentaries on different books of the Bible which are quite unequivocal in claiming that it "mandates free market capitalism. It is anti-socialist.[47]" North stands at the opposite end of the eschatological spectrum from LaHaye. He is a reconstructionist – in other words, he holds a very optimistic view of the state of

Christianity in the last days before the return of Christ, believing that during this period the majority of the population, including world leaders, will be converted. He has written extensively about how society should be reconstructed along Biblical lines when this happens, admitting that he is writing for the future rather than for the present. "This commentary appears on the surface to be a book without a market[48]", he states in the introduction to his first commentary.

Certain aspects of North's blueprint for Biblically-orientated government after the worldwide revival he anticipates have attracted controversy[49], and his adherence to the Austrian ideal of subjective value and the principle of non-intervention by the state in monetary matters have raised a few eyebrows. "The state," he writes, "is not to be trusted with the right to issue money[50]" and adds, "Government-issued money is a violation of customer authority sovereignty in money. It is a power that the State invariably violates eventually.[51]" In spite of coming to conclusions that have been distinctly unfashionable among economists in recent years, North, in attempting to design an economic system based on the Scriptures, has blazed a welcome trail which should challenge Christians to think biblically about all areas of life. Furthermore, whereas the impetus for drawing Schaeffer and Falwell into politics was their opposition to abortion and homosexuality – modern examples of issues relating to Christian compassion and Biblical moral restraint respectively – North, in arguing powerfully the Biblical case for private property, limited government and free trade, has focussed on the third component of the Christian worldview – liberty. Indeed, North claims that the Bible offers the only consistent defence against the big state. While agreeing with Mises and Hayek about the errors of socialism, he maintains that Hayek's defence of the market from an evolutionary standpoint is untenable. "He cannot demonstrate that the moral and legal rules of the game should not be changed in some future social order...Evolutionism is another variety of historicism and historicism offers man no fixed, reliable, universal

and perpetually binding principles of law, legislation and liberty.[52"]
A younger but highly influential individual whose contribution to Christian political thought should be mentioned is Al Mohler, president of the Southern Baptist Association, the man who has turned it round almost single-handedly to a conservative Calvinist position. While as unequivocal as Schaeffer or Falwell in his opposition to abortion and homosexuality, Mohler, like North, has also addressed economic issues, and come out in support of the free market as opposed to socialism. "The free market is not perfect, but capitalism has brought more wealth to more people than any other system. It rewards investment, labor, and thrift and rises on innovation. Better ideas and better products push out inferior ideas and inferior products. Given the reality of human sin, we should not centralize economic control in the hands of the few, but distribute economic power to the many. A free market economy distributes power to multitudes of workers, inventors, investors, and consumers.[53"] Such comments are not as in-depth as North's analyses, but this is hardly surprising given Mohler is a preacher and a theologian and not an economist. What is significant is that such a man should take such a public position on economic issues, for it would have been unthinkable in the America of the 1950s and would still be extremely unusual in Britain today. Still, at least in America, it is encouraging to observe how, over the last 30 years, a comprehensive Evangelical political worldview is slowly being reassembled.

However, it would be painting a very unbalanced picture to suggest that all American evangelicals support small government and condemn socialism. One of the best-selling books in the 1970s was Ronald Sider's *Rich Christians in an age of Hunger* which, amidst a wealth of statistics showing the incredibly uneven distribution of wealth between rich and poor nations, included a classic socialist call for wealth redistribution by the state. Sider is as opposed to abortion and homosexual marriage as any of the names mentioned above, being a fellow-signatory of the 2008 *Manhattan*

Declaration, a call to Christian Conscience with Mohler, but he supported Obama's healthcare policy, which Mohler did not. Like the theologically liberal Rauschenbusch nearly one hundred years earlier, Sider's encounters with poverty in the early days of his ministry drew him to the conclusion that state intervention and wealth redistribution were the only answer. Although feeling able at the time he wrote his book to square his Christian faith with socialism like Keir Hardie and Sir Stafford Cripps before him, by the 1970s growing evidence was proving that from a Biblical perspective, such a position was becoming untenable. In recent years, it is encouraging to note that he has back-pedalled from some of the positions he adopted in his book. He admitted, "My thinking has changed. I've learned more about economics" and the 20th edition was provided with a new subtitle, *Moving from Affluence to Generosity*[54].

In Britain, the beginnings of a revival of Evangelical political concern can be dated to the Festival of Light movement of 1970, which grew out of the vision of a young missionary couple, Peter and Janet Hill, who returned to England after four years in India and were shocked to find how the country had changed. As with many evangelical Christians in the USA, their concern about abortion and homosexuality, both of which had been legalised by the Wilson government during their absence, was the catalyst which inspired them to action, along with their opposition to the growing number of sex shops which were opening in towns and cities across the country. The Hills conceived the idea of ten thousand people marching on London to make a stand for Christian moral principles, and a year later, on 25th September 1971, Hill's ten thousand met at Trafalgar Square. What had begun as a grassroots movement had managed to attract the support of high profile names such as the journalist Malcolm Muggeridge, musician Cliff Richard and media campaigner Mary Whitehouse.

Out of this Nationwide Festival of Light emerged the Christian Action Research and Education organisation (CARE), which continues to campaign on moral issues. Other Christian campaign organisations have emerged in the UK in more recent times, such as the Newcastle-based Christian Institute, Christian Watch, Christian Voice, Christian Concern (formerly Christian Concern for our Nation) and the Christian Legal Centre, which has fought for Christians who have faced opposition or even dismissal from their jobs because of their Christian faith.

In Britain, the focus of most Christian campaigning has been the issues of abortion, sex education at schools, and in more recent years the right for churches to maintain a biblical stance on homosexuality. Christian compassion and moral restraint have therefore been resurrected as areas of concern to Evangelicals in the UK also, but the issues relating to liberty have yet to become mainstream on the British Christian political agenda. There are some promising signs of movement in this area, notably from the Cambridge-based Jubilee Centre, which has undertaken significant research into areas such as economics and health from a Christian viewpoint, and the Christian Party, a political party launched by Rev George Hargreaves in 2004, whose manifesto is strongly supportive of low taxes and cutting the size of the state. There is still considerable hesitation among many British Evangelicals about moving beyond the areas of compassion and moral restraint to follow the American model of Christian political activism. The editorial in the October 2009 *Evangelical Times*, a newspaper with unashamed Calvinist leanings, questioned the desirability of British Evangelicalism following the American pattern of a close alliance with any one political party. While rightly pointing to the divisive effect of members of a congregation disagreeing over which party to support, the editorial left a number of questions unanswered. In Britain, there is a wider range of political parties to choose from compared with the USA, and things are far less clear cut. Should Christians vote for a specifically Christian party? Could either the Conservatives or the UK Independence Party ever adopt a manifesto that Christians would be comfortable with if they were to replace their current leaders? What about tactical voting to keep out a particularly ungodly individual?

Christians may share a common ideology and yet hold differing opinions on these subjects, but on the other hand, as will be proven in a subsequent volume, Labour, the Liberal Democrats and the Green Party[55] are all so terminally infected with the pseudo-tolerance of postmodern socialism that Bible-believing Christians should be as strongly dissuaded from voting for them as they have been from voting for the neo-Fascist British National Party.

It is significant that until David Cameron was invited to give an address in Oxford's Christ Church Cathedral in 2011 to mark the 400th anniversary of the completion of Authorised Version of the Bible, Margaret Thatcher was the last British Prime Minister to address a gathering of Christian leaders. Brought up as a nonconformist, she felt no contradiction between the Bible and her political principles. In her address to the General Assembly of the Church of Scotland in Edinburgh on 21st May 1988 (often referred to as the "Sermon on the Mound") she said, "The Old Testament lays down in Exodus the Ten Commandments as given to Moses, the injunction in Leviticus to love our neighbour as ourselves and generally the importance of observing a strict code of law. The New Testament is a record of the Incarnation, the teachings of Christ and the establishment of the Kingdom of God. Again we have the emphasis on loving our neighbour as ourselves and to "Do-as-you-would-be-done-by". I believe that by taking together these key elements from the Old and New Testaments, we gain a view of the universe, a proper attitude to work, and principles to shape economic and social life. We are told we must work and use our talents to create wealth. 'If a man will not work he shall not eat' wrote St. Paul to the Thessalonians. Indeed, abundance rather than poverty has a legitimacy which derives from the very nature of Creation.[56]" It goes without saying that at the time of the speech, not all the assembled clergymen were impressed. What is more remarkable is that more than twenty years on the significance of a Prime Minister using the Bible to attack compulsory wealth redistribution – one of the hallmarks of socialism – has still not been appreciated by the majority of British Evangelicals. Mrs Thatcher, like Ronald Reagan, benefitted from Evangelical support during the 1979 election campaign that brought her to power, and showed considerable sympathy to Evangelicals during her premiership. In 1985, she appointed Brian Griffiths as her personal advisor. Griffiths is an evangelical believer who attended Westminster Chapel during the latter years of the pastorate of Dr Martyn Lloyd-Jones. Griffiths had previously caught her eye as a result of a series of lectures he had given on the moral basis of capitalism, or the market economy as he called it[57]. He is one of few British Christians in recent years to have drawn attention to the Biblical support for private ownership of property, albeit balanced by the Biblical responsibility to care for the poor[58]. A more ambivalent figure who has recently emerged onto the British political realm is Philip Blond, founder of the *Res Publica* think tank. Blond, who spent several years as a lecturer in theology at Exeter University and the University of Cumbria, is the man credited with originating David Cameron's *Big Society* project. He is a strong opponent of abortion, saying "I think it should become an unacceptable practice. I would probably want to limit it to only the most extreme cases: rape, or when someone was very young, or incest.[59]" He is also strongly critical of the expansion of the state in the post-war period, pointing out its destructive influence on community life. He is unafraid to say that Conservatism should be compassionate and people-focused. His vision is for communities to become more active – in other words, to make space for the bottom-up initiatives that has characterised Christianity from its earliest days and which developed right across society in Victorian Britain. He is particularly enthusiastic about "distributism" – an economic philosophy which favours widespread property ownership, but with an emphasis on collaboration and communality – for instance through co-operatives. This emphasis on communality unfortunately is accompanied by a strong antipathy to the free market. Blond is a strong critic of the Thatcher years, and such comments as "the state embodies in structured form a common concern – it represents the coalesced will of the people that there is a level below which you cannot fall and an undertaking that we as a body politic have a stake, a care and indeed a provision for you and every other citizen.[60]" suggest that he supports a much larger role for the state than the Puritans, Kuyper or Gary North.

A similar pattern of Christians starting to speak out over political issues, particularly but not exclusively in the moral sphere, can be found in Australia and Canada. John Howard, Prime Minister of Australia from 1996 to 2007, shared both Margaret Thatcher's Methodist background and much of her political ideology. He was strongly supported by a number of Christian pressure groups, as was Stephen Harper, Canada's Prime Minister since 2006, who is a member of an Evangelical denomination, the Christian Missionary Alliance Church. Harper also supports the free market and believes that Christian charity rather than the government should help the poor[61]. Regrettably, Harper's government has done nothing to reverse the damaging effects of legislation introduced in 2005 permitting same-sex "marriage", which has resulted in employees being dismissed and businesses being sued if they speak out against it[62]. One more positive development in Canada has been the formation of the Association for Reformed Political Action (ARPA), which states that, "In harmony with our Reformed theological tradition, we are grounded by our faith in the truth and authority of the Bible...and believe that the Lordship of Jesus Christ must apply to every sphere of life, including politics.[63]" The same approach to scripture which characterised Calvin and Puritans, and which has largely lain dormant since 1700 apart from Abraham Kuyper, is making a long overdue and welcome return.

Away from the Anglophone world, organised Evangelical involvement in politics is very rare and many of the parties involved are very small. The European Christian Political Movement (ECPM), recognised as a pan-European party by the European Union in 2010, includes over 20 affiliated parties from countries within and without the European Union. Few of these parties, however, are founded on Evangelical principles. Some are linked to the Roman Catholic Church, and only the Swiss Federal Democratic Union appears to endorse policies in line with historic Christian political thought as outlined in chapters 3 and 4. There is broad agreement over support for marriage and opposition to abortion, but the consensus does not extend to economic issues or the size of government – indeed, the only British member of this movement, the Christian People's Alliance, in its 2010 manifesto favoured such measures as a permanent 50% top rate of income tax on salaries over £150,000, new bonus taxes on bankers' salaries and support for the European Union-controlled carbon trading scheme[64] – all policies which no-one who understands the Biblical concept of liberty can possible endorse. It also now supports plans for the proposed levy on all currency exchange transactions (the so-called "Tobin Tax"), which, if ever implemented, would adversely affect the City of London, which is the world's leading centre for this business, and result in an exodus of skilled financiers to Singapore or Hong Kong, where the imposition of such a tax is not on the agenda[65]. Another member of the ECPM, the Dutch *Christenunie*, supports a significant role for the state, particularly in the area of healthcare and education.[66] Holland actually boasts two Christian political parties, the second being the Reformed Political Party (*Staatkundig Gereformeerde Partij*) which left Kuyper's Anti-Revolutionary Party (ARP) in 1918 in protest against women being given the vote. However, neither the SGP nor the *Christenunie* boast anything like the influence which the now-defunct ARP enjoyed in Kuyper's time.

So the Anglophone nations once again have found themselves in the vanguard of Christian political thinking, and notwithstanding the muddled thinking of the Christian Peoples' Alliance or the hesitation of many concerned Christians in Britain to broaden their agenda beyond the issues of homosexuality and abortion, it is to these lands that anyone desiring to see the final and irrevocable defeat of socialism must surely look to in the years to come.

Notes

[1] The term is in many ways synonymous with capitalism, and the two terms are often used in conjunction with each other. Unfortunately, thanks to Marx and other 19th Century socialists, the word "capitalism" still carries a lot of baggage from the days when it was associated with the more exploitative practises dating from the early years of the Industrial Revolution. See Chapters 5 and 6.

[2] See Chapter 2, pages 65–66.

[3] http://mises.org/daily/2799/Carl-Menger-Pioneer-of-Empirical-Theory Accessed 02/03/2012.

[4] Congdon, T, *Keynes, the Keynesians and Monetarism*, pp32, 47. Edward Elgar Publishing Ltd, Cheltenham 2007.

[5] Hayek, FA, *The Fatal Conceit* p7. The University of Chicago Press, Chicago 1989.

[6] http://en.wikipedia.org/wiki/The_Road_to_Serfdom Accessed 03/03/2012.

[7] Speech at Castle Kennedy, Scotland 24th July 1963. See Powell, E, *Freedom and Reality* p22, Elliot Right Way books, Kingswood, Surrey 1969.

[8] In actual fact, Powell never used this particular phrase. He was actually quoting from Vergil, who talked of "The River Tiber flowing with much blood".

[9] http://www.cps.org.uk/about/history/ Accessed 02/03/2012.

[10] Fukuyama, F *The end of History and the Last Man*, Hamish Hamilton London 1992.

[11] Kirkup,T, *A History of Socialism*, p7 Elibron Classics 2006 (originally published by A&C Black, London 1909).

[12] http://www.academia.org/the-origins-of-political-correctness/ Accessed 08/04/2011.

[13] http://www.marylandthursdaymeeting.com/Archives/SpecialWeb-Documents/Cultural.Marxism.htm Accessed 13/06/2012.

[14] Jay, M, *The Dialectical Imagination*, p xii, Institute of California Press, Berkeley 1973, 1996.

[15] http://www.wsws.org/articles/2010/jan2010/pers-j13.shtml Accessed 25/05/2011.

[16] Jay, M. *op cit,* p41.

[17] *ibid*, pxvii.

[18] Jay, M, *op cit,* p41.

[19] *ibid*, p47.

[20] Rivkin, J and Ryan, M: *Literary Theory: an Anthology*, p344, Black-

well, Oxford/Malden Massachussetts, 1998.
[21] Marcuse, H, *One Dimensional Man* (1964). On-line version http://www.marxists.org/reference/archive/marcuse/works/one-dimensional-man/ch02.htm Accessed 25/05/2011.
[22] Marcuse, H, *Repressive Tolerance*. (1965) On-line version http://ada.evergreen.edu/~arunc/texts/frankfurt/marcuse/tolerance.pdf accessed 25/05/2011.
[23] *idem.*
[24] Published by the St Martin's Press, New York City. 1991.
[25] Hattersley, R, *Choose Freedom, the future for democratic socialism*, p xix. Michael Joseph Ltd, London , 1987.
[26] Crosland, R, *op cit*, p195.
[27] Quoted in Naylor, F and Peach, R. *The Truth about Grammar Schools*, p4 National Grammar Schools Association, Brackley 2005,
[28] Crosland, R. *op cit*, p169.
[29] Crosland, R, *op cit*, p355.
[30] http://www.newstatesman.com/200205270012 Accessed 23/04/2011.
[31] Hichens, P, *The Abolition of Britain*, p256. Continuum Books, London & New York, 2008.
[32] Hattersley, *op cit*, p16.
[33] Smith, D.B. *Living with Leviathan*, p150. The Institute of Economic Affairs, London, 2006.
[34] Jay, M, *op cit*, p xx.
[35] Crosland, R, *op cit*, p343.
[36] Carson, DA, *The Gagging of God*, p33 Apollos/IVP Leicester 1996.
[37] http://www.telegraph.co.uk/news/6194148/Margaret-Thatcher-airbrushed-from-Harriet-Harmans-history-of-women-in-politics.html Accessed 01/04/2011.
[38] http://conservativehome.blogs.com/platform/2010/08/martin-parsons-did-we-alienate-christian-voters-at-the-election-.html Accessed 01/04/2011.
[39] Eagleton, T, *A response to Elaine Showalter"*, quoted in Richter, D, *The Critical Tradition* (3rd edition), p1597–8, Bedford/St Martins, Boston 2007.
[40] http://news.uk.msn.com/uk/articles.aspx?cp-documentid=152401327 accessed 01/04/2011.
[41] http://blogs.telegraph.co.uk/news/danielhannan/100028285/michael-foot-gods-englishman Accessed 01/04/2011.
[42] Readers interested in pursuing this subject should read Ian Murray's excellent book *The Puritan Hope* (Banner of Truth, Edinburgh, 1971).
[43] Ham, K *The Answers Book*, p119, Answers In Genesis, 1999 Acacia Ridge, Queensland Australia. The identity of Cain's wife is not recorded

in the Bible, but most Evangelical scholars suggest that is is likely he married one of his sisters. Sibling marriage was not forbidden until the time of the Mosaic Law.
[44] The lack of organised Christian support was not the only reason for Goldwater's failure. He opposed the 1964 Civil Rights Act, which outlawed racial segregation on the grounds that it was unconstitutional and an encroachment on the rights of private property owners. He did not believe that expansion of federal power would ever solve the race problem. However, his decision was misinterpreted as support for racial prejudice, and cost him many votes.
[45] Postman, N, *Amusing ourselves to Death*, p119, Methuen, London 1987 (Third edition).
[46] http://www.telegraph.co.uk/news/obituaries/4143579/Paul-Weyrich.html. Accessed 01/03/2012.
[47] http://www.garynorth.com/public/department57.cfm Accessed 01/04/2011.
[48] North, G *The Dominion Covenant: Genesis*, pxxxiii, Institute fo Christain Economics, Tyler , Texas 1982.
[49] For instance his support for high birth rates – see *The Dominion Covenant*, p166–176
[50] http://www.garynorth.com/HonestMoney.pdf p128. Accessed 03/03/2012.
[51] *idem*, p138.
[52] North, G. *op cit*, p336–337.
[53] http://www.albertmohler.com/2008/09/24/a-christian-view-of-the-economic-crisis/ (Original spellings retained.) Accessed 01/04/2011.
[54] http://reformed-theology.org/ice/newslet/bet/bet97.10.htm Accessed 09/03/2012.
[55] It is planned to include a detailed study of the Green movement, showing its incompatibility with Evangelical Christianity, in a second volume of this book.
[56] For the full text, see http://www.margaretthatcher.org/document/107246 Accessed 01/03/2012.
[57] http://www.banneroftruth.org/pages/articles/article_detail.php?1209 Accessed 03/03/2012.
[58] *idem*.
[59] http://www.guardian.co.uk/theguardian/2009/aug/08/phillip-blond-conservatives-david-cameron Accessed 05/03/2012.
[60] http://www.abc.net.au/religion/articles/2011/05/27/3229488.htm?topic1=&topic2 Accessed 05/03/2012.
[61] http://communities.canada.com/vancouversun/blogs/thesearch/archive/2008/09/10/why-stephen-harper-keeps-his-evangelicalism-very-private.aspx Accessed 01/04/2011.

[62] Quoted in an article by Philip vander Elst in *Freedom Today*, August 2012.
[63] http://arpacanada.ca/index.php/about-arpa Accessed 05/03/2012.
[64] http://www.cpaparty.org.uk/resources/CPA_Election_Manifesto_2010.pdf Accessed 01/04/2011.
[65] http://www.cpaparty.org.uk/?page=issues&id=20&further=1 Accessed 03/03.2011.
[66] A summary of the *Christenunie*'s policies (in English) may be found at http://www.christenunie.nl/l/library/download/436532.

Concluding thoughts – The credit crunch and its aftermath

Righteousness exalts a nation, but sin is a reproach to any people[1].

Governments seem particularly inept at doing what God has asked them to do, yet run to take over that which goes beyond their remit. As a result of believing they can legislate so widely and control so many areas of our lives where they really have no business to be poking about, this means they need to take more money than they ought to cover the extra expenditure.

David W. Norris
Bible League Quarterly, April-June 2012

Late summer 2008 ushered in a remarkable series of events that saw the world banking system come close to failure. The collapse of the American sub-prime mortgage sector, the bankruptcy of Lehman Brothers and similar events in the UK triggered a recession on a scale unseen since the Second World War. Boom rapidly turned to bust and governments round the world resurrected F.D. Roosevelt's New Deal and Keynesianism from the grave. Vast amounts of money were spent (or borrowed) to bail out troubled banks, mortgage lenders, motor manufacturers and other large companies in difficulty, leaving many government finances in a pretty parlous state.

In the USA, true to their belief in small government, a sizeable minority of Republican congressmen and senators stoutly resisted these measures, and insisted that failing companies must be allowed to go to the wall, but president George W Bush eventually forced the bailouts through against the wishes of many in his own party. Echoing Keynes over half a century earlier, he declared, "I've abandoned free market principles to save the free-market system.[2]" In the UK, shadow chancellor George Osborne and other Conservative MPs spoke out against Gordon Brown's big spend, only to be told that they were out of step with the rest of the world. Confidence in the free market, so strong in the immediate aftermath of the Cold War, began to evaporate. At the height of the banking crisis, some left wing Labour MPs even called for full nationalisation of all the banks – behaviour which ten years earlier would have been instantly dismissed as a throwback to a bygone era.

The Great Recession, as it has come to be known, cannot be blamed solely on socialism, but the socialist government of Blair and Brown unquestionably caused the UK to be hit particularly hard. It was not Britain's dependence on the financial sector but the vast increase in the number of public sector workers under New Labour and the profligate spending of Gordon Brown and Alistair Darling, particularly in the final years of New Labour, which left the Treasury with little room to manoeuvre. Predictably, socialists queued up to blame everyone but themselves for the recession, and defenders of the free market and a smaller role for the state found themselves on the back foot.

The scale of the problem

No Christian looking at the events of 2008–9 from a Biblical perspective can possibly condone some of the behaviour which led to the crash. A desire to own one's own property is commendable and perfectly Biblical, but reckless lending to people who were always going to struggle with repayments cannot be condoned by any stretch of the imagination. Nonetheless, however irresponsible some banks and buildings societies may have been, the bottom line is that it is the state, not the financial sector, which is ultimately responsible for the vast debts which taxpayers across the world are having to repay. Even if in the future the British government stakes in HBOS and the Royal Bank of Scotland could be sold to the private sector for a far more substantial sum than Sir Richard Branson's Virgin Money recently paid for Northern Rock, it would still leave the British taxpayer shouldering a substantial burden for the next few years.

The short-term solution, reducing government debt by spending less and increasing taxes, does not address the root of the problem, nor its scale. The root of the problem is the legacy of socialism. Socialism may have changed its emphasis over the years from state ownership of industry to compulsory wealth redistribution and then again to a broader equality agenda, but its adherents' belief in the state has survived intact through these metamorphoses. Governments in most advanced economies have become ever larger, less accountable and more intrusive. The debts which they have racked up in country after country and the austerity measures which have been forced upon their citizens to balance the books are therefore the ultimate proof of the fatal flaws common to every variety of socialism.

Let us consider in more detail the economic misery which socialism has inflicted, thanks to the big state. In Victorian Britain there was no VAT, no insurance premium tax, no national insurance, no stamp duty, no "green" taxes and no council tax. Death duties were only introduced in 1894, and before World War 1, income tax was only paid by a small percentage of the population, and the rate never exceeded 10%, yet the state was solvent. Now on average, even before the recession struck, every British worker had to work for the state for over 2 days each week – in other words, over 40% of his earnings were taken from him in one form or other by the state. This was some 10% higher than the percentage of GDP devoured by the 1945–51 Attlee government, but still insufficient to satisfy the voracious appetite of Gordon Brown and Alastair Darling for our hard-earned money. Something has gone very seriously wrong. Obscenely large sums of money are being taken away from ordinary, hard working people, who are given absolutely no say in the matter.

Sadly, the defeat of New Labour has not seen any significant cuts in the deficit. In early 2012, Britain's debt topped £1 trillion for the first time ever. George Osborne's desire to balance the books and cut the size of Britain's budget deficit as quickly as possible is highly commendable, and should be supported by every thinking Christian, even if the imposition of swingeing cuts in government spending will unquestionably be painful for the public sector in the short term. What is less commendable has been his failure to do so. Not only has Osborne failed to reduce the number of QUANGOs (Quasi-autonomous non-governmental organisations), most of which Britain could well do without, but he has allowed the costly taxpayer-funded HS2 high speed rail link to go ahead, and has also refused to adopt the one policy that would not only free up British industry and commerce but would save several billion pounds without any cost to the taxpayer – withdrawing Britain from the European Union. Instead, only in April 2012, he committed no less than £10 billion of British Taxpayers' money to the International Monetary Fund – most of which will be used in what could well be a futile attempt to prop up the Euro, and which may never be paid back. Such a move was wasteful in the extreme given the debts the British government is struggling to reduce. It is now apparent that it was God's providence that Britain was spared joining the Euro, and it is equally apparent that leaving the EU would be most beneficial. The net direct costs of the EU alone amounted to over £10 billion in 2010, while the additional costs of the Common Agricultural Policy, the Common Fisheries Policy and the myriad regulations imposed by Brussels (and transposed into British law in a most rigid way by Whitehall) are estimated to have cost the country a total amounting to 10% of GDP – roughly £150 billion in 2011.[3] The European Union, characterised by international compulsory wealth distribution and an overbearing bureaucracy which is most uncomfortable with democracy, is an institution whose ethos cannot be reconciled with Christian political thought. A more detailed study of the EU in the light of the Bible is planned in a second volume of this book, but the eurozone Sovereign Debt crisis is worth a brief look as it proves so conclusively that big government is very damaging. Even disregarding the peculiar features of the charter of European Central Bank, (which has made the problem worse by denying it the same role as national central banks) this crisis still illustrates graphically how a toxic situation can arise when governments overspend. Government spending nowadays does not merely include vast amounts of tax revenue which goes directly to fund healthcare, pensions and schools, but also includes debt repayment on extra money which has been borrowed from the markets. The idea of "live now, pay later" saddles future taxpayers with massive additional tax bills, particularly if the yields on that debt reach the levels currently demanded of Greece and Portugal – and the electorates, both present and future, have no choice in the matter.

Big-spending governments and contempt for the electorate so often go together, and this crisis has also taken the already significant democratic deficit in the EU to new levels by the suspension of the democratic process Greece and Italy. Elected prime ministers were replaced at the behest of Brussels by unelected technocrats, Lucas Papademos in Greece and Mario Monti in Italy. Some 150 years after Karl Marx railed at the bureaucratic government of 19th Century France, the principal legacy of the ideology which he helped create has been precisely the opposite of that which he desired. Government was meant to wither away; rather, it has become a vast, faceless monster that racks up huge debts and refuses to be accountable to its citizens.

The EU's proposed Fiscal Union, which does not include the UK, and which insists on balanced budgets, is not the solution to the crisis. In the short term it will trap the Eurozone periphery in a lengthy recession, while in the longer term, it will only force governments to avoid spending more than an agreed amount; it does not address the issue of whether the state should control so many areas of public life. Will the spending caps work? It is hard not to be cynical. Even in America during the Reagan years, with its commitment to reduce the size of the state, the federal budget deficit actually increased during his tenure of office. If national sovereignty among the Eurozone member states is undermined by unelected officials with the power to overrule the decisions of any democratically-elected government which ends up in the same position, the net result is likely to be violent street protests on a far greater scale than those which have recently taken place in Athens and other Greek cities. It is God's mercy to the UK that David Cameron, under pressure from his backbenchers, did not sign up to the new treaty, but he should go further and withdraw the country completely from this over-regulated, declining club of nations whose structure is so far removed from the guidelines found in God's Word,

The eurozone crisis – indeed, the EU in general – is not the only illustration of the connection between big, expensive government and liberty. The more money any state takes from its citizens, the more it imposes on them in other ways, even if it professes to be using that money for benevolent ends, such as healthcare or education. Ronald Reagan said, "Man is not free unless government is limited….as government expands, liberty contracts.[4]" David Smith has also noted that, "the high degree of government intervention in many western nations poses a threat to personal liberty.[5]" One place where liberty has particularly been eroded, certainly in Britain, is the classroom. British Christians are facing uphill struggles to prevent compulsory sex education being taught not just in secondary schools, but even to children as young as five. This is a violation of the Bible's teaching that the prime responsibility for a child's education rests with the parents[6]. While in most cases, they will wish to subcontract the teaching of cognitive skills to specialists, how many parents of 12-year old children would be happy with any school teaching them about "anal, oral and digital sex"?[7] – especially bearing in mind that in the name of toleration, socialism has ignored the widespread support for pro-marriage policies[8] and refused to promote sexual abstinence among schoolchildren. Meanwhile, academic standards in schools are deteriorating, in spite of Tony Blair's mantra,

"Education, Education, Education." Eight years ago, one child in every four could still not read by the age of eleven, [9] while a pass grade could be obtained in GCSE Maths by students who answered four out of five questions incorrectly[10]. The harsh truth is there for all to see: the state cannot be trusted to control education any more that it can control public spending.

It is not just schoolchildren who are suffering from interference from the state in their daily lives. A century ago, as A J P Taylor described so beautifully, British citizens were left largely to their own devices, with the state only interfering to punish lawbreakers and ban exploitative and inhuman practises. By contrast, we are now subject to all manner of interference from politicians who in many cases have never held down a normal job yet who think they know the answers to all our problems. Politicians may claim that they go into politics to do good to the people, but the influence of socialism all too often replaces that initial altruism with an intoxication for power and a know-it-all attitude that despises contrary opinions. Socialism has turned the Chartists' dream of salaried politicans into a nightmare. Three hundred years ago, Matthew Henry rightly observed that "those that have so much power over others as to be able to oppress them have seldom enough power over themselves as not to oppress.[11]" Socialism has practically buried the Augustinian and Calvinistic idea of servant leadership, accountable to the people and to God. While Europe and the Anglophone world are still a long way from the horrors of Nazi Germany or Mao's China, as Ronald Reagan was right to warn his fellow countrymen, "Freedom is never more than one generation away from extinction. We didn't pass it on to our children in the bloodstream. It must be fought for, protected and handed on for them to do the same, or one day, we will spend our sunset years telling our children and our children's children what it was once like in the United States when men were free.[12]" Interference by the political classes threatens the time-honoured rights of freedom of speech. In Britain, Christian objections to homosexual practises have been a particular target of over-zealous policemen and council officials, but the scale of the challenge to free speech is far larger, as a recent incident at Gatwick Airport illustrates. David Jones, the creator of the children's character *Fireman Sam*, was placing his scarf in a tray while passing through Airport Security, noting at the same time how quickly a Moslem woman, wearing a *hijab* head covering, passed through the security. He made a light-hearted remark to the effect that he wondered what would have happened if he had been wearing his scarf over his face instead of putting it in the tray, and this resulted in him being stopped by a security guard and accused of racism, as a Moslem member of the security team had taken offence at this remark. He refused to apologise, even when pressured into so doing by a policemen[13]. It is manifestly absurd, considering that blasphemy and insults to Almighty God are not (and should not be) punished by the state, that the taking of offence by an individual is treated in this way. Christians have long cherished freedom of speech, even if it means that we (or our Saviour) are insulted at times. In the latter instance, we can and should protest, but should not seek to invoke the state's power. "Vengeance is mine; I will repay", says the Lord[14]. It is truly tragic that individuals like this security guard so miserably fail to appreciate the hard-won freedoms they enjoy in the UK. The state should never compromise our liberties just because some individuals are over-sensitive. In an imperfect world, the behaviour of some will always be unacceptable to others, but state intervention should only occur when that behaviour becomes violent. It is very much the lesser of two evils. Britain needs to return to the days of Winston Churchill's premiership when, on being booed as he boarded a train in London, he urged his security staff to ignore the offender, stating his pride in living in one of the few countries where you could say "boo" to a head of state without being arrested.

The opportunities

These examples are only the tip of the iceberg. It is unsurprising and encouraging that there is a growing public realisation in Britain, Canada, the USA and elsewhere that big government is a curse rather than a blessing. They are correct. The "messianic state," which socialists (and europhiles) would love the rest of us to worship, is in reality a voracious money-wasting, freedom-denying monster that needs to be slain. Shrink the State to its Biblically-mandated size and the pseudo-tolerance and political correctness of postmodern socialism will crumble in its wake. The down side of the Deuteronomic principle discussed in Chapter 1 – namely, that a nation run according to political principles opposed to the Word of God is inevitably going to suffer miserably – has been conclusively proven in the last century. While the non-Christian element among the electorate may not accept this diagnosis, reality is beginning to dawn that something has gone very badly wrong. With this realisation comes an opportunity for drastic change – an opportunity which is probably as great as it ever has been since the end of the Second World War. Such is the widespread frustration with the cost of government overspending, political correctness and the perceived injustice of the welfare state in particular that it is only a matter of time before radical reform will feature prominently on the political agenda in these countries. A recent British opinion poll came up with the remarkable finding that no fewer than 74% of the respondents supported a substantial reduction in benefit payments[15]. The resentment about the benefit culture, which has replaced the resourceful make-do-and-mend mindset which characterised the Victorians, is understandable, especially in times of financial austerity. The opinion poll also reflects the realisation that the state is not very good at discerning between the deserving and undeserving poor – indeed socialism is in denial about the existence of the latter category. Such a change in attitude offers good grounds for hope that just as Crosland's confidence of the permanence of leftward shift in Britain in 1956 was proven wrong by Margaret Thatcher, so the seemingly immovable stranglehold of the welfare state and postmodernism may yet be broken. In America, the populist TEA[16] Party movement has sought to return to the founding principles of the American Constitution, and have demanded radical cuts in government spending and a downsizing of the state. The Republican Party had a long struggle before coalescing around a single candidate to challenge Barack Obama for the 2012 Presidential election, with Evangelical candidates Michele Bachmann and Rick Perry lacking the presentational skills and substance to last the course, in spite of their endorsement of the TEA Party agenda, but this radical movement is not going to go away. There is likely to be a considerable confrontation in the coming months between free-spending Democrats and the TEA party and their Republican allies in the shape of the so-called "Fiscal Cliff", whereby a deadlock over the US Federal budget during 2011 will result in simultaneous tax rises and spending cuts at the beginning of 2013. While some of America's $15 trillion budget debt can be blamed on Barack Obama, he inherited a fairly substantial deficit caused in part by the defence spending of earlier administrations – a function of government which would be supported by many on the Republican Right, especially the neo-Conservatives with their endorsement of war to spread democracy overseas, as in Iraq. From a Biblical perspective, such interference in the affairs of another sovereign state is hard to defend, although the Iraq war enjoyed substantial support among American Evangelicals at the time.

In Britain, the opening will most likely come when David Cameron leaves office, particularly if public borrowing has been brought under control by then. The British Prime Minister is now far to the left of the majority of Conservative party activists and many of the new intake of Conservative MPs first elected in 2010. The number of think tanks committed to reducing the size of the state has grown significantly since the 1970s, and useful policy documents are being produced. All that is needed is a leader who believes in them, can sell them to the electorate as Margaret Thatcher did, and who will implement them. Sadly David Cameron fails on all three points. Whether the Conservative Party will soon elect a leader more in tune with its rank and file membership, or whether some sort of split will need to take place, only time will tell. There is unquestionably substantial and growing support for any party who is prepared drastically to slim down the state, and it must be only a matter of a few years before something will emerge to satisfy that market.

The challenges we face

The solution to Britain's social and economic problems are to be found in God's Word. A second volume of this book is planned, which will develop these concluding thoughts and attempt to produce a Biblical perspective on some of the main policy areas where socialism has caused particular damage, drawing on helpful research and ideas from non-Christian and Christian thinkers – both past and present. It is encouraging that the writings of Hayek, Friedman and others are being supplemented by an ever-increasing stream of Christian political literature. Gary North and the Cambridge-based Jubilee centre have already been mentioned in this connection, and a welcome recent addition to this genre is *God and government: A Biblical perspective on the role of the State* by Cornelius van Dam from the Canadian-based Association for Reformed Political Action. Dr van Dam writes, "The general description of the duty of government in Romans 13 and elsewhere suggests that the task of the governing authorities is a relatively limited one. To a modern mind this may seem strange. Today government intrusion into the lives of its citizens grows continually. Virtually every aspect of our existence is touched by government controls and laws.[17]" It appears that there is already a consensus among those seeking to apply the Bible to every area of life that the state should be limited in size. These are still early days, however. No one at this stage can claim to have said the final word on a Christian approach to many of our contemporary problems; more debate is needed in most areas.

This is particularly the case when no help can be provided from Christian political thinkers from the 16th or 17th centuries. Take energy supply for example. When Christian thinkers of the Reformed tradition sought to apply God's Word to every area of life, and in the realm of politics, they were convinced that unless there is a clear Biblical mandate for the state to play a role in a given area, then it should not do so. It will be a major challenge to devise an effective energy strategy according to these criteria – in other words where the state's only role in the provision of cheap, reliable energy is to ensure that no price cartels develop and that lives are not put at danger by the generation and distribution processes. Christian thinkers will nevertheless need to address this issue as evidence proves that energy supply cannot be trusted to the state either. The current policy of the UK government has resulted in the absurdity of *reverse compulsory wealth redistribution* – in other words the poor are subsidising the rich. Lower-income and middle class households are having to pay a "green surcharge" in their already astronomical energy bills which, among other things, is paid as a subsidy to landowners (who are usually the wealthiest in society) who wish to erect wind farms on their estates. Even the installation of solar panels, which are also subsidised[18], is usually undertaken by the more affluent in society. Renewable energy is, in theory, a good concept, and under certain circumstances could be regarded as good stewardship of resources. However, technology has not yet developed sufficiently to allow it to generate anything like the majority of the energy requirements of a densely-populated country like the UK, which does not enjoy a great deal of sunshine. This premature dash for renewable energy is driven by a desire to combat global warming, which, according to a 2010 survey, only 26% of the British public believe to be both a reality and largely man-made[19]. Allowing the state to dictate energy policy has therefore resulted in a very serious democratic deficit.

The state must be drastically shrunk, but to what size? It is worth recalling the opinion of the prophet Samuel that tithing to the government – i.e. the state taking 10% of GDP

– equalled "big government.[20]" A state that managed on only 10% of a nation's GDP would be very small by today's standards, and to shrink government to this level would be very much a long-term objective, as too rapid a reduction in state spending would not only be hard to sell to voters, but would unquestionably cause hardship if sufficient time were not given for an orderly, well-planned takeover by communal and private enterprise of the responsibilities which the state has usurped.

However, 10% should be the goal, rather than the current figure of 40–50%. Societies as diverse as Old Testament Israel, New England in the 17th Century and the industrial Britain of the Victorian era all functioned well with small government. We can be confident that as God's standards do not change, even if circumstances may vary, a modern state run on Biblical lines can also live within these limited means. Even in the early 21st Century, a state that is restricted to its God-given role need not breach the 10% barrier. In spite of all the sophisticated modern equipment required by the police and armed forces, defence and law and order enforcement still account for a mere 5% of the GDP of a nation such as Britain[21]. This leaves a reasonable margin for the state to fill its other God-given tasks including facilitating (but not undertaking) compassion for the needy, while the provision of pensions for public sector workers – one of the biggest drains on Treasury coffers – would also cost less, as there would be far fewer of them. If such a radical downsizing is to take place, Evangelical Christians should be prepared to take the lead. With our confidence in God's word, we need not be afraid to "think the unthinkable" – to be the first to devise well-thought out plans for rolling back the state in areas such as energy supply which others have hesitated to consider. We can be sure that if very limited government is what the Bible teaches, it will not only be feasible, but beneficial for our fellow countrymen as a whole, for the Bible's teachings on government are part of God's gift of providence – blessings to be enjoyed by all mankind whether Christians or not.

Such a downsizing would inevitably be challenging. Firstly,

substantial opposition from the left-wing media, including the BBC, would need to be overcome. Secondly, in the UK, it would require a re-education of the public, who are unaware of how well the country functioned before the Attlee years, and for whom the scrapping of vast amounts of legislation passed since 1945 may seem daunting. Although support for cutting benefit payments may be on the increase, there are still some people who view the welfare state as a welcome provider of freebies and others view it erroneously as an essential safety net, seemingly suffering from amnesia as to who ultimately has to pay for it. The furore over Iain Duncan-Smith's benefit reform proposals is an indication of the mountain that needs to be climbed. It is hard to see any Biblical reason why anybody should expect to receive £25,000 per annum for doing nothing – especially when such high levels of benefit act as a deterrent to job seeking. In these circumstances, the resentment felt against supposed "scroungers" is understandable. Reassignment the task of supporting the needy to community groups and individuals would address this resentment inasmuch as it would restore the link between giver and recipient. "God loveth a cheerful giver,[22]" the apostle Paul informs us. Giving would be far more enjoyable without the state determining how much we have to give and to whom it must be given. It would also be more beneficial for the recipients, for as F D Roosevelt (of all people!) rightly pointed out in 1932, state welfare is "a narcotic... a subtle destroyer of the human spirit."

Historically Christians who have looked to be guided by the Bible to direct their political thinking have never found any support for state-funded healthcare either. It too, therefore, should be privatised. Tim Congdon's observation that "private supply of the vast majority of goods and services is technically and institutionally feasible, and it is invariably more efficient than government supply[23]" applies to healthcare as much as to any other commodity. The obstacles are political, not economic. The feasibility of healthcare privatisation has already been demonstrated in dentistry. Such was the frustration with NHS bureaucracy in the first years of the

21st century that the majority of dentists in England withdrew unilaterally from treating anyone but children and the elderly under the NHS. Private dental care has not proved particularly expensive, and the experience of your author and his wife (and, by report, of many others) is that the quality of treatment has improved, with the dentists appreciating their freedom from government-imposed targets. Likewise, the recent takeover of the NHS Hinchingbrooke Hospital in Cambridgeshire by a private company saw it score extremely highly in a patient satisfaction survey[24]. There is every reason to believe that privatisation of other aspects of healthcare could yield equally beneficial results, and a country like the UK with its long expertise in the field of insurance and its previous history of bottom-up friendly societies is well positioned to lead the way.

The welfare state, including the NHS, is likely to be the last creation of big state socialism to disappear. It is likely that Britain will be offered a referendum on membership of the EU within the next five years, and that the "Green" movement will be in its death throes by the end of the decade, but it would be very surprising if the NHS is phased out by then, let alone the welfare state as a whole. However, it is becoming increasingly apparent that any Western nation wishing to have any role to play in the 21st century needs to move beyond the welfare state. It is no longer a badge of enlightened progress, but rather a system that degrades its recipients and leaves an unaffordable economic millstone round the neck of any country aspiring for a meaningful role in a world where new players like China, India and Brazil will be calling more of the shots. With the demographic challenges of the coming years, it is likely to become even less affordable, unless it is financed by excessive long-term government borrowing – in other words, leaving a generation not yet enfranchised to pick up the tab. This is nothing less than immoral.

In the field, of education, the reforms of Michael Gove, such as the setting up of "free schools" which are subject to less government interference, have been one of the few commendable achievements of the Cameron government, alongside Duncan-Smith's benefit reforms. However, the reforms should go much further. The voucher system, proposed by Milton Friedman, and recently adopted by Sweden, offers a roadmap for liberating education almost completely from state control. Friedman suggested that the state provided vouchers equivalent to the cost of educating a child at a state school which parents were free to spend at a school of their choice – including using the voucher as part of the cost of school fees in more expensive private schools. (The Swedes have not implemented this part of Friedman's proposal). However, the voucher was designed to be an intermediate stage, which would ultimately be replaced by all schools charging a fee to most children, with free places offered to those unable to pay, so that the state would cease funding education at all. Its only function would be to ensure that children are not indoctrinated to support violent extremism and terrorism. If the Bible teaches that parents have the primary responsibility for educating their children, those who do not wish to home-school their children (which will probably always be the majority of parents) should have the freedom to delegate the cognitive aspects of education to institutions in line with their own beliefs, If there is a demand for schools which teach creationism, which wish to enter pupils for "O" levels rather than GCSEs[25] or which seek to uphold sexual abstinence before marriage, the state should not seek to suppress that demand. The competition that goes with a free market in education would drive up standards, and ensure that the schools that thrive would be those whose ethos is in accordance with parental wishes. It may be hard to achieve this in some of the more run-down inner city areas, but the pioneering work of Katharine Birbalsingh to attempt to start a Free School in South London proves that it is by no means impossible[26].

However, small government is not the sum total of the Christian political worldview. Liberty must be balanced by compassion and moral restraint if Christians are to be faithful to the Word of God – indeed, only thus can the big state be confined to history. It is all very well for men like Grover Norquist of *Americans for Tax Reform* to say, "I don't want to abolish government. I simply want to reduce it to the size where I can drag it into the bathroom and drown it in the bathtub," but if the state is to be seriously shrunk to its Biblically mandated level, something else needs to be in place, particularly in lieu of the welfare state, that can pick up the pieces in a downturn. Even in the good times, the poor we will always have with us[27], and for all the obvious advantages of a market-driven economy for most people, some vulnerable groups will suffer if there is no one to address their needs. Christians therefore need once again to take the lead in the area of compassion. This is where Philip Blond's community-based "big society" vision has a role to play, but with the proviso that if the state is involved in helping to set up grass roots initiatives, it must then step back and leave them alone.

Politicians will never be redundant. We do not need so many of them, particularly at local/regional government level, which has too many tiers, but those that have a genuine role to play should be more accountable to us. It will be quite a challenge to find politicians genuinely committed to a reduction of their power, but Switzerland's widespread use of the referendum illustrates how well a country can call its elected leaders to account. Referendums are useful tools of restraint, clipping the wings of politicians with an excessive lust for power, but offering no threat to those with a true servant heart. Their introduction would also help rebuild the trust between politicians and the electorate, which has been shattered by the expenses scandal, broken promises and resentment over "nanny state" interference. Rebuilding this trust is essential, as government does have a positive, God-given role to play in certain areas. In recent years, particularly among students, there has been a rise in support for libertarianism, or Anarcho-Capitalism, as it is sometimes known. Libertarians are welcome allies for Christians wishing to see a drastically shrunken state, but there is a sharp ideological divide in their underlying philosophies. The agnostic philosopher Herbert Spencer (1830–1903) is regarded by many libertarians as their ideological mentor. Spencer's views on the state accord in many ways with the Bible's teaching. In his 1884 work *The Man Versus the State,* he wrote, "What, then, do they want a government for? Not to regulate commerce; not to educate the people; not to teach religion; not to administer charity; not to make roads or railways; but simply to defend the natural rights of man – to protect person and property-to prevent the aggressions of the powerful upon the weak – in a word, to administer justice. This is the natural, the original office of a government. It was not intended to do less: it ought not to be allowed to do more.[28]" On the other hand, he also stated that, "Every man has freedom to do all that he wills, provided he infringes not the equal freedom of any other man,[29]" and many of those claiming to be his ideological descendents have taken this to include complete sexual freedom, along with the legalisation of drugs and prostitution. Indeed, libertarianism, while eschewing violence and supporting the right to private property, otherwise appears to share many of the objectives of anarchism, being based on the same false premise as socialism. There have to be restraints in society due to man's sinful nature. A complete removal of restraints would not bring equality, freedom or happiness, but rather exploitation, violence and a collapse of society, as the Bible so graphically depicts in Judges 17–21.

Libertarians would agree with Christians that the state should protect individuals against injustice, for instance by passing and enforcing legislation ensuring that weights and measures are correct or by punishing such practises as forced marriages, female genital mutilation or paedophilia. There are, however, profound areas of disagreement between other aspects of the Bible's teaching and the opinions of some libertarians. Ayn Rand (1905–1982), another important influence on the libertarian movement, argued that the freedom to do what one wishes includes the freedom to have an abortion. Unlike God's Word, which teaches that life begins at conception rather than birth,[30] Rand denied any rights to the most vulnerable in today's society. To his credit, Ron Paul, America's most prominent libertarian, is opposed to abortion. Libertarianism is likewise divided over whether the defence of Biblical marriage is a legitimate function of the state. Christians, on the other hand, can look at both the Bible's teaching and the experience of history and should not be in any doubt. The French Revolution and the early Soviet years have proved that an attack on marriage is inevitably followed by disorder, crime and the breakdown of society. It is hardly surprising that the petition against the British government's plans to redefine marriage organised by the *Coalition For Marriage* in early 2012, attracted some 600,000 signatures. An opinion poll conducted by ConRes in March 2012 found that 70% of the public oppose the plan to give equal rights to same-sex unions, agreeing that marriage should remain a life-long exclusive commitment between a man and a woman[31]. It is therefore not just Christians who are wiser than David Cameron (and wiser than some libertarians, most socialists and virtually the entire Green Party) in recognising that past failure to support traditional, Biblical marriage has played a large part in creating the "broken society" so many bewail today.

Four hundred years ago, our Puritan forebears were concerned that time was running out for England, and that God's judgment was looming. They would be horrified to view their land today. Are we actually already under judgment? Is the big-state legacy of socialism and our subservience to Brussels part of that judgment? Does Romans 1:18–32, which talks of God giving a people up (or over) sound uncomfortably like our land today? If so, we must be thankful that there is still mercy mixed in with judgment, for we are still a long way from the horrors of the French Revolution, which must surely be understood as God calling a nation to account for its protracted rejection of His Word from the days of Calvin through to the revocation of the Edict of Nantes and its aftermath.

As this book has sought to point out, wherever the Bible has been influential in a nation's politics, the nation has been blessed. The withdrawal of Christians from the political sphere has had the opposite effect, and hence we have arrived at the present situation in a number of countries where hard-won freedoms are under threat in a way that would have been considered unthinkable 50 years ago. However, the principal reason for having written this book with its call for Christians to think seriously about political issues was not a desire to avoid persecution or even a desire to preserve the freedom to proclaim the Gospel. Neither was it inspired by a desire for a higher standard of living. While the Bible teaches that "the love of money is the root of all evil[32]", the culture of aspiration engendered by the free market is surely less inimical to the Word of God than the widespread jealousy of success and wealth and the curse of welfare dependency which has resulted from socialist compulsory wealth redistribution. Unlike the works of many 19th century socialists, this book most certainly does not suggest that any paradise can be created on earth. Until Jesus returns, this world will always be populated by – and ruled by – sinful men and women in need of restraint and for all the improvements in our standards of living and advances in medical knowledge, will always include vulnerable people in need of care.

The reason for writing this book is first and foremost to challenge Christians to following the footsteps of our Saviour, who loved righteousness and hated wickedness[33]. My hope is that it will inspire Christians to work actively towards a government in their nation that will be characterised by that righteousness which comes through obedience to the Word of God. If this challenge is taken up, socialism may well indeed be viewed by succeeding generations as a strange unbiblical aberration like the Divine Right of Kings or emperor worship which has been confined to the dustbin of history where it belongs. In practical terms, it behoves younger readers to consider their future career carefully. Christians are needed in the field of education – both as teachers and school governors – to counteract the influence of socialism among the young. Likewise, Christians are needed in the legal professions and the media. As for older Christians, those who have been successful in business should consider using their wealth to fund new think tanks and pressure groups committed to rebuilding society along the lines of the Christian worldview set out in this book, along with more Christian schools. Following the foundation of the first independent British university in Buckingham, it would be most beneficial for an independent Christian university to be established. For those feeling a direct call to serve God in politics, Christian organisations such as the Lachlan Macquarie Internships in Australia or CARE in the UK provide valuable training. No fewer than 20 British MPs have benefitted from staff provided by the latter organisation. All Christians over the age of 18, even if they may be too old, or do not feel the call to political activism on the front line, have a vote, which needs to be used wisely. Christians should read party manifestos and study the profiles of their candidates, to ensure they do not elect men or women who despise our Christian heritage. MPs are very aware that they need their constituents' support if they are to be re-elected, and while not everyone has the time or the inclination to write to their MP, those that do so have an opportunity to show that Christians are concerned about the way the country is going. Organisations such as the Christian Institute and Christian Concern often provide helpful guidelines for letter writers.

Finally, all Christians should pray earnestly for their country. The final, irrevocable defeat of socialism will be a great blessing in terms of liberty and prosperity, but what we need above all is a gracious outpouring of the Holy Spirit – another great revival that will bring many to repentance, turn back evil in the land and bring in its place a godly society. Anne Steele's marvellous hymn of national repentance was written some 250 years ago, but it wonderfully sums up the sentiments of God's people today as they pray that God will show mercy on their country in these dark times:–

See, gracious God, before thy throne
Thy mourning people bend;
'Tis on thy sovereign grace alone
Our humble hopes depend.

Tremendous judgments from thy hand
Thy dreadful power display;
Yet mercy spares this guilty land,
And still we live to pray.

Great God! and why is Britain spared?
Ungrateful as we are;
O make thy awful warnings heard,
While mercy cries, Forbear!

What numerous crimes increasing rise
Through this apostate isle!
What land as favoured of the skies,
And yet what land so vile!

How changed, alas, are truths divine,
For error, guilt and shame!
What impious numbers, bold in sin,
Disgrace the Christian name!

Regardless of thy smile or frown,
Their pleasures they require;
And sink with gay indifference down
To everlasting fire.

O turn us, turn us, mighty Lord,
By thy resistless grace;
Then shall our hearts obey thy word,
And humbly seek thy face;

Then, should insulting foes invade,
We shall not sink in fear;
Secure of never-failing aid,
If God, our God, is near.

Notes

[1] Proverbs 14:34.

[2] Levin, M.R. *Liberty and Tyranny*, p194 Threshold Editions, New York 2009

[3] See *How much does the EU cost Britain?* (Fifth edition) by Tim Congdon. Published by the author, 2012.

[4] http://quotes.liberty-tree.ca/quotes_by/ronald+reagan Accessed 05/04/2011.

[5] Smith, D B, *op cit*, p18.

[6] See, for example, Deuteronomy 6:5–9.

[7] Article in the *Daily Telegraph*, 16th November 2005, Quoted in *Campaign For Real Education* Winter 2005 bulletin.

[8] According to a Press release by the Christian Institute, a 1997 national opinion poll revealed that 75% of those questioned believed that marriage should be positively promoted in schools.

[9] Figure quoted in 2004 by Prime Minister Tony Blair.

[10] Green, B, de Waal, A and Crockett, P, *Education:Better results and declining standards*, P10. Civitas on-line briefing 2005.

[11] Henry, M, A commentary on the Whole Bible, Volume 1, p52 (Genesis 6:4–5) World Bible Publishers Iowa (originally published 1708)

[12] Quoted in Levin, M R *op cit*, p205

[13] http://www.dailymail.co.uk/news/article-2106631/Fireman-Sam-creator-Dave-Jones-detained-branded-racist-burqa-joke-airport-security.html Accessed 06/03/2012.

[14] Romans 12:19.

[15] http://www.dailymail.co.uk/debate/article-2109526/Why-Britains-fallen-love-welfare-state.html Accessed 06/02/2012.

[16] Taxed Enough Already

[17] http://www.arpacanada.ca/attachments/731_God%20&%20Government%20(ARPA%20Canada).pdf Accessed 06/02/2012.

[18] Although subsidy levels were significantly reduced in early 2012.

[19] http://news.bbc.co.uk/1/hi/sci/tech/8500443.stm Accessed 05/03/2012.

[20] 1 Samuel 8:15,17.

[21] http://10years.reform.co.uk/essays/The-case-for-halving-the-size-of-the-state.pdf Accessed 06/03/2012.

[22] 2 Corinthians 9:7

[23] *idem.*

[24] http://www.bbc.co.uk/news/uk-england-18612396 Accessed 14/08/2012.

[25] British examination boards still produce "O" level examinations for use in several Comonwealth countries including Singapore, Malaysia,

Malta and Pakistan, However, British pupils may not be entered for "O" levels.

[26] https://en.wikipedia.org/wiki/Katharine_Birbalsingh. See also Katharine Birbalsingh's articles in *Standpoint* magazine.
[27] Matthew 26:11
[28] Quoted in http://www.libertarian.co.uk/lapubs/libhe/libhe026.htm. Accessed 08/03/2012.
[29] *idem.*
[30] See, for instance, Psalm 139:13, 15 and Luke 1:41.
[31] http://www.christianconcern.com/our-concerns/social/70-per-cent-of-the-public-oppose-same-sex-marriage Accessed 09/03/2012.
[32] 1 Timothy 6:10.
[33] Psalm 45:7.

Bibliography.

Abbott, D and Glass, C *Share The Inheritance,* The Inheritance Press, Lake Oswego Oregon/Shawford 2010.

Adair, A *Puritans – Religion and Politics in Seventeenth Century England and America,* p218 Sutton Publishing, Stroud 1998.

Brother Andrew, *God's Smuggler,* Hodder & Stoughton, London 1968.

Augustine, *City of God,* translated by Marcus Dods, Eerdmans, Grand Rapids, 1988.

Bakunin, M, *God and the State,* On-line translation: http://www.marxists.org/reference/archive/bakunin/works/godstate/ch03.htm

Bartholomew, J *The Welfare State we're in,* Politico's London, 2004.

Baxter, R *The Reformed Pastor,* Banner of Truth, Edinburgh 1989 (Originally published in 1656).

Baxter, R *A Holy Commonwealth,* Edited by William Lamont, Cambridge University Press, Cambridge 1994.

Beeke, J R, *365 days with Calvin,* preface, Day One publications, Leominster, 2008.

Beyer, William C, (1959) *The Civil Service of the Ancient World,* Public Adminstrative Review XIX (3) American Society for Public Information.

Bible League Quarterly, April-June 2012.

Bieler, A *La Penseé Economique et Sociale de Calvin,* Librarie de l'Université Georg & Cte S.A. Geneva, 1959.

Booker C and North, R *The Great Deception,* Continuum Books, London 2003.

Booth, P (ed.) *Sharper Axes, Lower Taxes,* Institute of Economic Affairs, London 2011.

Breen, T.H. *The Character of the Good Ruler,* Yale University Press New Haven, 1970.

Brook, B, *Lives of the Puritans,* Soli Deo Gloria Publications, Morgan Pennsylvania (reprint – original published in 1813).

Cairns, E E, *Christianity through the Centuries,* Zondervan Corporation, Grand Rapids 1954

Calvin's commentaries, (22 volumes) Baker Book House, Grand Rapids, Michigan (originally published in French and/or Latin from 1540 to 1564.)

Calvin, J, *Institutes of the Christian Religion*. Translated by F. L. Battles. *The Library of Christian classics* Volume XX. The Westminster Press, Philadelphia 1960 (Based on Calvin's 1560 French edition)

Carson, D A, *The Gagging of God*, Apollos/IVP Leicester 1996.

Catechism of the Catholic Church, (English edition) Geoffrey Chapman, London 1999.

Chadwick, O, *The Reformation, Pelican History of the Church* Volume 3. Penguin books, Harmondsworth, 1964

Clark, S (ed) *Tales of two cities – Christianity and Politics*, IVP Leicester 2005.

Cockett, R, *Thinking the Unthinkable*, Harper Collins London 1994.

Congdon, T, *Keynes, the Keynesians and Monetarism*, Edward Elgar Publishing Ltd, Cheltenham 2007.

Congdon, T, *How much does the European Union cost Britain?*, 2012 Edition. Published by the author.

Coupland, D, *Generation X: Tales for an accelerated culture,* St Martin's Press, New York City. 1991.

Cragg, G R, *The Church in the Age of Reason 1648–1789*, Penguin Books, Harmondsworht, Middlesex, 1960.

Crosland, C A R, *The Future of Socialism*, Schocken Books, New York 1957

Dabney, R L, *Discussions of Robert Lewis Dabney*, Benner of Truth Trust, Edinburgh/Carlisle Pa, 1982 (originally published 1892)

Dallimore, A *George Whitefield, Evangelist of the Eighteenth Century Revival*, the Wakeman Trust, London 1990.

Dickens, C. *Oliver Twist*, (originally published 1838) on-line version http://www.literaturecollection.com/a/dickens/oliver-twist/50/

Dwight, S (ed) *The Works of Jonathan Edwards*, Banner of Truth, Carlisle, Pa 1996.

Ensor, Sir R. *England 1870–1914*, The Oxford History of England, Volume 14. Oxford University press, Oxford, 1962.

Fraser, Lady A, *Cromwell, our Chief of Men*, Mandarin Paperbacks, London 1993.

Fukuyama, F *The end of History and the Last Man*, Hamish Hamilton London 1992.

Gay Marriage in All but Name, The Christian Institute, Newcastle 2004.

Green, B, de Waal, A. and Crockett, P, *Education:Better results and declining standards*, Civitas on-line briefing 2005

Grudem, W *Systematic Theology*, Zondervan, Grand Rapids/ IVP, Leicester 1994.

Ham, K *The Answers Book*, Answers In Genesis, 1999 Acacia Ridge, Queensland Australia.

Hattersley, R *Choose Freedom – the Future for Democratic Socialism*,

Michael Joseph Ltd London 1987.

Hayek, F A, *The Fatal Conceit*, University of Chicago Press, Chicago, 1988.

Hayek, F A. *The Road to Serfdom*, University of Chicago Press, Chicago 1944.

Held, D *Models of Democracy*, Polity Press, Cambridge 2006.

Henry, M *A Commentary on the Whole Bible* (6 volumes) World Bible Publishers Iowa (originally published between 1706 and 1714).

Hitchens, P, *A Brief History of Crime*, Atlantic Books, London 2003.

Hichens, P, *The Abolition of Britain*, Continuum Books, London & New York, 2008.

Jay, M, *The Dialectical Imagination*, Institute of California Press, Berkeley 1973, 1996.

Johnstone, P *Operation World*, OM Publishing, Carlisle, 1993 (5th edition) .

Kirkup, T, *A History of Socialism*, Elibron Classics 2006 (originally published by A&C Black, London 1909).

Kuyper, A, *Lectures on Calvinism*, Eerdmans, Grand Rapids, 1987 (reprint).

Levin, M R, *Liberty and Tyranny*, Threshold Editions, New York, 2009.

Lives of the British Reformers (anonymous), Religious Tract Society, London. Date of publication unknown

Lloyd-Jones, M *Studies in the Sermon on the Mount*, Eerdmans, Grand Rapids 1959–1960.

Luard, E, *Socialism without the State*, Macmillan, London, 1979.

Marcuse, H, *One Dimensional Man* (1964). On-line version: http://www.marxists.org/reference/archive/marcuse/works/one-dimensional-man/ch02.htm

Marcuse, H, *Repressive Tolerance*. (1965) On-line version: http://ada.evergreen.edu/~arunc/texts/frankfurt/marcuse/tolerance.pdf

Marx, K: *The critique of Hegel's philosophy of right*, Cambridge University Press, 1970.

Marx, K and Engels, F, *The Communist Manifesto*, Translated by Samuel Moore, Merlin Press, London 1998.

Murray, I, *D. Martyn Lloyd-Jones, the First Forty Years 1899–1939*, Banner of Truth Trust, Edinburgh 1982

Murray, I *The Puritan Hope*, Banner of Truth Trust, Edinbugh, 1971.

Naphy, W, *Sex Crimes from Renaissance to Enlightenment*, Tempus, Stroud 2002.

Naylor, F and Peach, R. *The Truth about Grammar Schools*, National Grammar Schools Association, Brackley 2005

Neill, Bishop S, *A History of Christian Missions*, Penguin Books, London

1986 (second Edition).

North, G, *Genesis, The Dominion Covenant*, Tyler, Texas. 1992.

Orna-Ornstein, F, *France—Forgotten Mission Field*, European Missionary Fellowship, Watford (undated).

Open Doors Magazine.

Postman, N, *Amusing ourselves to Death*, Methuen, London 1987 (Third edition).

Powell E, *Freedom and Reality*, Elliot Right Way books, Kingswood, Surrey 1969.

Ramsbottom, B A *William Gadsby*, Gospel Standard Trust Publications, Harpenden, 2003.

Richter, D, *The Critical Tradition* (3rd edition), Bedford/St Martins, Boston 2007.

Rivkin, J and Ryan, M: *Literary Theory: an Anthology*, Blackwell, Oxford/Malden Massachussetts, 1998.

Robbins, J, *Ecclesiastical Megalomania*, The Trinity Foundation, USA 2000.

Rousseau, J J *Discourse on poverty*, (1754). On line translation http://www.constitution.org/jjr/ineq.htm

Rousseau, J J *Social Contract*, (1762). On line translation: http://www.constitution.org/jjr/socon.htm

Rutherford, S, Lex, Rex, (1644) On-line version: http://www.lonang.com/exlibris/rutherford

Ryle, J C, *Expository thoughts on the Gospels,* James Clarke, Cambridge Reprinted 1983

Schaff, P, *History of the Christian Church*, (8 volumes) Scribner 1910/Eerdmans Grand Rapids 1989.

Skidelsky R *John Maynard Keynes*, Pan Macmillan, London 2003.

Skidelsky, R, *John Maynard Keynes Fighting for Britain 1937–1946*, Macmillan London, 2000.

Smith, D B, *Living with Leviathan*, The Institute of Economic Affairs, London 2006.

Southern, R W, *Western Society and the Church in the Middle Ages*, Penguin Books, Harmondsworth 1970.

Taylor, A J P, *English History 1914–1945,*(Oxford History of England) Pelican, Oxford 1965.

Tudur Jones, R, *The Great Reformation*, Inter-Varsity Press, Leicester, 1985.

Vassilev, A. *Spies, the rise and fall of the KGB in America,* Yale University Press, New Haven, 2009

Vidler, A, *The Church in the age of Revolution*, Penguin Books, Harmondsworth, 1961.

Watson, L *The Citizenship of Women* in the *Girls Own Annual,* Volume

XL London 1919.

Watson, T, *The Ten Commandments*, p155 Banner of Truth, Edinburgh 1995. Originally published posthumously in 1692 as part of *A Body of Practical Divinity*

Weber, M, *Die protestantische Ethik und der Geist des Kapitalismus* (1904–5). English on-line translation http://www.archive.org/stream/protestantethics00webe/protestantethics00webe_djvu.txt

Whelan, R, *The Corrosion of Charity*, Insititute of Economic Affairs, London 1996.

Wheen, F, *Marx's Das Kapital*, Atlantic Books, London, 2006.

Woodward, Sir L, *The Age of Reform*, The Oxford History of England, Volume 13. Oxford University Press, Oxford, 1962.

Wurmbrand, R, *In God's Underground*, W.H. Allen/Hodder & Stoughton, London 1969.

Index of individuals

Index of subjects, places, organisations, etc.

INDEX OF SUBJECTS, PLACES, ORGANISATIONS, ETC.